Exploring Oregon's
Historic Courthouses

Exploring Oregon's Historic Courthouses

Kathleen M. Wiederhold

❖

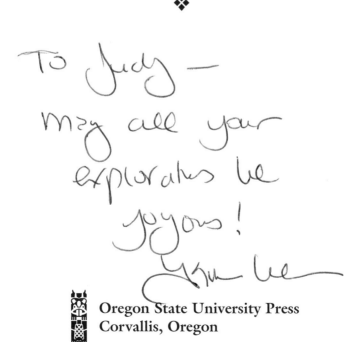

To Judy —
may all your
explorations be
joyous!

Oregon State University Press
Corvallis, Oregon

The paper in this book meets the guidelines for permanence and durability of the Committee on Production Guidelines for Book Longevity of the Council on Library Resources and the minimum requirements of the American National Standard for Permanence of Paper for Printed Library Materials Z39.48-1984.

Library of Congress Cataloging-in-Publication Data
Wiederhold, Kathleen.
   Exploring Oregon's historic courthouses / Kathleen Wiederhold. — 1st ed.
     p. cm.
   Includes bibliographical references and index.
   ISBN 0-87071-436-8 (pbk. : alk. paper)
   1. Historic buildings—Oregon—Guidebooks.
2. Courthouses—Oregon—Guidebooks. 3. Oregon—Guidebooks. I. Title.
F877.W54   98-15704
917.9504'43—dc21   CIP

Oregon State University Press
101 Waldo Hall
Corvallis OR 97331-6407
541-737-3166 • fax 541-737-3170
osu.orst.edu/dept/press

Contents

Acknowledgments

THIS BOOK HAS BEEN A LONG JOURNEY along a winding path. It would not exist without the help of many, many people.

I wish to thank those who had an impact very early in my life. Nellie Wiederhold instilled important values, not by word but by example. I miss her still. Jeanette Baker, in her abundant kindness, made it easy for me to excel. I love her zest. James T. Walker encouraged a shy ten-year old to write. Jeffrey Gray listened. Brigitte Patrick taught me an important lesson. My siblings, Theresa Wiederhold, Patrick Wiederhold, and Mary Catherine Wiederhold, stuck with me through the years.

Genevieve McCullough and Garrick Ducklard helped me with my writing very early in the project. Sylvia McFarland provided sound advice through the years.

While I was writing the book, Arlene Rand was a source of wisdom. In the last few months before its completion, she and David Rand generously shared their lives with me and helped me to start anew.

I am grateful to the people at the historical societies throughout the state who welcomed me and shared their information. I also thank the staff at the Oregon Historical Society Library, who have helped me throughout the years. The work the historical societies and the library do is critical in preserving our past.

People throughout the state helped me understand their counties and their courthouses. They shared their perspectives, told me their stories, and, many times in the process, gave me a glimpse of their lives. I wish to specifically thank:

In Baker County, Judge Bill Jackson, Judge Milo Pope, and Gary Smith.

In Benton County, Daniel Burke, Judy Juntunen, Charles Goodrich, Nancy Hoffman, Judge Richard Mengler, Bob Miller, and Stewart Wershow.

In Clackamas County, Ailsa Werner.

In Clatsop County, Bill Ballard, Irja Curtis, Arnold Curtis, Judge Thomas Edison, Millie Edison, Bonnie Susan Oathes, and Mark Tolonen.

In Crook County, Grace Bannon, Dee Berman, Fred Farrish, Gorden Gillespie, Leona Puckett, and Judith Windsor.

In Deschutes County, Michael Houser.

In Douglas County, Gerald Bacon, Doris Bacon, Sharon Burril, Fred Reenstjerna, and Iola Simon.

In Harney County, Avel Diaz, Maria Iturriaga, Eugene Luckey, Irv Rhinehart, and Dee Swisher.

In Jackson County, L. Scott Clay, John French, Carol Harbison-Samuelson, Judge James Main, Luella Main, Nancy Myrick, Stephen Terry, Sue Waldron, and Jerry Wilson.

In Josephine County, Juanita Clark, Marlene Gorman, Edna May Hill, Judge Gerald Neufeld, Clyde Mulrooney, and Carolyn Sieger.

In Linn County, Craig Brokaw and Rosalind Keeney.

In Morrow County, Barbara Bloodsworth, Andrea Denton, and Marsha Sweek.

In Multnomah County, Barb Bremler, Jackie Jurkins, and Esther Lugalia.

In Polk County, Eldon Bevens, Lois Bevens, Judge Charles Luukinen, and Mike Propes.

In Sherman County, Dan Bartlett, Ramon English, Sarah Irsyk, Sherry Kaseberg, Lee Langston, County Judge Michael McArthur, Patty Moore, Nancy Smith, and Richard Stradley.

In Tillamook County, Wayne Jensen.

In Wallowa County, Grace Bartlett, Claudia Jones, Marjorie Martin, Charlotte McIver, Jeff Oveson, and Rich Wandschneider.

In Wasco County, Walter Ericksen, Marilyn Ericksen, Judge John Kelly, Philip Klindt, Karen LeBreton, Carl Long, Freda Webb, and Jerry Webb.

In Washington County, Barbara Doyle.

In Wheeler County, Louise Becket, Merle Becket, Barbara Sitton, George Brindle, Doris Brindle, Bob Britt, Marille Britt, Marion Bumcrot, Jeanne Burch, Ortho Calverce, Carol Calverce, Gordon Dunn, Bud Hayes, Betsy Ray, Gerald Ward, and Robert Welsh.

Judge Donald Kalberer's humorous stories were a cornerstone of the sample chapter and helped me set the tone of my work.

Larry Roumpf, who did not live to see my book completed, gave me the unforgettable experience of riding a horse and driving cattle. He also showed me that one can have dignity no matter what the circumstances.

Writing this book was risky both personally and professionally, but some persons, through their interest in the project, told me I was on the right track. Bruce Taylor Hamilton saw the first attempt and gave me encouragement. Judge Charles Crookham listened to my proposal and helped open those early doors. Paul Nickell went out of his way to promote the book. Terrence O'Donnell and Richard Ritz each gave me an afternoon filled with information.

Carolyn Buan made wonderfully creative suggestions that helped me craft the sample chapter and cover letter.

I salute the Oregon State University Press, without which many books about the state would not be published. Specifically, I wish to thank Jo Alexander and Tom Booth, whose interest was an incentive to continue working on the book through long hours and times of doubt. Warren Slesinger patiently answered my thousand questions, and Roxanne Nelson worked to find fiscal support.

Alan Viewig shared his photographic expertise and never balked about the pre-dawn meetings to photograph a courthouse in the early morning light.

I am forever indebted to two people who supported me throughout the entire project. Sieglinde Smith generously gave her time and her exquisite wit. Through the years, she was a tireless champion of the book. Bruce Ostly shared his wide-ranging insights about building construction and town landscapes. He believed in me even in times when I did not. My words of thanks to both of them seem inadequate.

Introduction

They gathered at the Burns church one January night in 1891. The election to determine the county seat was full of fraud, the commissioners had said; the records must go back to the town of Harney. If the records were moved, Burns would not be the county seat and the town could fail. The leaders roused the throng to action; they called them to arms. The hardware merchant supplied weapons to those without guns or rifles. They posted sentinels outside the building that housed the records with instructions to shoot anyone who tried to take them. Armed, determined, they vowed that no other town would be the county seat. Burns would have the courthouse.

An episode like this might seem absurd today, but as the West was settled, competition for economic supremacy pitted town against town, and fortunes were made by winning a railroad depot or county courthouse. The courthouses in this book are at the center of many intriguing stories. Their tales are about people, revealing how they fought for the county seat, built their edifices, and treated the courthouse in subsequent years. Some of these stories are recent history, some took place more than one hundred years ago, but many explain what we see today.

The courthouses in this book have endured for well over fifty years, and one for more than a hundred years. Each is unique and speaks of a particular time and place. The architect for the 1909 Baker County courthouse, for example, vowed that it would be the finest on the Pacific coast; certainly it was a fitting acquisition for what was then a rich mining town. Tillamook County residents, many of them farmers, constructed their courthouse during the Depression, and even as their austere building was being erected, they eliminated county positions in order to save money.

Several broad themes revolve around Oregon's historic courthouses, and although many have faded from our consciousness, they still shape what we experience. People wanted the courthouse to be in their town because it was socially and politically prestigious. In addition, being the county seat ensured a level of business activity that helped a town endure and prosper. County workers and attorneys tended to live in the county seat. Out-of-town citizens would shop with the local merchants before or after conducting their business at the courthouse.

While a few counties had just one leading town that clearly would be the county seat, others had several towns fighting for the position. And fight they did. Citizens wrote to their local newspapers, advocating this or that town, but other tactics also were employed. Dallas citizens helped fund a railroad to come to their town so that they would have advantages equal to their rival, Independence. In the Heppner-Lexington contest, someone reportedly drugged a guard posted to protect the election results and stole the ballots.

Courthouses served as the crossroads of the community. There citizens paid taxes, sat on juries, and talked to their commissioners. They recorded the significant events in their lives: births, marriages, and deaths. Social events, such as picnics, took place on the courthouse lawn. On the square or in the building, neighbor met neighbor. While people went to separate churches or joined different fraternal groups, the courthouse belonged to all.

The first courthouses were modest wooden structures, but later citizens built the best brick and stone buildings they could afford. Residents believed their courthouse embodied the economic prospects of the county seat and the county. The *Oregon Mist* newspaper in St. Helens proclaimed that any newcomer sailing up the Columbia River would see their handsome edifice and know that this was a successful community in which to live and invest.

Of course, courthouses were not solely for impressing the newcomers. Years ago, the buildings were perceived as representing the people themselves. Just as people once dressed for dinner, so they built courthouses with the finest materials and attention to detail—even if no one might notice. In Wasco

County's courthouse, a visitor probably would not notice the corners in the lobby, yet workers added half-pilasters to maintain the pattern on the walls. The eagles on the Jackson County courthouse, high above the ground, are so detailed that even the skin on the talons is defined.

Even with a small construction budget, communities wanted their courthouses to appear grand. It was important that the courthouse appear progressive, but not avant-garde, and so Oregon's historic courthouses today display a range of architectural styles as preferences changed. Courthouse architects generally practiced within the state, and some designed courthouses for several Oregon counties. While they did not design nationally recognized architecture, they did create monumental structures that frequently were better than any other building in the county.

Despite changing building styles, courthouses still had to look like courthouses. For the earlier buildings in this book, this meant a tower. If the county could afford it, they installed a clock on the tower, making the courthouse the authority on time when pocket watches were expensive and not everyone had one. This symbol of affluence was so important to the residents of Linn County that, although the architect suggested they build a fireproof vault to protect the records, they chose to fund a clock tower instead.

After the turn of the century, courthouse styles shifted toward classic embellishment, displaying Greek- and Roman-styled columns and cornices. Later, exterior embellishment became more subdued. Regardless of the style, if the county could afford it the exterior was adorned with symbolic decorations. On the classically styled Clatsop County courthouse, for example, the heads of alternate columns exhibit what appears to be a clerk's ledger, depicting a basic function of county government. The Clackamas County courthouse was constructed during the Depression, but a reporter for the local newspaper at the time defended the courthouse's decoration because it added meaning. The courthouse exterior displays sculptures of two men, each holding an omniscient eye, which, according to the reporter, should inspire the sheriff to watch out for "monkey business."

Many counties followed a national tradition and built their courthouses on a square. The locations of these blocks vary; some are in the center of town and others on the edge of development. A few lay prominently on a hill. For some Oregon county seats today, the courthouse square is the only park-like setting among the town's buildings, and maintaining the landscaping is an important part of keeping up appearances.

Over the years, courthouse squares have become a place for community mementos. The square usually serves as the place to commemorate local men and women killed in the country's wars. Other items, telling of some aspect of the county's past, also are set on the square: a set of logging wheels, a pair of grist mill stones, a cornerstone from a demolished courthouse.

Since courthouses are open to the public, one can explore the building interiors. Like the exteriors, the lobby or main hallway can be opulent or economical, depending on the construction budget. Here, many of Oregon's historic courthouses are relatively true to their early design, so that one can view a classically interpreted or Art Deco finish. Some have been refurbished in an attempt to "modernize," but most retain a sense of their original appearance.

Equipped with just a little background knowledge, a visitor sees nuances in the community mementos displayed. Albany was a town divided by its Republican and Democratic political beliefs; although the Republicans symbolically claimed the square by placing a bench there, the Democrats captured the building by displaying a picture of President Franklin Roosevelt in the lobby. Medford started as a railroad town, and the train station benches in the courthouse tie the town to its early beginnings. In the Morrow County courthouse, a photographic display of the 1903 flood in Heppner reveals an important event in the town's history.

To the careful observer, the courthouse also can disclose attitudes, both past and present. The doorways to the restrooms in the Wallowa County courthouse are smaller than those of a typical office, suggesting some modesty in concealing these necessities. In Wasco County's courthouse, the interest in preserving the historic atmosphere of the building was so great that modern trash containers have plastic laminate surrounds that match the marble wainscoting.

The main courtrooms are formal rooms where interior decoration and symbolism were made as grand as the budget would allow. Courtrooms served as a place to administer justice and sometimes as a site of general community meetings. Even if they initially may have appeared similar, courtrooms have evolved into distinct places. The same architect designed the courthouses in Wheeler and Sherman counties, but today the jury in the Wheeler County courthouse sits on what appear to be old movie theater seats, possibly salvaged from the defunct theater in Fossil. In the Sherman County courthouse, by contrast, the jury sits on brightly colored high school stadium pads that read "Sherman County Huskies."

Over the years, courthouses have undergone some alterations. Modern glass doors have replaced wooden ones; aluminum windows have supplanted those with wooden sashes. In Clatsop County, the glass and copper dome was removed; in Sherman County, the tower. In Polk and Baker counties, stairways were eliminated when additions were constructed. For many counties, newer additions reflect changes in attitudes about county buildings: they should be constructed as inexpensively as possible. This belief makes the older courthouses more valuable than ever.

The goal of this book is to help the reader appreciate courthouses on a deeper level. Rich in meaning, courthouses represent the nation's political ideals, a county's aspirations, a community's pride, and a people's gathering place. This book explains these buildings, suggesting where to look and what is important. After exploring this book, the reader will be able to look at courthouses, either in Oregon or elsewhere, with a more developed eye. Furthermore, he or she will be more aware of how other buildings, not just courthouses, communicate through their design and embellishment.

Oregon's historic courthouses exist in a civic setting, and to examine the courthouse without understanding the county seat is to limit one's experience of the building. The courthouse has influenced the county seat, but in turn the county seat has influenced the courthouse. In many towns, the ties between the two began when the community was very young. Each of the county seats in this book is unique. Although Astoria and St. Helens both stand beside the Columbia River, they are different due to distinct histories. Corvallis and Albany stand in the Willamette Valley just twelve miles from each other, but they have different personalities because of their past. To understand this influence on the courthouse, this book explores the events that fashioned the county seat. How did it start? What made it grow?

The past shapes what we see today in these towns. A town's history gives it personality. In Baker City, nearby gold discoveries led to a wealth of downtown buildings. St. Helens with its industries once was called "Payroll City," and today its Main Street leads directly to what was its first great lumber mill. In Grants Pass, turn-of-the-century structures still line the street opposite the site of a demolished train depot.

It also is important to understand how the courthouse evolved. Although this book explores the early county buildings, it places particular emphasis on the issues and attitudes about the present courthouse when it was built. The buildings often were the center of great controversy, some of it amusing in retrospect. While records of county meetings tend to be sparse, the newspaper in the county seat generally followed the courthouse's progress from preliminary discussion to final dedication.

With an understanding of the county seat and the history of the courthouse, this book investigates courthouses today. These are living buildings that can be explored and admired. For many of us, history is most vivid when we can experience its legacies personally. Fortunately, change occurs very slowly in courthouses, and many people throughout Oregon protect the historic integrity of their courthouse.

A few counties, such as Jackson, have former courthouses that are still standing. Although the book discusses these former courthouses, my emphasis is on the operating courthouse. Other tenants occupy the former courthouses and significant alterations have occurred to some.

This book explores only Oregon's historic courthouses, which I have defined as those completed before 1950. During the 1950s, a wave of courthouse construction occurred in Oregon, but the design of these new buildings, following then widespread architectural trends, displayed bland, simplified facades that bore a strong resemblance to generic office buildings. Consequently, many lost the affection of the public.

Each chapter in the book is devoted to one county and is self-contained, allowing the reader to explore that county without consulting prior chapters. Each chapter is divided into four sections: the history of the county seat, visiting the county seat today, the history of the courthouse and the courthouse today.

I used a variety of sources for this book: local histories, clipping files of various historical societies and public libraries, and county seat newspapers. I interviewed judges, county employees, local historians, and knowledgeable citizens. I toured the courthouses extensively. Sometimes during my inspection I was joined by a custodian or maintenance person, generally the person who knows the courthouse the most intimately.

Courthouses are open during regular office hours. Courts may be in session, requiring respectful behavior from visitors, and a few places such as private offices or the clock towers may be closed to the public. But for the most part, the mysterious marked tiles in the Baker County courthouse or the fresco in the Tillamook County courthouse are accessible to all. The visitor should move slowly through a courthouse, as there is much to see.

I welcome stories and comments about Oregon's courthouses. Please visit me at my web site at

http://www.teleport.com/~courthse

or write to me at

courthse@teleport.com

Northwestern Counties

Benton County's courthouse clock tower rises 110 feet, and is a landmark in Corvallis. The maintenance person has the harrowing job of raising and lowering the flag from a small trapdoor in the roof. *Credit: author*

Benton County

County Seat: Corvallis
Courthouse Address: 120 NW Fourth Street
Year Completed: 1889
Architect: Delos D. Neer
Date of County Formation: December 23, 1847

"Were the cows prohibited from running at large within the corporate limits of this city, then those steps at the three entrances of the court house yard would not be required. It is certainly delightful (!) to be compelled to go up four steps then down in order to get into the square."

—*Corvallis Gazette*, July 19, 1889

In the summer of 1887, officials dedicated the cornerstone of the first permanent building at Oregon's agricultural college. Almost two years later, the May 17, 1889 *Corvallis Gazette* reprinted an article forecasting that "the influence of this institution will be wide and consistently increasing." The prediction came true. While many other late 19th-century Corvallis industries disappeared, the college continued to grow. Today, Benton Hall, the first enduring building of the state school, still represents a time when they *thought* the college would have an impact on Corvallis.

Corvallis's recorded history begins in the winter of 1845 when Joseph Avery staked a claim along the Willamette River, just north of the confluence of Marys River. After returning to Oregon City for his wife and children, Avery began growing grain and kept the surplus in a log storeroom near his cabin. Like many other Willamette Valley settlers, Avery traveled to the California gold mines, but on his second trip there he realized that a greater wealth could be made by selling to the miner along the route rather than being one. He contracted goods from a San Francisco firm and began a store in his former granary.

In 1851, the first steamboat docked in Corvallis. Eugene, farther upriver, proved to be inaccessible by boat during part of the year, thereby making Corvallis the head of navigation on the upper river above the Oregon City falls. When gold was discovered in southern Oregon, prospectors disembarked at Corvallis before taking the overland route south.

In order to start a town, Avery chained off twelve acres of his claim, which was soon called Little Fields. In 1851, he filed a plat of Marysville, which included twenty-four full blocks, but reserved the ferry rights to six fractional blocks that bordered the Willamette River. Early surveying was sometimes imprecise; portions of three Avery blocks later would be determined to be located in the claim of his northern neighbor, William Dixon, who had settled there in 1846.

Corvallis soon consisted of two towns. Upper Town, positioned around Avery's claim on Second Street between Washington and Jefferson avenues, included Avery's store, a blacksmith shop, a grocery store, and a hotel. Lower Town, located around Dixon's claim on First Street between Polk and Van Buren boulevards, boasted of a blacksmith shop, a store, and a school. Both towns featured ferry landings. Madison Street, the dividing line between the two towns, gradually grew to be Middle Town.

Because of possible confusion with the town of Marysville in California, Avery renamed the community Corvallis in 1853, compounding the Latin words meaning "heart of the valley." For a few months in 1855, the oft-moving territorial government made Corvallis its home. Concerns rose over whether the body had the right to move without federal approval, particularly since the U.S. Congress had appropriated funds for a nearly completed state house in Salem. The legislature met in December and passed just one bill, an authorization to move them back to Salem.

Although Corvallis was not on the direct route to the 1860s gold discoveries in eastern Oregon, it profited indirectly by the demand for agricultural goods from the surrounding area. Corvallis's economy, however, suffered when the Oregon & California railroad built a line through Albany in 1870. The Western Oregon Railroad finally reached the town in 1880, although for years it ran only between Corvallis and Portland.

Optimism swept through the town in 1885 when the Oregon Pacific Railroad finally finished laying track to Yaquina Bay. The plan was to cut the travel time from Portland to San Francisco by one to two days, thereby usurping Portland's role as the state's major trading center. The railroad also was to connect with the mainline at Boise, giving direct access to the rest of the nation. However, in December 1887, the first of two steamers sank in the Yaquina Bay. Wheat shipments, a major source of anticipated revenue, did not meet expectations. To the east, the railroad finally reached the present-day Detroit Dam area and then stopped. Investors lost confidence in the rail line and cash shortages developed. The railroad went into receivership, legal battles lasted for years, and many Corvallis citizens lost their investments.

According to the June 27, 1957 *Benton County Herald,* both Corvallis and Yaquina City were "dry" towns, "but an enterprising bartender anchored a barge outside the [Yaquina] city limits at the bay and did a thriving business. It is said that the term 'train sickness' became synonymous in Corvallis with a hangover."

In 1885, the state assumed full control of a college then operated by the Methodist Episcopalians. The first substantial building, now called Benton Hall, was soon constructed, and by 1940 thirty-five more buildings had been added. *Oregon, End of the Trail,* published that year, touted Corvallis's "numerous industries based upon the extensive agricultural and timber resources of the region," but then concluded, "However, Corvallis remains essentially a college city."

The "college city" had a population just under 8,400 in 1940. Half a century later, with a population more than five times larger, Corvallis still was essentially a university town. Oregon State University has been a consistent provider of jobs, and the students, faculty, and staff ensure a market for the community's goods and services. The university has attracted high technology industries, another significant source of local employment. Aided by the university, the county has enjoyed an unemployment rate lower than the state average for several years.

Visiting the Seat of Benton County Government

EARLY INDUSTRIES SUCH AS THE CREAMERY, the planing mill, and the grain warehouse no longer stand along the Willamette, and with the overgrown foliage along the river bank, it is difficult to imagine that working buildings once operated there. One of Avery's early mercantiles, thought to have been constructed in the mid-1850s, still stands at 400 S.W. Second Street, but over the years this building has been modified so many times that little of its original appearance remains.

The 1882 Crawford and Farra Building at 344 S.W. Second Street replaced the wooden structure that served as the territorial capital for a brief period. Further north at 311 S.W. Second Street, the lavishly appointed post office seems out of place amid Corvallis' older downtown. It was built in 1931 during the Depression, when the government was one of the few entities that had construction funds. Far from a plain, cautious building, the post office features green marble pilasters and hanging bronze lanterns. Ornamental gargoyles, originally functional pieces designed to throw off water from a roof, project along the front of the building. Were the gargoyles operable, postal customers would be drenched regularly.

At 205 S.W. Second Street, the 1927 Hotel Corvallis displays its name repetitively on emblems near the top of the building. With a bronze crest displaying "House of Cheer" on one side of the entrance, this once-lavish hotel even offered its guests a stenographer. President John F. Kennedy once stayed there, and for years afterward his room was preserved unchanged. The building has been converted to apartments, but a black-and-white photograph of Kennedy, caught in an awkward drinking pose, hangs in the manager's office.

At 146 S.W. Second Street, the Kline Building, built in 1889, is the only downtown building that retains a lavish cast-iron facade on the second story. When the building was being built, the August 2, 1889 *Corvallis Gazette* wrote, "Its architecture will be very nice." Downtown Corvallis began to move east to Third Street in 1910, when Gus Harding constructed a two-story red and tan brick structure at 301 S.W. Third Street. Nolan's Department Store, the first occupant, enticed Corvallis citizens away from Second Street by advertising, "It paid to walk a little farther." Apparently, a one-block walk was insignificant, because within two years, two more buildings were erected, on the southeast and southwest corners.

Corvallis first grew along Second Street because it paralleled the Willamette River, an early source of commerce. By 1912, a Sanborn map shows that commercial structures were developing east along Madison Street, which at that time led to the front gates of the college. The map indicates that a bridge crossed Marys River at Third Street, which undoubtedly helped this street develop into Highway 99 and become commercially important.

A History of the Courthouse

EVEN BEFORE CORVALLIS WAS DEVELOPED, the legislature created Benton County in 1847 out of Polk County. The new entity honored Senator Thomas Benton, who along with his friend Senator Lewis Linn (after whom Linn County is named) was a staunch supporter of U. S. control over the Oregon Territory. County officials met in various locations until 1851, when Avery and Dixon each donated forty acres to secure the county seat. To finance a courthouse, the county sold lots, and with the terms of one-third down, one-third in six months, and the remainder in a year, its coffers held $3,549 by the summer of 1853.

In 1855, the county completed a wooden courthouse with a porch featuring four two-story pillars supporting a pediment. Shortly after the courthouse was constructed, the county decided to add to the building's stature by constructing a cupola on the roof. To beautify the grounds, the county planted 150 broadleaf maple trees on the square in 1861. Beauty apparently was a more pressing matter than building insurance, which was not purchased until 1867.

The completion of the Oregon Pacific Railroad to the coast started a movement to replace the building, as citizens believed that such a growing county should have a more flamboyant courthouse. The December 30, 1887 *Corvallis Gazette* reported that the proposed courthouse would cost $40,000, but then on January 13, 1888 reported that "Benton County's new court house will cost nearly $75,000. So says the Oregonian. Whew!" The February 29th, 1888 edition proudly asserted that "the new court house for Benton County, when completed, will be the handsomest building in the state. Whew! And then, just think! That new public school building yet to come, and the new agricultural college now nearly finished. Boom! Boom!"

Not all were pleased. The March 9, 1888 *Corvallis Gazette* related, "The proposed meeting of the farmers . . . for the purpose of remonstrating against the building of such an expensive court house . . . was not held." Although no further protests were reported, the newspaper itself changed its boosterish position during the 1888 election campaign of county commissioners. Two positions were open, but the men who had held the office were not renominated. On March 30, 1888, the Republican-leaning *Corvallis Gazette* stated, "The democrats have in the nomination of these [new] gentlemen endeavored to make restitution and atonement for the ridiculous expenditure of $80,000."

Of the Republican candidates, the June 1, 1888 issue promised that "they would consider well the measures before them and if of an extravagant nature and liable to place a heavy debt on the taxpayers, would properly give the necessary notice." A memo written by A. L. Strand relates the story that a friend later asked one of the routed county commissioners about "what he got out of it [the courthouse]." He replied, "I'll tell you what I got out of it. I got a hell of a good licking at the next election."

The 1888 Fourth of July celebration was an opportunity to lay the cornerstone. The exuberant festivities began early with the firing of a cannon at sunrise, and according to the July 6th, 1888 *Corvallis Gazette*, the cannon "fired out nearly all the glass panes in the windows of the engine house and cracked and shattered a number of others." Corvallis streets were crowded; more than seven thousand people were in town. After hearing speeches on the courthouse lawn, it was time for lunch, but feeding the crowds became a problem. The newspaper later stated, "A grand rush was made for the different hotels and eating houses, but a large number were compelled to go without their meals. Some of the grocerymen turned their stores into eating houses by turning boxes upside down and supplying oysters and crackers to the hungry throng." Afterward, officials dedicated the cornerstone, and then the crowd attended a staged battle held by the local militia near the junction of the Willamette and Marys rivers.

Early in the courthouse planning stages, the use of local materials was advocated. Although Neer was quoted in the February 24, 1888 *Corvallis Gazette* as saying Benton County's stone was "no good," apparently a quarry at the Witham place, then two miles east of the town, was of suitable quality. To save cost, the first-floor exterior walls were changed from stone to brick, which then was covered with plaster to simulate stone. Benton County's courthouse would use approximately 800,000 bricks; Linn County's 1865 courthouse used only about 300,000 bricks.

A view of the courthouse before it was painted and when chimneys lined the roof. In early days, a wooden fence surrounded many courthouses to keep cows off the square. *Credit: Oregon State University Archives*

When local sand was not considered fine enough for the inside plastering, sand from the Lewis River in Washington Territory was ordered. Its transportation was not easy. The sand was shipped to Portland on a barge, then sacked and carted almost a city block to a steamer, then shipped to Albany. There, it finally was placed on railroad cars and brought to Corvallis.

As the courthouse progressed, the November 16, 1888 newspaper reported that the "lawyers will have a large chance to show what are the size of their vocal chords." When the statue of justice was placed on a pedestal, the March 8, 1889 *Corvallis Gazette* predicted that "there the old lady will stay until the end of the world, probably." Finally, on July 12, 1889, the building was almost completed. The new courthouse and the old building, which had remained on the site, stood side by side, until blocks and tackles were hitched to the older structure's cupola and it was pulled down.

The Courthouse Today

THE REMAINDER OF THE BROADLEAF MAPLE TREES, planted around the first courthouse, contribute to the park-like setting on the square today. Unlike some counties where the custodian works on the grounds as part of his or her many duties, in Benton County a gardener cuts the grass and weeds the flower beds, helping to create one of the finest courthouse grounds in the state. Augmenting the garden theme is a brass drinking fountain shaped like a flower on the south side of the building. Although people occasionally lounge on the benches, the square was not always such a placid setting. One resident related that during Prohibition, her great-grand aunt and other women in the Women's Christian Temperance League would circle barrels of illegal liquor confiscated by the sheriff, singing their songs while smashing the containers.

Private parties can sponsor benches and other garden furniture, and in return have a plaque commemorating their gesture. On two benches, the dead impart wisdom to the living. Near the front of the square, a plaque commemorating Carl Maxey displays his favorite phrase, "You bet you can." Near the south side of the block, Cindy Sandrock's plaque says, "You may not be able to choose your circumstances, but you can choose the colors in which to paint them."

The Benton County courthouse features an Italianate architectural style. Characteristic of the style is the courthouse's arched windows and the quoins on the corners of the building that simulate stone. An oft-repeated phrase is that the building exhibits a "military influence." Perhaps this refers to the narrow single windows on the second and third story and those on the tower, which mimic castle openings from which arrows were shot.

Though county offices have outgrown the courthouse, this was not always true. When retired judge Richard Mengler came to Corvallis for the first time in 1938, he was struck by the size of the three-and-a-half story, 110-foot high courthouse. He later related that, at the time, "I wondered, 'Now how did that ever happen? That there should be such a large building in such a small town.'"

Like many other Oregon courthouses, the county had stopped flying the flag on the roof and instead began using a flagpole on the grounds in 1953. The June 27, 1957 *Benton County Herald* noted that before the improvement, the flag was "pulled through the trapdoor of the rickety, bat-infested tower." When Judge Mengler campaigned to restore the flag to the tower in the 1980s, he reported in a later speech that a custodian had to cut another trapdoor in the clock tower roof. Now, during national days of mourning, the maintenance person still has the harrowing job of extending his or her body out onto the tower roof to raise and lower the flag.

Just below the roof, a single word on each side of the tower spells out "The Flight of Time." The clock bell, which adds an audible reminder of the passing time by ringing every hour, was reported to be heard six miles away in Philomath. The bell has had periods of quiet, such as in 1938. The February 3, 1938 *Benton County Herald* reported that a clock without a bell was "in a class with the odorless skunk, the tailless dog and the hornless cow." A number of old-timers were saying "the old town ain't the same since the 'ticker' quit chimin'."

On the front of the building, a statue of Justice, with a sword in one hand and a scale in the other, stares off into the distance. Justice, one of the seven Virtues, is more frequently represented

The June 27, 1957 *Benton County Herald* reported the clock needed repair in 1939. "The tone had become so clamorous that citizens complained that the clanging disturbed their slumbers, as the clock unaccountably became particularly noisy at one o'clock. But while [William] Konick was muffling the guilty gong by tying buckskin over it, the citizens again complained that during the time of the repair, the absence of the hourly chimes was equally disconcerting."

blindfolded, but according to the June 27, 1957 *Benton County Herald*, an early day judge once stated, "It's high time that Justice saw what she is doing." Two other faces appear on the front of the courthouse. In the keystone above the porch opening, a horned male face, with lips pursed, presents a droll appearance. Beyond, in the keystone above the main doorway, a maiden modestly looks downward; one interpretation is that it represents "Justice Asleep."

Through the arched double doors, the foyer suggests the Victorian splendor of the courthouse. The walls have not always shown their natural wood appearance, however, as they were once "updated" with white paint. In the main hallway, plastic laminate once covered the fir and pine wainscoting. As noted in the July 1, 1988 *Corvallis Gazette-Times*, "The courthouse was collecting tacky renovations as quickly as an old house gathers dust." The construction of the jail in the late 1970s on the north side of the building was the unlikely impetus to remodel the courthouse. The July 1, 1988 newspaper reported that "because of the flak that the commissioners took for the [jail] project," a preservation committee was formed with Judge Mengler as the chairman. Some remodeling work was left as it was. Originally, two staircases were positioned on either side of the hallway, but one was removed when the elevator was installed in 1960. Now, only one staircase displays the newel post, which has multiple wooden pieces fitted together without a single nail, like a three-dimensional jigsaw puzzle.

Off to the right is the district court jury room, which displays the ornate leather-covered jury chairs originally located in the courtroom. The glass case exhibits treasures recovered in 1988 from the cornerstone, which includes a Talmud and a peach

pit. Buildings of this vintage did not have drinking fountains, and thirsty jurors must use the water cooler.

When the courthouse was constructed, the building had so much extra space that offices were rented out. The city held their council meetings in the jury room. Elsewhere in the building, the horticulture society and an insurance and real estate man rented offices. Doubtless, few Corvallis tenants could boast of such posh quarters whose central hallway had a sixteen-foot ceiling and sculpted feminine faces over the rounded doorways.

The county clerk, the official recorder of deeds, once occupied an office on the first floor before moving to the basement quarters. According to Edwin Johnson, in 1956 S. Edward Burrier purchased three quitclaim deeds from the short-lived Interplanetary Development Corporation. Each deed entitled the owner to a one-acre plot on the moon, and included a helpful map. Burrier asked the clerk to record his deeds, and although the property was clearly out of the Benton County jurisdiction, the clerk accommodatingly recorded them under "Miscellaneous."

Early photographs of courthouse offices were relatively rare. This one, taken about 1919, shows the latest technology of the time. The sign on the wall on the right offers money to children for catching moles and gophers. *Credit: Oregon State University Archives*

Two basement offices offer peepholes to the past. In No. 12, two holes in the rubble wall reveal an enclosed, once-hidden room still filled with construction debris from the 1880s. One recognizable item is an old wooden barrel. According to a photograph exhibited in the basement hallway display, such barrels supported the first level of scaffolding for the stone workers.

On the stairway landing between the first and second floors, the window is covered with the original wooden shutters, their ornamental hinges indicating that no detail was too small for the Victorians to leave unadorned. The escutcheon on the closet door housing the public telephone is similarly adorned. Although one hopes to find an old-fashioned telephone, instead there is a modern replacement. At the turn of the century, officials decided to equip the courthouse with this newfangled invention, but installed only one telephone for the entire building. The sheriff and other officials were notified of a call by a bell wired to their offices.

A grand courtroom was once located on the second floor. A well-meaning circuit court judge, in order to make room for the newly elected Judge Mengler, divided this once-spacious courtroom into two in 1955. Each room was further "modernized" with such furnishings as vinyl tile over the wooden floor and plywood veneer in front of the original judge's bench. Judge Mengler in the July 1, 1988 *Corvallis Gazette-Times* reported, "It really made me ill that they were remodeling that thing for me."

One decision made in the restoration was to keep the two courtrooms due to the county's expanded judicial needs. Both Courtroom No. 1 and No. 2 are similar, but No. 1 displays the original judge's bench, considerably more demure in size than those in later courthouses. As he did in the Polk and Baker courthouses, Neer added stature to the judge's position by placing a soaring wooden panel behind the bench, but the current location of this piece is unknown. Also gone is the sawdust that once lined the floor, later replaced by papier maché spittoons, and then by brass spittoons. According to Judge Mengler, the removal of the spittoons in the mid-1950s did not stop one attorney. "Tom would look around this way, and he'd look around that way, and then he'd just go 'phlllt.'"

The judge's robing room, dedicated to Judge Mengler, is located beyond the courtrooms, and contains the red "fainting" couch which was suitable for napping during the lunch hour. When Judge Mengler wanted to decorate this office, the county supplied the wallpaper, but he had to hang it himself. One Saturday, while the judge was papering his office, a reporter took a photograph of him at work. Mengler later related, "And the thing was run in newspapers . . . all over the United States, because a friend . . . in Vermont wrote to me when he saw this picture of the 'hanging judge.'"

Official tours of the district attorney's offices show the grandeur of the old courtroom. This extra floor, which is eight feet high, was created out of the space provided by the courtroom's original twenty-four-foot high ceiling. In the center of the hallway ceiling is the wooden medallion with lace-like ornamentation that once formed the centerpiece of the courtroom ceiling.

The employee lounge, once empty attic space, is located above the third floor. It is not a place for napping, as the clock tower bell overhead rings hourly. Five men calling themselves the Corvallis Bell Ringers ushered in the new year by signing their names on a wooden truss and dating it December 31, 1891 and January 1, 1892. A bank donated the carillon, which once could play Westminster Chimes.

A wooden stairway leads to the clock tower bell. Another unused bell sits off in the corner, and stories conflict as to whether this came from the Central School or was an old city fire bell. According to one story, a cord once hung from the tower down to just inside the front courthouse doors, allowing anyone to hurriedly ring the bell to call the volunteer firemen.

On the next floor are the clock mechanisms, once controlled by weights but now by an electric motor. Each of the four clock faces has a one-foot by two-foot removable wooden rectangle so that one can adjust the clock hands. Therefore, it is possible to spy on the pedestrians along Fourth Street below, but this vantage point also gives extensive views, reportedly the best in town. From the Benton County courthouse, one can see the places that define Corvallis: its downtown, the Oregon State University campus, and the countryside beyond.

The Art Deco-styled Clackamas County courthouse has an unusual location with Singer Falls cascading down a cliff a block away and with the Willamette River directly behind the building. Unfortunately, for security reasons the side entrance is the only way into the building. *Credit: author*

Clackamas County

County Seat:	Oregon City
Courthouse Address:	801 Main Street
Year Completed:	1937
Architect:	F. Marion Stokes
Date of County Formation:	July 5, 1843

"Debris from the wrecked [courthouse] building must be removed from the premises and can not be dumped into the river canyon back of the courthouse [block] as originally estimated."

—*Oregon City Enterprise*, November 26, 1935

Looking west from the McLoughlin Promenade on top of the Oregon City bluff, one can survey different aspects of the area's past. Water gushes over the falls, a significant power generator in the early history of the town. Two paper mills sprawl along both sides of the river, but the now-closed Simpson mill on the west side is bereft of activity. On the east side of the river, the historic downtown, once home to the territorial government, lies along Main Street north of the Smurfit paper mill. Old Oregon City seems weathered, but perhaps that is so because the town has seen so much history.

In 1829, John McLoughlin, the chief factor in charge of Fort Vancouver, claimed a site at Willamette Falls, a promising source of water power. McLoughlin had three cabins constructed on his land, but, according to *Empire of the Columbia,* plans for a sawmill were soon abandoned because of the then limited market for lumber.

Others eventually saw the potential at the falls. In July 1840, McLoughlin wrote a letter to the Rev. Jason Lee stating that he would not prevent the Methodists from building a store there, but that he wanted to keep the rights to his claim. In 1841, the Methodists constructed a sawmill on an island in the river which was part of McLoughlin's land, and so, to protect his interest, McLoughlin had his property surveyed for a townsite. According to some sources, the work was done by Sidney Moss, a settler who was qualified largely because he had a pocket compass. Jesse Applegate resurveyed the townsite in 1844, reportedly to correct some of the inaccuracies of the first survey.

Settlement in the Willamette Valley fostered the first localized governmental organization south of the Columbia River in 1843, and the legislative committee of the provisional government decided to meet in Oregon City. By this time, the town had at least three stores, but the nine committee members had to be content to meet in a room in the Methodist granary.

In 1849, William Eddy, the surveyor of the "Town of San Francisco," gave his map of San Francisco to Captain William Irving to be taken by boat to the territorial capital, Oregon City. The journey took three months, and today Clackamas County is the owner of an original San Francisco plat.

Pioneers journeying west on the Oregon Trail surged into Oregon City. The California gold rush temporarily diverted the flow of settlers, but like many other communities, the town benefited by shipping food and goods to the miners. With no established currency, local citizens decided to establish a mint in the town. Just before it opened, however, Oregon became a territory, and the first territorial governor, Joseph Lane, arrived in Oregon City and informed the people that the manufacture of money was a federal activity. However, in his opinion, the mint would be legal if it was private, and so for several years it produced gold coins.

Oregon City began to lose its commercial eminence when Portland, aided by its accessibility to ocean-going vessels, began to grow. Oregon City's attraction as a source of water power, however, remained. In 1864, a woolen mill was started along the falls, and a year later, a paper mill. On completion of the paper mill, citizens celebrated with a huge dinner and danced through the night. But the machinery would not work properly, and the mill soon closed.

Transportation improved when the Oregon & California railroad began regular service through Oregon City in 1870. Locks were built in 1873, which allowed ships with a deeper draft to travel farther up the Willamette. The falls soon were harnessed for electricity. In 1889, the first long-distance transmission of electricity took place from Oregon City to Portland.

According to the March 11, 1900 *Oregonian*, businesses that depended on the falls for water power created 1,037 jobs and $3,150,000 annually in products. (Included in the figure is Willamette Pulp and Paper, located on the west side of the falls, which employed 500 and generated $1,725,000 in products.) Although the newspaper forecast a prosperous future for the town as a manufacturing center, it spoke about its residential advantages in relationship to Portland. "The great scenic beauty, the salubrity of the climate . . . and the close proximity of the town to the metropolis [Portland] unite to make this an ideal home city. . . . As Portland continues to grow, so will the population of Oregon City increase."

Today, the only major employer still located near the falls is the Smurfit Paper Company, a descendant of the Hawley mill begun in 1908. As the March 11, 1900 Sunday *Oregonian* article insinuated, Oregon City's fortunes are tied to Portland, and it is considered part of the Portland Metropolitan area. Although the city has climbed the bluff and spread to the east, the compact downtown is still reminiscent of its earlier life.

Visiting the Seat of Clackamas County Government

DOWNTOWN OREGON CITY, SQUEEZED between the river and the bluff, is only two blocks wide. The railroad and State Highway 99E, both older transportation routes, take up some of the limited room and add train whistles and car noise to the downtown sounds. Now, less automobile traffic flows through old Oregon City since the modern-day Interstate 205 freeway on the opposite bank of the river avoids the downtown.

Along Main Street, layers of remodeling have hidden the original appearance of its seasoned structures. One of the oldest commercial buildings still in use in the state is believed to be the Caufield structure at 723 Main Street. Now one-story with a stucco exterior, it was constructed as a general store around 1850 and featured two stories with an outside staircase. The February 28, 1984 *Oregonian* reported that hand-hewn beams joined by wood-pegs formed the unfinished basement. According to a subsequent owner, the beams were cut at John McLoughlin's sawmill. Jane Caufield ran this store while her husband was mining in the California gold mines, and shrewdly sent an agent out on the Molalla Road to intercept farmers and buy wheat from them before they could come to town and sell it to someone else.

Another of Oregon City's early roles is exemplified in the four-story Masonic building at 707 Main Street, which displays the date "1846" on the parapet near the northeast corner. The *Oregon Spectator* ran an advertisement for members in its first issue in February, 1846, and the fraternal group became the first organized west of the Mississippi River. An oxen team carried its charter to Oregon City. On the southeast corner, the parapet displays "1907," the date the cornerstone was dedicated. The February 7, 1908 *Oregon City Courier* reported that "in Oregon City it was a veritable skyscraper." No other building in downtown Oregon City has exceeded its four stories, and almost ninety years later, it still is a "skyscraper."

The original town of Oregon City was centered farther south. At the southeast corner of Sixth and Main Streets, a marker denotes the Legislature's meeting place when the town was the capital of the Oregon Territory. Farther south, the sprawling Smurfit Paper Mill has gradually expanded and enveloped several older buildings over the years. While the John McLoughlin house was saved when it was moved up onto the bluff, other buildings, including the old mint, woolen mill, and opera house, have been demolished.

Oregon City citizens once climbed wooden stairways to ascend the bluff; today a concrete stairway stands near the end of Seventh Street. A more effortless route is via the adjacent municipal elevator, one of the few in the nation. The first elevator was constructed in 1915. Water initially powered the mechanism, which caused the water pressure for home owners at the top of the bluff to drop when the elevator was used.

Part of living in a mill town was hearing the mill whistle. The August 12, 1958 *Enterprise-Courier* noted the replacement of "Old Pooper," a steam whistle which blew at 7:55 a.m., 8 a.m., noon, 12:40 p.m. and 4:45 p.m. "For years [the retiring whistle] has set the dog population in Oregon City and West Linn and Willamette howling."

A History of the Courthouse

THE PROVISIONAL GOVERNMENT DIVIDED the Oregon County into four districts: Clackamas, Tuality, Yamhill, and Champoeg. (Later, the government would call these districts counties.) The first Clackamas County courthouse was constructed in 1850 on the bluff just east of the present-day Library Park, but it burned seven years later, reportedly the work of an inebriate. Succeeding officials apparently did not believe they needed their own courthouse, as over the next twenty years they met in various buildings in the downtown.

When officials finally did commission a courthouse, they selected the firm of Neer & LoRomer. One of the partners, Delos Neer, would later design the still-standing courthouses for Benton, Polk, and Baker counties. When the cornerstone ceremony was held in June 1884, crowds coming from Portland and the rest of the Willamette Valley patiently endured the rain to hear speeches made by local dignitaries.

The construction of the tower on the brick and stone courthouse was not a simple matter. In order to install a tin roof, a man was suspended by a rope more than two stories above the ground. One evening after completing his soldering, the roofer decided to leave the charcoal bucket in the tower rather than carrying it down to the ground. Early in the morning, a high wind began fanning the coals, whipping up a flame. A carpenter boarding with the courthouse contractor saw the danger, climbed the scaffolding on the new building, and likely saved the courthouse.

The courthouse, described in the March 20, 1937 *Oregon City Enterprise* as "mighty and pretentious," featured an H-shaped plan, tall arched windows, and numerous pediments. One of the most notable features was the statue of Justice on the roof. County Judge White had asked an Italian stonemason to carve the statue, which then was nicknamed "Colonel White's Mary Anne."

The jail was located in the basement of the courthouse. The March 1, 1901 *Oregon City Enterprise* reported, "Night watchman Ed Reckner arrested a half dozen hobos last Monday night for being drunk and begging in the streets. They were taken before Recorder Curry, who gave them, in addition to a lot of fatherly advice, a fine of $10.00 each for three of them, and a smaller fine for the others. As they had no money they will be allowed to work it out by cleaning out the jail; something that hasn't been done in the memory of the oldest inhabitant."

The courthouse, described in the March 20, 1937 Oregon City Enterprise *as "mighty and pretentious," featured an H-shaped plan, tall arched windows, and numerous pediments. Author's collection.*

By 1935, overcrowding in the courthouse offices prompted the Planning Board to investigate the construction of a new facility. The county learned that they could apply to the federal Public Works Administration (PWA) for funding to cover forty-five percent of the cost of a new courthouse, provided that they could come up with their share of the money. To do this, citizens needed to approve a levy. The October 31, 1935 *Oregon City Enterprise* printed a statement from the county court attempting to persuade the voters, arguing that "the courthouse is antiquated and dangerous" and in language revealing how they perceived the federal government, "Uncle Sam is yet Santa Claus and offers a straight gift of $90,000."

Perhaps one of the most persuasive arguments came a day before the election when a delegation representing the Kiwanis Club, Breakfast Club, and Business and Professional Women's Club inspected the proposed plans. According to the November 5, 1935 *Oregon City Enterprise*, the group determined that in comparison with the old courthouse's limited facilities, "Adequate rest room and toilet facilities available to the public are provided." The article went into detail, describing the women's restrooms as "14 by 16 feet, connecting with adequate toilet and wash basin equipment." For the men, there were "large toilets." Voters passed the measure by almost a two to one margin.

Despite county officials still waiting to move out of the old courthouse, the December 15, 1935 newspaper reported that "souvenir hunters, looking for keepsakes from the historic old building, got in some licks ahead of the wreckers yesterday, removing some floor tiling, some stairway bannister heads and other pieces such as slats from balustrades." While the court was considering which firm to hire to raze the building, Jack Mollard in the December 17, 1936 *Oregon City Enterprise* suggested turning the building over to the army of souvenir hunters, who "could do the work in three days" at no cost to the county. Envisioning the "royal battle" over the statue of Justice, he speculated that someday, someone would tell the story that 'By cracky, I'm proud of that stone. . . . Maw had me polish it up and put it over the mantle where we could always look at it. I had to knock down seven fellers before I got away with it.'"

In January of 1936, a small gathering at the old courthouse came to watch Frank Glennon, the same mason who had cut the cornerstone, open it fifty-two years later. Unfortunately, the copper box in the stone had loosened, and much of its contents were deteriorated. The January 9, 1936 newspaper reported that one of the speakers at the event, J.E. Hedges, stated that the old building reminded him of "a body from which the soul has fled."

Approximately one thousand people gathered to watch the members of the Masonic fraternal group perform the cornerstone ceremony in September 1935, and about two thousand gathered for the building dedication six months later. As part of the celebration, the March 21, 1937 *Oregon City Enterprise* listed "Interesting Facts On New Courthouse Taken From Record," which noted that the building was constructed with 20,000 sacks of cement, 350,000 board feet of Clackamas County-grown and manufactured lumber, and 90,000 bricks from Yamhill County. More importantly, as a PWA project geared to create employment, the project required 83,121 hours of labor, and the average wage was 0.956 cents per hour, "one of the highest in the state."

The Courthouse Today

THE SETTING OF THE CLACKAMAS COUNTY courthouse is unique in Oregon. One block east, Singer Creek Falls drops down the bluff, producing a natural sound in an urban environment. Along the Willamette River behind the courthouse block, the Oregon City Transportation Company steamer once had a landing for passengers and freight. Although this was gone by the time the present courthouse was erected, steps behind the courthouse still extend under McLoughlin Boulevard to the water.

While other Oregon courthouses typically have their own squares, the Clackamas County courthouse shares its block with other commercial buildings. An adjacent building to the north, now storage space, once was a theater that could seat almost a thousand people. A perfunctory stretch of grass with a few bushes along the front of the courthouse distinguishes

it from the other structures along Main Street. The site includes two memorials in the form of bronze tablets affixed to rocks. One commemorates the end of the Oregon Trail; the other, William U'ren, an Oregon City attorney who campaigned for Oregon's initiative and referendum laws, the direct primary, and the recall. (Doubtless, many politicians throughout the years have regretted the crafting of the recall.)

Because downtown Oregon City was already well developed by the time the courthouse was built, it is one of the youngest structures in the central business district. Constructed during the Depression, the courthouse exhibits a style which some informally call "P.W.A. Modern" because of its similarity with so many Public Works Administration buildings across the nation. The more formal interpretation of the courthouse's architectural style is Art Deco, based on its polychromatic facade and motifs such as the chevron which encircles the building above the second story windows.

The rear and sides of the Clackamas County courthouse, like those of most buildings, were generally left plain. *Credit: Alan Viewig*

Another characteristic of this and other Art Deco buildings is stylistic sculpture. A reporter in the March 20, 1937 *Oregon City Enterprise* rationalized this expense during the Depression by saying the sculptures were not "useless trimmings" but had a purpose. The stone eagles surmounting the columns were to remind elected officials that this was a free county, and that "they should exercise care in trespassing too far on the rights of the citizenry." The scales, the symbol of justice, "should inspire judges, juries and such to weigh carefully all evidence." Each man above the two piers was dubbed "The Old Man of the Mountain" or "Aztec sun god." Each holds an "All Seeing Eye" which "inspires the sheriff and other such peace officers to keep an omniscient eye on the county, quickly detecting any monkey business."

The most significant alteration to the building has been the raising of the front of the roof when the former jail was converted to courtrooms in 1959. Other changes have included an awning over the front entrance, which hides the metal door surround displaying another chevron pattern. The awning is now redundant; for security reasons, the side door on Eighth Street is the only public entrance to the building. Although two eagles on top of columns flank the entry, it is not as grand.

The metal detector just inside the entrance is one indication of the changes that the county has experienced over the years as its population has grown and the number of crimes has increased. Once the entire county administration fitted into this building; now county offices are spread over several structures across the town. The needs of the judicial department alone have increased from one courtroom to eight today.

Although the courthouse was initially projected to cost $200,000, expenses began to exceed the budget. With the approval of the PWA, the county eventually spent $273,000 on the courthouse. The county was able to keep the oak trim, terrazzo floor with rose speckles, and the pink-tinged Tennessee marble wainscot, all visible today in the lobby. Deschutes and Harney Counties, which tried but failed to receive PWA funding for their new courthouses, could not afford such lavish appointments in their buildings.

Furnishings from years ago, now largely overlooked, still connect the courthouse to an earlier time when local pride was more evident. A wooden suggestion box reading, "For Better County Government," is now obscured by a vending machine on the first floor lobby. A leather resting couch remains in the first floor women's restroom. Despite the bland remodeling in the once main courtroom, Room 1, a picture shows portraits of long-ago Oregon attorneys and judges with the label "Bench and Bar of Oregon-Pioneer and Distinguished Dead."

In the March 21, 1937 *Oregon City Enterprise*, the chief inspector for the PWA said that "it was one of the finest building jobs he had seen in his tour of such projects in the United States." Even the contractors described the marble work as "the best matched job [of the seams] they had ever seen." With many of the county offices moved to other quarters, a smaller section of the community enters the building, and now even fewer notice the workmanship of the courthouse.

The Clatsop County courthouse subtly conveys messages to those who stop to look. Every other pilaster displays a ledger, perhaps alluding to the county clerk's duty to record important events such as births and deaths. Above the words "Clatsop County," two horns of plenty signify abundance. *Credit: author*

Clatsop County

County Seat: Astoria
Courthouse Address: 749 Commercial Street
Year Completed: 1908
Architect: Edgar Lazarus
Date of County Formation: June 22, 1844

*"The exterior of the building is to be plain and
substantial, without any of the 'gingerbread' work
that is expensive and of no use."*

—*Astoria Daily Budget*, February 22, 1904

International container ships, fresh from their ocean voyage,
make their way past Astoria up the Columbia River to
Portland. Once, the land around Astoria was the focus of
attention, not Portland. High on Coxcomb Hill, the shaft of
the Astoria Column records the area's great events: Gray's
discovery of the Columbia River, the Lewis and Clark
expedition, and the Astor fur-trading endeavour. Unique
aspects of Astoria's later history can be seen elsewhere.
Uniontown and Uppertown resulted from the Scandinavian
immigrants who came to fish and work at the canneries. The
Victorian houses lining the hills suggest Astoria's former
maritime wealth. The downtown, replete with mid-1920s
concrete buildings, points to the 1922 fire. What is not visible
is Astoria's years of struggling as a town dependent on natural
resources with their fluctuating markets. Astoria today has a
rich past, but fishing and logging no longer provide abundant
prosperity.

The area's natural resources attracted John Jacob Astor, a
wealthy New York entrepreneur, who sent his men to establish

a fur trading post on the site of present-day Astoria in 1811. After the War of 1812 began, a Canadian from a rival fur trading organization, the Northwest Company, appeared at Astoria warning of the impending arrival of a British warship. Unprotected and fearing a British seizure, Astor's men agreed to sell the post's "furs and stock on hand" to their rivals. By the time the British arrived and "captured" the fort with a single sloop, it was already in friendly hands. Nevertheless, the British took down the still-flying American flag, and raised their own.

At the end of the war, seized land was to be exchanged, but England argued that the post should be excluded. The United States in turn contended that only the inventory had been sold, that the fort had been captured by the British military, and the American flag had been replaced. When the fort was finally returned to U.S. possession, Astor was no longer interested in his western venture. The fort remained in the hands of the Northwest Company, which later merged with the Canadian Hudson's Bay Company in 1821. After 1825, when the company's principal trading center moved to Fort Vancouver, Astoria gradually lost its early commercial significance.

In 1840, Methodist minister Reverend Joseph H. Frost and Soloman H. Smith, a teacher, constructed a mission on the Clatsop Plains. Soon other pioneers, hearing of the farming possibilities near the established settlement, moved to the area. At the request of the settlers, the legislature formed the Clatsop District (later county) out of a part of the larger Tuality District in June, 1844. Lexington, once located on the Clatsop Plains, was the designated county seat.

In the mid-1840s, John Shively, a civil engineer, claimed land along the bank of the Columbia River and surveyed an ambitious 121-block plat of a town he named Astoria. Journeying east to advocate U.S. possession of the land south of the Columbia, Shively also procured the commission of the first post office west of the Rocky Mountains. The federal government soon established the first custom house west of the Rocky Mountains just east of Shively's claim to handle the international ships entering the Columbia River.

As the population grew north of Lexington, Clatsop citizens began to debate moving the county seat. In February 1854,

John McClure, hoping to secure the courthouse on his property, filed an optimistic sixty-five-block plat on his land to the west of Shively's claim. As an incentive, he offered to donate two acres of land to the county for the new courthouse. Despite an offer of free land by yet another competitor, McClure won the county seat position in the election held in June 1854.

After establishing itself as the county seat, Astoria grew slowly with an economy based on exporting lumber and salted and pickled salmon. In the mid-1870s, salmon canning became widely accepted and Astoria began to grow. In 1876, Astoria had five canneries, but by 1883, the number had grown to twenty-four. Astoria's waterfront became lined with long sprawling buildings that extended out onto the river on piers, and several hundred fishing boats dotted the river at one time. According to the *Astoria Downtown Historical Resource Survey*, in 1891 the leading salmon packer, the Marshall J. Kinney Cannery, produced 67,000 cans, sixteen percent of the year's salmon catch. Kinney, with his three canneries, also owned 138 fishing boats. Three hundred men were needed to run his fleet. Astoria was the self-described "salmon capital of the world."

Initially, Chinese immigrants worked grueling hours at the cannery, but were barred from fishing in the river. Scandinavian immigrants soon labored in the canneries, but they were allowed to fish. Of the Scandinavians, those of Finnish descent were the largest group, comprising almost thirteen pecent of Clatsop County's population in 1905. While the Norwegians and Swedes typically lived in a small community east of Astoria called Uppertown, the Finns generally lived west of Astoria in Uniontown, named after the Union Packing Company. A subsequent Uniontown entity, the Union Fishermen's Co-operative Packing Company, was a business formed by two hundred fishermen. Their label, "Gillnetters Best," was once world famous.

Foreign sailers, adding more international flavor to the town, frequented the saloons and brothels. According to the *Astoria Sesquicentennial* official program, "Competition was keen among the latter [the brothels] and there were occasional price wars." Some local entrepreneurs also made money on shanghaiing; apparently any able-bodied man straying into the wrong side of town was not safe. Vera Whitney Gault wrote in *A Brief History of Astoria, Oregon* that one woman even sold her husband for two hundred dollars. Galt also related that shanghaiers once even jumped a local Methodist minister while he was in the belfry ringing the bells to call the faithful to evening prayer. His former profession, boxing, served him well and he was able to conduct the service in torn clothing.

Astoria's geography of a narrow strip of flat land lying between the river and steep hills limited its building placement. Astorians consequently constructed their structures on piers over the river, and tides rose and fell underneath a part of the Astoria business district. One resident recalled that "the tide coming up under the stores as far up . . . as 13th Street . . . made a good garbage dump as the tide carried out refuse, rotten vegetables from grocery stores, and whatever they didn't want."

After years of discussion and debate, the city began constructing a seawall in 1917. In the process, streets in the flat section were raised one story, making the ground floors of buildings effectively basements. Initial plans were to construct concrete retaining walls separating the blocks and streets above a sand fill, but taxpayers balked at the expense. Instead, many of the streets consisted of asphalt on top of a timber deck supported by girders and posts, with an open passageway remaining underneath the streets.

This inexpensive method proved to be the town's downfall. On December 8, 1922, a fire starting in a pool room quickly spread through the downtown. The mayor called fire departments as far away as Portland for assistance. When the flames were out, buildings on more than twenty-four downtown blocks had been destroyed. According to an Oregon Insurance Rating Bureau report, the open area under the streets was a significant factor in allowing the fire to spread rapidly. The report noted, "Analysis of the situation arouses surprise; not that the fire occurred but that it did not occur sooner."

Funds to assist in the rebuilding poured into the town; a descendant of the Astor family even sent $5,000. To prevent looting, the December 14, 1922 *Astoria Evening Budget* related, "The police department is watching every incoming train and boat to guard against disreputable characters gaining an entrance." The city council imposed an ordinance to license merchants, which allowed them to delay the approval of nonresidents coming to work. The December 14, 1922 newspaper predicted that this would give "Astoria men and firms an opportunity to regain their feet before being forced to meet the competition of outside rivals." While store owners had set up temporary quarters, the first permanent structure was started in early January. The January 8, 1923 edition stated that "architects are working day and night."

According to the reminiscence of one resident, after the fire, "Nobody received enough insurance from their fire loss, so it was a slow hard start for the merchants." In the 1930s, with declining salmon runs, Astoria canneries began packing tuna, and augmented the local stock with tuna caught in the west Pacific Ocean and shipped frozen to the town. During World War II, the economy was buoyed when the navy expanded its operations at the naval air station on Tongue Point. Log exporting gained prominence in the 1960s, and Astoria gained a new title when the August 7, 1966 *Oregonian*, called the town "the largest shipper of logs in the world."

Astoria's optimism during the 1920s showed both in its buildings and its advertising; the 1927 Polk directory for Portland carried an advertisement boasting that Astoria was the "New York of the Pacific."

Thirty years later, the October 25, 1996 *Oregonian* announced "Astoria's wood-shipping days are past." Although the canneries have long closed, the largest private employers in Astoria today are processors selling fresh and frozen fish. Many Astoria residents work at the paper mill at Wauna, the largest employer in the county. With such a rich, varied past, and a spectacular setting, the town is looking to tourism to bolster its economy.

Visiting the Seat of Clatsop County Government

AT THE SIXTH STREET VIEWING PLATFORM, one frequently sees dockside fishermen, but the massive canneries and the river crowded with gill-netters are part of the past. Behind the viewing deck, the 1894 M. J. Kinney building at 1 Sixth Street was once a cannery, replacing one that had been burned in a fire. The *Astoria Downtown Historic Resource Survey* reports that large mounds of melted tin cans, destroyed in the fire, still remain beneath the structure.

Fishing was a dangerous livelihood; in the August 1958 *Mainstream*, Kathleen Cronin wrote that Astoria had more widows per capita than any town on the Pacific Coast. On a memorial under the interstate bridge by Bay Street, fishermen and those connected with the river have their names etched in "Starbright Black" granite. Small phrases, such as "Gillnetter," "Commercial fisherman," or "Founder Union Fishermens Cooperative Packing Company," succinctly describe past lives, while a small anchor indicates a watery death. In addition to Swedish and Norwegian names, many are of Finnish descent.

Directly south of the memorial, Astoria Finns still gather at Suomi Hall at 244 West Marine Drive. Walter Mattila, writing in the May 1959 *Finlandia Pictorial*, called Astoria the "Helsinki of the Northwest." With so many Finnish emigrants, Astoria could support two halls. While the Suomi was for the church-goers, another hall for socialists stood in Uniontown until it burned in a 1923 fire.

After the 1922 downtown fire, rebuilding began quickly. The *Astoria Downtown Historic Resource Survey* found that more than sixty structures were built in 1923 and 1924, and since so many were constructed within a very short period, the buildings are homogeneous in style. Many have concrete, fire-proof exteriors with parapets and mezzanine windows. Commercial Street remained the main business street, but several important structures were rebuilt on adjoining streets, such as the Labor Temple at 934 Duane Street.

Astoria has a long labor history. The Columbia River Fishermen's Protective Union, organized in 1884, is one of the oldest unions in the Northwest and once had offices in the

Labor Temple; they now are located at 322 Tenth Street. Unions made up of pile drivers, meat cutters, and motion picture operators also had offices in the second floor, while the third-floor ballroom was used for strike meetings and contract explanations. As Joyce Morrell wrote in the fall 1991 *Cumtux*, Astoria's Labor Temple "stands as a monument to the working man, past and present."

With the streets widened after the fire, new structures such as the Labor Temple were built to the new lot lines. The exterior walls of the 1916 Young Building at 1360–1380 Commercial Street were a survivor of the fire, and today the second story hangs over the sidewalk while the first floor is in line with its neighbor. The street widening also required the reconfiguration of the foundation for the Hotel Astoria at 342 Fourteenth Street, which had just been completed before the fire. As a sign of faith in the future of the town after the conflagration, the investors added more rooms. Today, this eight-story, former long-struggling hotel, now an apartment building, is reputed to be the tallest commercial structure on the Oregon Coast.

Hotel rooms facing north toward the river had a view of the hills in Washington State and the ferry landing at the end of Fourteenth Street. Responding to the increasing automobile traffic, Captain Frizt Elfving, a Swedish immigrant, began transporting cars across the river in 1921. In 1932, after a competitor drove pilings in front of the landing, the captain rammed into them with one of his ferries. Fittingly, the floating debris disabled his competitor's ferry for several days. Ferry service was discontinued after the interstate bridge opened in 1966.

A History of the Courthouse

THE FIRST COURTHOUSE, A WOOD-FRAME structure with a gable roof, was built in 1855. In addition to county matters, the townspeople also used the building as a theater, ballroom, and church. After the building had served for almost forty years, the January 31, 1891 *Morning Astorian* called the building "a disgrace to the city." At that time, the commissioners

An early view of the courthouse before mementos were added to the square and the side entrance was removed. *Author's collection.*

contemplated building a new courthouse on a more prestigious hillside site with a view.

Officials delayed action until 1902, when they began interviewing architects. They selected Edgar Lazarus, who later would design the Morrow County courthouse and the Vista House in the Columbia Gorge. By March of 1904, Lazarus had the plans ready, and on August 23 of that year the county dedicated the two-ton cornerstone. Festivities included a parade that started from the Masonic hall and wound its way to the courthouse. After the dedication ceremony, the people returned home, doubtless thinking that the courthouse would be completed within the next year.

Construction halted abruptly three months later. The county had sold warrants to fund the courthouse construction, so it had exceeded the state limit of allowable debt. The warrants were deemed worthless and the construction contract illegal. In order to resume work on the building, the legislature passed a bill to increase the ceiling on the county's debt, but several Astoria business owners filed a suit with the Oregon Supreme Court challenging the new law. The court decided that the new law was unconstitutional. The April 25, 1905 *Astoria Daily Budget* noted that Multnomah County also was operating well over its legal debt limit, but Multnomah was allowed to do so "because she has no moss backs possessed of such infinitesimal souls that they are ever ready to block any public improvement unless there is a graft in it for them." The newspaper went on to lament, "our prospects of securing a new public building in Clatsop County have faded into the distant future."

In July of 1906, the Clatsop County court ordered that the courthouse's basement windows be boarded up until the funds to complete the building could be raised. In August, the newspaper reported a plan in which local property owners would finish the building and lease it to the county for three years until sufficient tax money was raised.

The March 9, 1906 St. Helens *Oregon Mist* reported, "The Grand Jury in Clatsop County finds that the county road master is a partner in the Astoria Crushed Rock Company. The company furnishes crushed rock to the county and the road master approves the bill. Great system."

The county court finally was able to raise the money through a special levy. A few days before officials awarded the contract to complete the construction, the January 2, 1907 *Astoria Daily Budget* reported that the delay had cost an additional $30,000. The reason for this, according to the newspaper, was "because a few knockers saw fit to take advantage of an antiquated provision in the state constitution which the people in other counties in the state have ignored for years." In February 1908, almost four years after the plans were ready, the courthouse finally was completed.

The Courthouse Today

THE BLOCKS ADJACENT TO THE COURTHOUSE are linked to significant aspects of Astoria's past. The 1922 fire had burned out in the court yards of the courthouse and the post office directly north. The post office building also displays the words "Custom House," tying it to Astoria's position as having both the first post office and custom house west of the Rocky Mountain.

Parking lots, including one used by the county, occupy the block directly west of the post office. For years the *Toveri*, a socialist newspaper, was printed in one of the wood-frame buildings lining the street. This paper had subscribers in all states west of the Mississippi except the Dakotas, and besides advocating socialist ideals, it printed reports from various Finnish communities in America. Just as the paper was shutting down in 1931, government authorities arrested six men associated with the paper in order to deport them for their "subversive" ideas.

Mementos on the courthouse square also tie it to the area's history. On the northeast corner of the block, a plaque on a concrete bench commemorates Civil War soldiers from Clatsop who fought on the Union side. The Japanese World War II howitzer cannon standing directly behind the bench appears ready to protect anyone who stops to rest. Similar to many on courthouse grounds, this World War II cannon replaced a World War I cannon melted for scrap metal during World War II. On the northwest corner of the site, a colossal Douglas-fir log, over ten feet in diameter, represents the old-growth trees once plentiful in the county. When installed in 1937, this log was from a tree estimated to be 624 years old, making it 179 years old when Christopher Columbus landed in the Americas.

Near the rear parking lot stands a two-story jail constructed in 1914. Even a jail could not go unadorned, and the county embellished it with classical elements such as a dentils and a pediment. Closed in 1976, it is believed to be the longest operating free-standing jail in Oregon. Today, the structure is used for storage.

The Clatsop County courthouse has an American Renaissance style, as evidenced by its symmetrical design, flat roof, and smooth-dressed exterior materials. The courthouse's brick, however, varies in color on the southwest corner above the first floor, probably because of the work stoppage. When the county resumed building, the original brick manufacturer was reportedly out of business, forcing the county to buy from a different firm unable to match the shade exactly.

Terra cotta encircles the window frames and embellishes the bases and capitals of the pilasters. Some capitals display a unique ornament—a clerk's ledger—alluding to a basic county function. The greatest concentration of terra cotta moldings, however, is above the front entrance. Under the pediment, two

horns-of-plenty, signifying abundance, flank the words "A. D. 1904"—the year construction was started. Below the words "Clatsop County," a lion's head, commonly used to symbolize authority, gazes at the citizens entering the courthouse. A terra cotta garland, another symbol of abundance, hangs just above the front door opening.

It is common to incorporate symbols into the architecture of courthouses.
Credit: author

The two gray marble pilaster shafts framing the front entrance appear to clash with the tan tones of the brick and terra cotta, but they do provide an introduction to the marble inside the building. In the hallway, marble extends up almost eight-and-a-half feet to the top of the doorways, and marble tile covers the floor, sometimes slippery during Astoria's frequent rainy weather. Even the lone table, standing in the center of the hallway, has a matching marble base.

Although the original plans show unusual arched ceilings similar to a Gothic cathedral, the large beams dividing the ceiling doubtless provided a lower-cost finish.

A memorial made of metal from the U.S.S. Maine, commemorating those who died in the Spanish-American War, is on one wall near the front entrance. Another memorial, this one to good marksmanship, is the elk and deer heads hanging on the wall. A large moose head also once hung on the wall. Judge Johnson, now deceased, was known to place unlit cigarettes in its mouth.

Judge Johnson presided in the district courtroom when it was located on the first floor, instead of its present site in the basement. According to a retired judge, "to calm everybody down" during the typically tense court proceedings, Johnson kept a jar of candy on his bench which he would solicitously offer to the witnesses, prosecutors, and defendants. Perhaps as another soothing measure, he kept a cat in the courtroom.

After the fire, insurance adjustors and three of the city's four banks occupied space in the courthouse. After the courthouse closed each day, according to the December 14, 1922 *Astoria Evening Budget*, a "competent" sailor with a "very competent" machine gun guarded the banks' money. The newspaper noted, "These are trying times, but there's one place in the city that people had better not be trying."

Perhaps the banks used the clerk's large two-story vault, which has an ancient elevator to access the basement. The February 27, 1947 *Astoria Evening Budget* reported that one night an employee locked the vault door at closing time, failing to note that the clerk and immigrations examiner were in the basement. An hour later, children playing on the courthouse lawn heard shrill sounds emitting from a ventilator. Aided by the city police and others, the two men were finally released. The county clerk was heard to say, "There'll be no 'keep off the grass' signs posted on the courthouse lawn this year, if I can help it."

Situations unique to Astoria have occurred at the courthouse. When Oscar Mannisto, the *Toveri* printer, was held pending deportation, the September 19, 1934 *Astoria Evening Budget* reported that a large crowd gathered at the courthouse,

including "a number openly affiliated with the Communist party." The group asked the county court for food and medicine for his wife and children, but were told there was nothing the court could do. The crowd dispersed, only to return later and learn that arrangements for food had been made through the Red Cross. Mrs. Mannisto was apparently so desperate, according to the newspaper, that she "was in a highly hysterical state and wept during most of the proceedings."

Even the newel post had to be extravagant in the Clatsop County courthouse.
Credit: author

Oak newels flank the grand staircase at the far end of the main hallway. At the stairway landing, a large window frames the Flavel House, which the Summer 1991 *Cumtux* called "one of the finest surviving examples of this type of [Queen Anne style] architecture in the Pacific Northwest." Captain George Flavel, who had the house built, was the first licensed Columbia River bar pilot and was referred to in the *Cumtux*

Excluding the spectators' benches, the original furniture in this courtroom was carefully coordinated, such as the Ionic columns on the judge's bench matching the Ionic pilasters on the wall. *Credit: Alan Viewig*

as "Astoria's own version of J. P. Morgan and John D. Rockefeller."

The courthouse originally featured a copper and glass dome, which was removed in 1958 when it became too costly to maintain. Although the building appears complete from the exterior, the hallway ceiling shows a circular outline now covered with boards. Another skylight, elliptical in shape, was located in the circuit courtroom.

The decoration in this county courtroom makes it one of the most elegant in Oregon. On the walls, pairs of Ionic pilasters, standing above the marble wainscot, feature a clam shell in their capitals, perhaps alluding to the nearby Pacific Ocean. Molding continues above the pilasters, curving at the coved ceiling to join the ceiling beams. Somewhat lessening the courtroom dignity are the baby blue acoustical tiles covering not only the ceiling but the walls.

Excluding the pew-like spectator benches, the oak furniture is subtly matched. The Ionic columns forming the legs of the table for the plaintiff and defendant conform to those on the judge's bench. The fret design on the pedestal on the panel behind the judge's bench corresponds with that on the side of the jury box. Despite the elegant furnishings, the county has constructed a needed "temporary office" out of wood paneling in one corner of the room.

When the courthouse was completed, Astoria was the third largest city in the state; today, it is the forty-first largest. Throughout the town, clues to Astoria's former economic prosperity can be found in its Victorian houses and its rebuilt downtown buildings. The courthouse, with its matching courtroom furniture, marble walls, and oak finish also tells of Astoria's former greatness.

Columbia County's courthouse was constructed on the bank so that people sailing up and down the river could catch a glimpse of it. Although the front of the building faces the street, the architects replicated the building's front on the rear to fool river travelers.
Credit: author

Columbia County

County Seat:	St. Helens
Courthouse Address:	Plaza Square
Year Completed:	1907
Architectural Firm:	Hendricks and Tobey
Date of County Formation:	January 16, 1854

> *"[St. Helens] is the county seat. The noble structure rising on the river's bank settles that question forever."*
>
> —*Oregon Mist,* August 17, 1906

From Portland to St. Helens, Highway 30 winds past industrial warehouses and cargo docks, mobile homes and houseboats, truck farms and vacant fields. Along the way, the road also passes the ghosts of river towns—towns that tried and failed to overtake Portland's early lead in the race to become the region's metropolis. Two of these places, St. Johns and Linnton, now are only neighborhoods of Portland, their roles as separate villages mostly forgotten. Others, like Milton, have disappeared. But St. Helens, which also lost to Portland, survived to develop a distinct identity as a city and as a county seat.

In the mid-1840s, as waves of American settlers arrived, farming increased in the Willamette and Tualatin valleys, and trade with other places such as San Francisco became important in boosting the region's prosperity. Because water transportation was still the easiest, fastest, and least expensive method of freighting produce and goods, villages sprang up wherever boats could be loaded and unloaded easily. Soon local

Henry Knighton was a flamboyant, gregarious person. Even the local newspaper, *Oregon Mist*, once described the founder of its town as "active, dashing and speculative," and wrote that "he went to parties and gave parties." One major social event of 1846 was his gala celebration of Washington's birthday, to which he invited British soldiers from nearby Fort Vancouver even though Britain and the United States were disputing the ownership of the Oregon Territory. In 1848, despite his arrival in the Northwest only three years earlier, he was well connected enough to be appointed marshal of the Oregon provisional government.

business people realized that if their town became the metropolis, their businesses would flourish and their land values would rise.

One such business person was Henry Knighton, an immigrant of 1845 who owned a hotel in Oregon City and a ferry service across the Willamette River. Knighton knew that if he started a town that grew to be "the metropolis," he would become far wealthier by selling town lots than by running a hotel or a ferry service. The site he selected was the present-day St. Helens on the Columbia River, which had outstanding potential as a natural deep-water port. To design his grand city, Knighton hired surveyor P. W. Crawford and Army artist W. H. Tappan. However, apparently neither the surveyor nor the artist knew the site well, for they laid out the blocks in a perfect grid, disregarding the area's rocky outcroppings and irregular terrain that would make through streets an impossibility except on paper. Knighton's city contained more than 2,600 lots on 143 blocks—grander than Portland, which had started with a mere sixteen blocks.

After his city was surveyed, Knighton concentrated on improving its transportation routes so that farmers could easily bring their goods directly to his dock. Portland had already established this advantage by building a wagon road to the Tualatin Valley, but the long and difficult route consisted of many stretches that were no more than ruts through the forest. In the summer of 1850, Knighton joined Captain Nathaniel Crosby and Thomas H. Smith, developers of the nearby town of Milton, to construct another wagon road, one from St.

Helens and Milton to the Tualatin Valley. Portland leaders soon announced plans to build a railroad to the Tualatin Valley, and Knighton and his colleagues publicized their intention to do the same. However, neither railroad was undertaken.

Road and rail routes from the valley to the wharf were important, but so were shipping routes from the wharf to other parts of the country. When Knighton persuaded the Pacific Steamship Company to move the northern terminus of its San Francisco run from Portland to St. Helens, he finally seemed to have the winning edge. Without a shipping route to the major markets in California, Portland definitely would be second to St. Helens. However, Portland's leading citizens convinced another company to provide regular service to San Francisco, and goods continued to be shipped, causing demand at the terminal in St. Helens to fall short of local expectations. When Pacific Steamship officials decided to end their run at Portland, the battle was over.

In the 1870s, Charles and James Muckle bought a St. Helens sawmill at a sheriff's sale and began expanding its business. The sawmill burned in the 1904 fire which destroyed most of the business district, and was not rebuilt. The March 8, 1907 *Oregon Mist* fretted over the town's lack of a sawmill: "And still St. Helens is without a mill. Why? Here is the finest mill site between Portland and Astoria. . . . It is probable that if one is not put in here within the next year, that there never will be a saw mill on the old site."

The newspaper had no cause to worry. In 1908, two wealthy brothers from San Francisco, Hamlin and Charles McCormick, started a lumber mill at the end of First Street on the site of the old mill. Because the McCormicks required a riverside location and considerable acreage, the city fathers closed several streets south of the downtown and dedicated the land to the mill.

With jobs plentiful at the mill, the population in St. Helens more than doubled from 258 in 1900 to 742 in 1910, and then almost tripled to 2,220 in 1920. The McCormicks started several other related businesses, including a ship-building facility for transporting their lumber, and a broom handle plant utilizing the scrap wood. The legacy of one McCormick endeavor, a pulp and paper mill, remains by far the largest private employer in St. Helens today. The McCormicks were instrumental in transforming St. Helens from a struggling village to "Payroll City," its nickname for several decades.

The August 17, 1906 *Oregon Mist* prophesied that "St. Helens is . . . sure to become in time a manufacturing village." The forecast came true, as today St. Helens has attracted several other industrial companies. Ironically, given St. Helens's old rivalry, many residents now travel to Portland for employment.

Visiting the Seat of Columbia County Government

FROM A PLANNING PERSPECTIVE, ST. HELENS is a rarity among towns in Oregon because First Street, its main street, comes to an abrupt dead end at the Boise Cascade veneer plant, the descendant of the old McCormick mill. The mill and the wealth it brought into the community shaped today's downtown, which now provides a glimpse of how a main street in a small town would have appeared before the onset of the Great Depression.

Although First Street businesses have suffered from the competition along Highway 30 to the west, one can still see the institutions that were the cornerstone of a small town. The two-story Masonic Lodge building at 231 S. First Street was considered "an ornament to the town." The 1928 movie theater in St. Helens, appropriately named the Columbia, was proclaimed by Swepson Morton in the June 23, 1939 *St. Helens Sentinel-Mist*, "as good as any in cities of similar size in the state." (The same issue printed an advertisement from the theatre stating, "No show is too good for the Columbia.") Despite the pulp and paper workers union now occupying a former bank quarters, the structure at 230 S. First Street displays a false sense of permanence by declaring "First National Bank" above the door.

The former courthouse once occupied a central position along First Street before it was sold and the land converted to a plaza. A 1911 Sanborn map shows that the block facing north toward the plaza served as the hub for town services; here stood the post office, telegram office, and a public library. A basalt-clad bank, at 265 Strand Street, was constructed in 1908 just

after the courthouse, but the bank failed during the Depression and the city hall later moved into the structure. Near the corner of the building at Plaza and Strand Street, the 1894 Columbia River flood forced a druggist to load his merchandise on a fisherman's scow and tie it to an oak tree there. He conducted his business with customers who rowed to his "floating drug store."

Movie theaters standing on main streets still draw residents to the downtown. *Credit: author*

From the very start, the McCormick mill stimulated local businesses, as the first section of the 1908 Orcadia Hotel at 30 Cowlitz Street and the 1909 St. Helens Hotel Annex at 71 Cowlitz Street both were constructed to house workers building the mill. Later, these facilities undoubtedly housed many of the single mill employees.

After the 1904 downtown fire, the town rebuilt first along Strand Street. Although the buildings on the east side of Strand Street now are gone, a 1921 Sanborn map shows that more than ten buildings, including a creamery, undertaker, and confectionery store, once stood on pilings built over the water. Today, land on the east side of the street is owned by the plant, which uses it for log storage. Further north, today's restroom facilities just south of the courthouse have a dubious ancestry. The 1921 map shows restrooms built on pilings over the river; apparently, the sewage went directly into the Columbia.

A History of the Courthouse

WHEN THE TERRITORIAL GOVERNMENT FORMED Columbia County in 1854, St. Helens was not made the county seat; that honor was given to Milton. However, the Columbia River repeatedly flooded that town, and in 1862 the citizens moved the records to St. Helens, thereby informally designating it the county seat. Officials occupied a rented building, and county business apparently was low key. According to Judge McBride in the June 7, 1907 *Oregon Mist*, the clerk "lived out in the county and came and went in a boat. If he missed a day now and then, nobody noticed it."

For the first courthouse, the county purchased in 1870 a combined store and dwelling that stood on the present-day plaza. In 1903, talk of a new courthouse led to a vote as to whether to move the county seat. Four towns—St. Helens, Rainier, Clatskanie, and Vernonia—wanted the honor, but when neither of the top contenders, St. Helens and Rainier, received a clear majority, a run-off was held.

On the day of the election, St. Helens women served an all-day dinner with roasts, beans, biscuits, pies, and cakes, all provided by local sawmill owners. The St. Helens *Sentinel-Mist Columbia County Progress Report—1939 to 1949* related that "the story is told that Rainier attempted to import voters as hands on the steamer *Iralda*, which made the round trip to Portland each day, but that they were taken off at St. Helens, induced to vote for this place and kept here till the polls were closed." The ploy worked and St. Helens was victorious.

County debt delayed the construction of a new courthouse, but undoubtedly St. Helens residents were relieved when they read in the January 12, 1906 *Oregon Mist* that officials had decided to proceed with building the new quarters. The newspaper stated that the delay had "afforded a pretext to interested parties to urge the commissioners to delay as long as possible, with the hope that enough dissatisfaction could be created to create a demand for another county seat election." Perhaps to appease readers outside of St. Helens, the newspaper also noted "Columbia County will at last have a public building of which it can be proud, instead of a miserable old shack [the old courthouse]."

The February 16, 1906 issue reported "County Court met Wednesday (St. Valentine's Day), and the people are hoping the valentine will be a fine new courthouse." The residents did receive their valentine, as the court soon chose the architects and accepted the bids. A planning committee for the cornerstone dedication ceremony soon decided to serve a dinner of roast beef, boiled ham, and lemonade. To finance the celebration, two men contributed a total of $220, but more money was needed. The July 27, 1906 newspaper promised as an incentive that if others donated money, "after the celebration there will be a detailed statement made of receipts and expenditures."

More than a thousand people attended the ceremony in August, 1906, many coming by train from Portland, Scappoose, Astoria, Rainier, and other towns. Governor George Chamberlain, journeying to St. Helens on a steamer filled with prominent Portland business people, gave one of

It is relatively common to see residents proudly standing in front of their courthouse in older photographs. *Collection of Donald Kalberer*

the principal addresses. More than six hundred dined at the huge banquet. According to the August 17, 1907 *Oregon Mist*, "The arrangements for the dinner were entirely in the hands of the ladies, and it is simple justice to say that they were as near perfection as mortals ever get." Boats raced on the Columbia, and residents and guests danced until midnight at two balls.

Construction continued on the building over the next seven months, and the court finally accepted the new courthouse on March 6, 1907. At the first circuit court proceedings, the June 7, 1907 *Oregon Mist* recounted that Judge Thomas McBride spoke about a time in the not-so-distant past when officials lived out in the country and journeyed to St. Helens only on Saturday to transact business. At one time, the county "had no jail and very little use for one." McBride related one story concerning an otherwise outstanding citizen who had pled guilty to assault with a deadly weapon. The judge, pronouncing the sentence, stated, "It is the judgement of the court that you be imprisoned for a period of three months but as there is no jail in this county and the jail in Multnomah County is full already, you will go home to your farm and consider yourself in jail there. . . . At the end . . . come down and report to the sheriff and get discharged from the jail."

The Courthouse Today

THE COURTHOUSE, THE FOCAL POINT of the downtown, is visually connected to First Street by the grass- and tree-covered plaza that serves as the courthouse square. Around the plaza, a small one-way street gives automobiles access to the courthouse in a manner similar to a grand circular driveway. The plaza, outfitted with several wooden benches, the usual flagpole, and a retired fog bell, now is generally vacant, unused by tenants living in the nearby apartment buildings and ignored by strolling pedestrians. During hot summer months, an occasional group of teenagers congregates in the plaza, or a gaggle of county workers eats lunch in the shade.

When the courthouse opened, it likely was the first building in St. Helens with a basalt exterior. Because of the 1904 fire,

The plaza acts as a great front lawn for the Columbia County courthouse, and contains a memento usually found on a courthouse square. *Credit: author*

the county court had wanted a sturdy, fire-resistant building that would help protect the official records. A quarry located one-half mile away provided the basalt, which was cut into blocks of varying sizes.

The courthouse exhibits aspects of the Georgian style with its windows with fan-shaped transoms on the second floor and its classically styled columns on the porch. Parts of the building appear ill-fitting, such as the oversized dentils on the building and porch cornice. Although the tower appeared in a 1906 newspaper sketch, its pyramid-shaped roof with the gable-roofed clock faces make it seem dissimilar in style to the rest of the building.

Overall, the courthouse design is not extravagant, indicating that the county had limited funds when it was constructed. The total cost was $35,795, but the March 8, 1907 *Oregon Mist* boasted that it was "doubtful if the building could have been built for less than $50,000 anywhere but here." The newspaper also went on to say that the basement jail was solidly constructed, as "anyone who goes to the trouble of getting locked up in the jail will have a good substantial place to reside."

Although materials typically are economized on a building's rear, the Columbia County courthouse expenditures included designing the back to replicate the front. When the building was constructed, the Columbia River still was an important transportation route and those who viewed the courthouse from the river could see only the rear elevation. The January 12, 1906 newspaper proclaimed that the courthouse "will be about the first handsome edifice the newcomer to Oregon will see. It will attract favorable attention to our county, and convince the newcomer that there is life and enterprise here."

When the courthouse opened, the March 8, 1907 newspaper proudly stated that it featured "steam heat and was equipped with hot and cold water throughout." The sewer line ran from the building to the river, a fact noted by one local vagrant named Captain Rivers. According to one story, during Prohibition local officials were pouring wine down the urinal when somebody heard a noise out behind the courthouse. There was Captain Rivers at the sewage outlet with cup in hand.

Some items of upkeep—removing the Christmas lights, rebuilding a leaning retaining wall, adequately repairing crumbling mortar—have been delayed or overlooked as the county has struggled to find tax dollars. However, the county decided to keep the courthouse when they built the annex in the late 1960s immediately to the north. Today, almost all of the county offices are in the newer building, and only the parole and juvenile services departments, both serving those with specific needs, occupy the formerly busy first floor of the courthouse. Evident to a visitor by the supermarket-type front doors, the historic atmosphere in the main hallway is gone. The March 8th, 1907 *Oregon Mist*, though sparse on the interior description, did mention the Oregon fir, oak stained and varnished, which is now painted gray.

Due to more recent fire regulations, the central stairway, usually a striking feature in a courthouse's hallway, now is hidden behind a wall. The delicate balustrade and round newel cap, over seven inches in diameter, attest that such woodwork was not meant to be hidden from view. Renovation has not extended to the second floor, where a sense of the original building still prevails. Much of this is attributable to an increase in the hallway dimensions: high ceilings, wide hallways, tall doorways. Off the hallway, the women's restroom overlooks the Columbia River and provides an exceptional view.

The judge's chamber once was furnished with the original horsehair couch, which has been described by a retired judge, Donald Kalberer, as both "historic and historically uncomfortable." The chamber includes a balcony that faces the Columbia River, an amenity that has helped speed up the judicial process. Kalberer related that when two attorneys wanted to settle a case, he would send them out on the balcony under the guise of privacy, but the often cold and rainy weather would motivate them to form an agreement quickly.

In the early days when Kalberer was judge, the men's restroom was in the basement. During breaks in a trial, men would race down two flights of stairs, in the hopes of reaching the lavatory before the bailiff closed it off for the jury's use. In a 1991 television interview, he matter-of-factly discussed the original porcelain urinals as being so tall that "you could stand there and your chin would almost rest on the top of them. And every time I used those restrooms, I loved those old urinals because I often thought when they dig this building out of the rubble a thousand years from now, someone is going to say, 'God, those men were big in those days.'"

Although the men's restroom arrangement has been altered, the courtroom is generally true to its original appearance. The color scheme of the courtroom was kept simple with ivory

Judge Kalberer also owned a pizza parlor on First Street, where he would occasionally serve as the delivery driver. One time, after approving a search warrant that day, he went to his restaurant to pick up a pizza to deliver and "darned if it wasn't the same address as the search warrant. So I knew if I didn't get there before the police, I wouldn't get paid for my pizza. I hopped in my car and scooted over there, and was glad not to see any police cars when I drove up!"

The furnishings are modest in the original courtroom. The plaintiff and the defendant share the same table (which can make it difficult to confer confidentially with one's attorney) and the distance between the jury, witness, and judge is minimal. On the left stands a brass spittoon.
Credit: Alan Viewig

white walls against dark stained fir pilasters, ceiling beams, and window surrounds. Other touches, such as bentwood coat racks and an old clock behind the judge's desk, add to the room's character. The original jury chairs and spectator benches, not ornate by turn-of-the-century standards, testify to the county's thrift. However, proper respect for the court was still important. In the railing, one of the posts is hollow with a removable top that reportedly held the deputy's weapon during trials.

While the judge in the 1908 Clatsop courthouse has a wooden panel behind the bench to emphasize his or her stature, the wall behind the judge here is not so adorned. The architects, however, used the Columbia River as the backdrop by placing the judge's bench between two windows with fan-shaped heads. The windows also provide a diversion during trial: if the proceedings become slow, one can appear to be paying attention yet gaze out the window.

The courtroom evokes memories for those who worked there over the years. One retired judge tried a case there as a young attorney and vividly remembers the courtroom as sparse. "The windows were open, and it seemed like everyone had hay fever. The chairs were old and not too comfortable." Another long-time St. Helens attorney recounted in the 1991 television interview that "in those days, a lot of the lawyers and some of the judges and most of the juries chewed tobacco . . . and sometimes during the trial you wouldn't get back to your seat or anything, so if the plug got a little old and stale you kind of backed up to the radiator . . . and while the judge was talking to the jury or other lawyers, you'd slip that tobacco out and drop it behind the radiator." Stories are also told about several visiting judges who leaned back in the chair during trial, failed to catch their feet on the desk, and tipped over.

The 1912 *Oregon Almanac* stated that the "court house, three-story brick business block and new bank building would be a credit to a much larger city." Today, St. Helens is a larger city, but the courthouse remains the center of the old town and its 20th-century history. From one of the courtroom windows, a visitor can easily dream of the past when puffing steamers transported freight up and down the river, newly cut lumber was loaded onto locally made ships, and tired mill workers leaving their shift swarmed the streets.

Instead of traditional Greek-styled capitals, the Linn County courthouse pilasters exhibit five-pointed stars, which allude more to the federal presence. *Credit: author*

Linn County

County Seat:	Albany
Courthouse Address:	300 Fourth Avenue S.W.
Year Completed:	1940
Architectural Firm:	Tourtellotte & Phillips
Date of County Formation:	December 28, 1847

*"We don't need a new court house. What good
would it do but to enable the people of the county
to puff up with pride."*

— Former Senator S. Garland, quoted in the
Albany Democrat-Herald, February 16, 1937

T he latter part of the 19th century profoundly shaped the Albany of today. Exuberantly decorated cast-iron buildings from that time period line the numerous downtown blocks. South of the downtown, Victorian houses occupy the many residential blocks. Optimistic over the railroad and the new canal system, the 1878 city directory boasted that in ten years, Albany would be a town of ten to thirteen thousand people, which would have made it the second largest in Oregon. The expansion moderated, and Albany never became a leading city. The building legacy, however, gave the town three National Historic Districts, one for the downtown, and two named after the early settlers, Monteith and Hackleman.

In 1845, Abner Hackleman reserved two donation land claims on the southern bank of the Willamette River, and after asking Hiram Smead to hold them, returned to Iowa to bring his family out west. Although Abner died on the return journey, his son, Abraham, secured one of the claims. Within a year,

Smead sold the other claim to Walter Monteith, formerly of Albany, New York, for $400 and a cayuse pony. Walter's brother, Thomas, took up a claim directly west of his property.

The Monteiths platted the seventy-one-block Albany townsite in 1850, naming it after their former place of residence. A general store opened in the townsite, but the proprietor soon sold his stock to L. C. Burkhart, who then moved the store to Hackleman's claim. The Monteiths knew if they were going to have a town, they needed a store, and so joined with a partner to purchase goods in San Francisco. The mercantile was not the only Monteith venture; they also erected a flour mill near the confluence of the Calapooia and the Willamette Rivers. A steamboat soon docked near their mill, providing a new transportation route for Willamette Valley products.

One of the original requirements of securing title under the 1850 Donation Land Claim Act was that one live on the land for four years. Although Thomas and Walter lived in the same house, it straddled both their claims, thereby fulfilling the condition. According to lore, the dining table was placed so that when the two brothers had their meals, each was on his own claim. At dinner time, politics likely were discussed, for the Monteiths were both staunch Republicans.

Politics undoubtedly were a topic of conversation at the Hackleman house, for Abraham was a fervent Democrat. Hackleman also wanted to develop a town, which eventually was named Lower Albany. His supporters, however, persuaded the legislature to change the name of his town and Monteiths' to Takenah, an Indian name referring to the deep pool created by the Calapooia River where it joins the Willamette. Detractors protested

The Oregon Republican party started in Albany in 1856. In those early days, according to the August 25, 1948 *Albany Democrat-Herald*, "When victory came to the party, the torchlight parades which were then the vogue terminated on the corner of the lot where the Monteith home stood." The daughter of Thomas Monteith, Lottie Pipe, remembered that "her mother always placed lighted candles in the north and east windows of the house on these occasions as a welcome to the paraders."

that the town would become known as "hole in the ground." In 1855, both communities were renamed Albany.

Sawmills and flour mills developed on the river bank, and steamboats took their products to bigger markets. With the growing population, rival newspapers espousing divergent political beliefs started during the Civil War. Politics extended even to the schools. According to Dr. J. L. Hill in the November 25, 1925 *Albany Democrat-Herald*, when a Democratic school board hired a strongly Democratic teacher, Republicans started their own school in the Monteith area. Town leaders eventually settled their differences in order to incorporate the town, which reportedly had been delayed because of the dissimilar political beliefs. The government positions were equally divided between Democratic and Republican officials.

The residents apparently were able to reach a consensus in 1870 on the necessity of attracting the Oregon & California Railroad to their community. Ben Holladay, the railroad magnate, had threatened that his railroad was going to bypass Albany; when the residents raised $50,000, Holladay ran the railroad line through the town instead of locating it a few miles east.

Townspeople also raised $62,000 to finance a twelve-mile canal that ran from the Santiam River north of Lebanon to their town. Chinese laborers, who previously had worked on the railroad, dug the waterway, and numerous feeder lines soon branched off the main canal near the downtown. Power sources were critical, and the canal propelled Albany's industrial development. In 1878, approximately fourteen factory and mill turbines generated power from the canal. Dr. J. L. Hill in the November 25, 1925 *Albany Democrat-Herald* called the canal "the greatest enterprise ever engaged in by Albany people."

The town's location near the center of the Willamette Valley, with railroad lines soon extending in all four directions, earned Albany the title of "Hub City." Rail connections improved even further in 1912, when the electrical railway connected Albany to other points in the valley. The townspeople celebrated for two days, and a large picture of the line's owner, James J. Hill, hung amid bunting in the middle of a downtown street.

The population surged after World War II. Following the nationwide building boom, the August 25, 1948 *Albany Democrat-Herald* reported that the number of "modern" sawmills in the county grew from forty-nine in 1942 to ninety-three in 1947. In 1948, four large plywood mills were operating in the area, including one in Albany. With the timber industry becoming a powerful force in the Oregon economy after World War II, the same issue recognized that "the coming of the M and M Plylock division provided the impetus which started Albany on its way to becoming one of the leading cities of the valley."

Today Albany is the eighth-largest city in the Willamette Valley. The plywood mill has closed, and like other towns in Oregon, the expansionist times fueled by the timber industry did not last. A rare-metals manufacturer, Teledyne Wah Chang, is now the leading employer in the area (the plant is located in Millersburg, just north of the Albany city limits). Although Albany workers are employed with manufacturers of paper, frozen food, and mobile homes, many travel to other towns for employment.

Visiting the Seat of Linn County Government

VIEWED FROM THE PIER NEAR THE INTERSECTION of Water and Broadalbin streets, the Willamette River winds slowly past downtown Albany, making it easy to imagine steamboats plying lazily up and down the river. The Willamette, however, was more than just a source of commerce to Albany citizens, as it has played a part in the city's politics and entertainment. In 1861, local Democrats dumped a cannon into the river to thwart the Republicans who were going to fire it to celebrate an election victory. The cannon was finally discovered and raised by a dredging company in 1933. In 1908, thousands watched twenty-four Barnum and Bailey circus elephants frolic in the river after parading through the downtown. It took eight hours to round them up.

By the pier stands the oldest remaining river warehouse, the 1866 Avery Building at 213 Water Street. Now converted to offices, the structure first started as a warehouse, then became a flour mill for Willamette Valley wheat. In its long history, it also served as both a steamboat and a railroad ticket office.

An extension of the Albany-Lebanon canal once powered the Avery mill, just as one did the Albany Iron Works, a manufacturer of cast iron pieces that decorated many of the downtown buildings. Although bank structures tend to be conservative to suggest prudent money practices, the Flinn Building at 222 First Street S.W., constructed to house the First National Bank, displays an extravagance of cast-iron decoration. Between the second-story windows, garish faces with horn-like protrusions seemingly howl in pain. The window openings themselves are exaggerated with cast iron pieces, including pedimented hoods. This structure, like others on the block, is now noted for its embellishment, but such building styles were not always in fashion. Fred Nutting, writing in the November 7, 1936 *Albany Democrat-Herald* about the Flinn block in the 1890s, noted the structure was "characterized by artistic embellishments, then generally sought, now out of date."

Older buildings tend to be remodeled on the street level, so the best way to view them is to look up.
Credit: author

Cast-iron finery was even added to the Straney & Moore Livery Stable at 321 Second Street S.W. Carriages occupied the main floor, but horses were relegated to the basement with a grooved concrete floor to keep the horses on a sure footing. After the turn of the century, a hardware store moved into the building, and sold, among other things, "horseless carriages": Studebaker wagons. Today, the building stands on one of the few downtown blocks without a parking lot, thereby giving a sense of downtown Albany's earlier appearance.

Four blocks southwest runs the main branch of the Albany-Lebanon canal, although the roar of the water as it falls into the Calapooia River can be heard at least a block away. Water-powered industries are now a thing of the past, but a collection of red brick buildings, including the water treatment plant, stand by the canal at 300 Vine Street. Albany's drinking water still comes from this canal.

A History of the Courthouse

ALBANY WAS BARELY SETTLED WHEN the legislature created Linn County in 1847. The legislature named the new county after Missouri Senator Lewis Linn, a strong proponent of the American settlement of the land south of the Columbia River. Initially, officials met near present-day Brownsville before the legislature designated Albany as the county seat in 1851. The Monteiths proposed to donate ten acres to the county, which were resurveyed into lots and blocks and then sold to fund a courthouse. Three years later, the county constructed an octagonal-shaped courthouse that copied the design of a nearby Albany residence. Despite the standing courthouse, citizens from around the county remained agitated that the county seat location question had not been put to a popular vote. With so much public pressure, the legislature passed a bill that required the commissioners to appoint three citizens to select a new site which would compete with Albany in an election. The three selected the Raphael Cheadle homestead claim, a site about twelve miles southeast of Albany that was improved at the time with a single house.

Supporters of the Cheadle's site named it "Sand Ridge" and offered to donate lots so that the county could fund another courthouse, just as the Monteiths had done in Albany. As a ploy, Sand Ridge's champions had a load of lumber delivered to the site the day before the election, giving the appearance that building activity was already taking place. Their ruse was successful as Sand Ridge emerged the victor. The new county seat, however, was a town in name only, and according to the March 25, 1945 *Oregon Journal*, was "a lonely spot without inhabitants and with nothing to recommend it."

Architectural features such as turrets and towers were a subtle way to convey the message that this was a prosperous county. *Author's collection*

In order to sell Sand Ridge lots, an advertisement in the *Oregon Statesman* touted Sand Ridge's advantages, including the availability of several fine springs, but an episode in the summer helped kill Sand Ridge as the county seat. Colonel Lawrence Helm decided to have maneuvers of the Linn militia at the new county seat, and he unmercifully drilled the men in the hot summer sun. The "fine springs" had by that time dried up, and after the exercises were over, the parched men went home, undoubtedly cursing the location.

The county court tried to dispel the myth of no water by commissioning a well to be dug, but Albany factions continued their efforts to move the county seat back to their town. They finally succeeded as the legislature passed another bill in 1856 for an election to determine the county seat location. Sand Ridge, Brownsville, and Lebanon also contended for the honor, but Albany won by a small margin. Sand Ridge never became a legitimate town, and today the area is a cemetery.

The octagonal building once again served as the courthouse until it was destroyed by fire in 1861. The county constructed a second courthouse, this one of bricks, which featured a porch with two-story columns supporting a gabled pediment. In 1899, the county consulted architect Charles Burggraf about designing another addition to the courthouse. He later was quoted in the August 3, 1937 *Albany Democrat-Herald* as having advocated the construction of fire-proof vaults to protect the official records, but his advice was disregarded. Instead, the county wanted a third story and a clock tower. According to Burggraf, "Everyone was crazy at that time about town clocks . . . and Linn county had to get on the band wagon." A large, four-story high tower with a clock as well as a turret subsequently was added.

By the 1930s, the courthouse was showing its age. The August 3, 1937 newspaper speculated that with the wooden interior, the building could "become a roaring mass of flames." The floors sagged. Furthermore, "a few days ago one of the sash cords broke in one of the windows in the sheriff's office and the weight plunged through the floor as if the board were made of paper."

Despite the Depression, the commissioners believed they could afford a new courthouse, especially if they were to get a grant by the Public Works Administration (PWA), which typically funded forty-five percent of the construction cost of county courthouses. Although the courthouse measure passed in an election, the county missed the deadline to apply for the PWA funding. One year later, with more money in the county coffers, citizens again passed a measure approving the courthouse. This time, the county learned it would receive PWA funding. Discussions soon arose over where to locate the courthouse: on the old courthouse square, on the city's

Takenah Park, or on a two-block square encompassing both, which would require vacating a section of Broadalbin Street. The officials decided on the last choice, which would create a park at both ends of the new building. The August 13, 1938 *Albany Democrat-Herald*, which had campaigned extensively for the demolition of the old courthouse, now tried unsuccessfully to save the clock tower by arguing that adding a new clock to the new courthouse would "spoil its appearance."

Two judges broke the ground on August 22, 1938, and in a year and a half, county officials were moving into their new quarters, which cost approximately $310,000. The dedication, attended by more than one thousand people, was held on July 3 as part of the Fourth of July festivities. State Supreme Court Judge Percy Kelly, formerly of Albany, spoke to the crowd and noted that the courthouse was a "magnificent structure which will stand for all time."

According to the May 3, 1899 *Moro Leader*, when "the four great columns to the front of the Linn county courthouse were toppled to the ground, preparatory to the enlargement of that ediface. . . . Considerable interest was taken in one of the columns, in which was placed by the then county clerk, James Elkins, a package containing a list of the county and town officials in manuscript."

The Courthouse Today

ALTHOUGH THE WADING POOL AND THE sand pit are gone, the abundance of trees on the eastern portion of the site suggests its early use as a park. A rock with a tablet commemorates J. K. Weatherford, a director of Albany schools for fifty years. *Oregon End of the Trail*, published in 1940, noted that the rock was "beneath a young Douglas-fir tree, planted by Mr. Weatherford," but today no such tree is apparent. A sign announcing the Applegate Trail stands on the northeast corner of the site, although the trail never went through Albany. An editorial in the May 10, 1968 *Albany Democrat-Herald* told that the Trail Memorial Association placed it on the courthouse square because "the marker placed near Lewisburg was so situated that it would be seen by relatively few persons."

On the northwestern section of the square, a green metal cover in the grass marks an old well. According to the June 27, 1956 newspaper, a well was believed to be on the courthouse block since at least 1861. Many people, preferring well water to city water, brought jugs and buckets to the hand pump every night. Although a drinking fountain was added in 1956, now only the metal cover remains of this long-standing tradition.

Both the old and new blend to form the courthouse's architectural style, called "Half Modern." Like earlier Oregon courthouses, two-story high columns distinguish the entrance and dentils embellish the cornice. Although the exterior has the segmented appearance of blocks, it actually is poured-in-place concrete. The fluted pilasters between the windows display capitals with three five-pointed stars—not a typical Greek or Roman design. This alteration subtly changes the courthouse symbolism from links with abstract democratic political ideals to a more tangible representation of the federal government.

The aim of the PWA funding was to create employment during the Depression. In the March 26, 1993 *Albany Democrat-Herald*, one construction worker, Luther Shanks, recalled how his finances were improved. At that time, he received seventy-five cents per hour, fifty cents per hour more than from many of his previous jobs, and with such "rich" pay, he said his family "got ahead pretty fast. We paid off some bills." Shanks noted that "it was hard work. If you weren't sweating under your suspenders by 10 o'clock, he'd [the boss] send you home."

Because of the townspeople's outcry over the clock, the architects added a timepiece to the front face of the courthouse. However, this new clock did not compare favorably with the old courthouse's four-sided timekeeper. A former Albany resident wrote in the May 18, 1947 *Oregonian* that unlike the old one, "you can't see it [the new clock] except for one block, straight down Broadalbin Street," and that it was "more like a lady's wrist watch than a clock."

Twenty-two years after the county moved into the building, officials finally commissioned the cornerstone, now located on the northeast corner, to be set properly. The county moved quickly to construct the addition on the western side of the site, doubtless because the donor of the funding, L. L. Swan, stipulated in his will that the county must decide whether they would build it within six months. (Mr. Swan apparently had an understanding of the usual speed of government.) A prominent local attorney and former justice of the peace, Mr. Swan was such a fastidious man that he often would weed on the courthouse grounds on his way to work or home. When the county dedicated the building in 1968 amid considerable fanfare, Mr. Swan's sister reported in the November 2, 1968 *Albany Democrat-Herald* that if he had been alive, he would have hated the commotion.

The lobby exhibits a traditional courthouse interior individualized with Art Deco touches. The marble wainscot is gray, but the marble trim is green-black. Credit: author

Although a fountain dedicated to L. L. Swan marks the entrance to the annex, the original bronze entry doors on the courthouse still function as the main entrance to county offices. Just inside, on each side of the stairway, are two restroom doors, modestly designed to be almost a foot narrower than the standard doorway. Up the stairs, the hallway originally extended to the opposite end of the building, where a window provided light to the five-color, eight-pointed star in the center of the terrazzo floor. An office now occupies this space, and a display case stands in front of the wall. The glass case exhibits, among other items, a 1944 receipt for a two-dollar donation to the "Linn County War Chest."

While the exterior displays a Half-Modern style, the interior features Art Deco, which sometimes is referred to as Modernistic. However, like the exterior, the courthouse's interior is tempered with a traditional courthouse finish. The walls feature the usual gray marble wainscot, but this is offset by a rich, green-black marble trim—a common Art Deco color. Another characteristic is its curved surfaces, which are found in the rounded bronze stair handles. The Art Deco vertical signs announcing the various offices are reminiscent of miniature theater marquees.

Even though the Republicans placed a bench commemorating their Civil War efforts on the square, the courthouse stands as a monument to the Democrats. Without the PWA funding during the Depression, it is unlikely that such a grand courthouse would have been constructed. On the northern wall in the main hallway hangs a print of President Franklin D. Roosevelt, a tribute to his programs to alleviate the effects of the Depression. Adjacent to it is a photograph of Judge Owen Denny, a one-time Linn County resident who was the first to import Chinese pheasants. Ironically, according to Virginia Holmgren in *Chinese Pheasants, Oregon Pioneers*, Denny was "firmly Republican."

Besides the addition, L. L. Swan also left his mark on the inside of the courthouse. Part of his estate included a promissory note from a local furniture factory, and in order to pay down the loan, the factory supplied solid maple chairs to the county, some of which are in the county commissioners' meeting room. Hanging on the meeting room walls are pictures of important county structures: covered bridges, and an architectural drawing of the courthouse.

The most decorated place on the second floor of the building is the original circuit courtroom, now called Courtroom No. 1. Upon entering the double doors, one's attention is directed to the bronze grillwork on the windows on the far wall. The grillwork features a five-pointed star similar to those on the outside of the building, again symbolizing the federal presence in the county courtroom. These windows give the impression of opening directly to the outside, but when they are opened, the courthouse's true exterior wall is revealed along with regular rectangular windows to keep the outside symmetry.

In addition to stars on the windows, stars also appear on capitals of the pilasters and overhead between the recessed lighting. The careful design shown in the walls and ceiling might lead one to expect the judge's bench, usually the focus of the courtroom, to be similarly well considered. However, the bench, standing only about four feet high and six feet wide, appears diminutive for its function, and it has been moved off its traditional center to allow access to the judge's office. Although the dusty pink marble extends further up the wall behind the bench, the seal of Oregon stuck on the wallboard is an apparent afterthought—another suggestion that the federal presence predominates.

Walnut was used throughout the courtroom, including the spectator benches. Although the benches are among the most elegant of Oregon's historical county courthouses, the maintenance person reported that they are renowned for being uncomfortable. Before the benches were refinished, during warm summer days a spectator's clothing would stick like gum to the finish.

Black-and-white photographs of Sheriff Wheeler and his wife grace the wallboard in the back of the room. While his wife has the steely gaze common in pioneer portraits of the time, Mr. Wheeler has a kindly face, and one can imagine his difficulty in arresting a lawbreaker.

The July 3, 1940 *Albany Democrat-Herald* described the courtroom as being "the showplace of the court house," yet called it "exceptionally plain." At that time, "plain" was in style, although the newspaper could not foresee just how nondescript courtrooms and buildings would become over the succeeding half century. Today, embellishments such as bronze grillwork and figured stars on the ceiling are anything but plain.

The *Oregonian* billed this building as the "finest courthouse on [the] Pacific coast" when it was completed in 1914. With a budget of $1.6 million, it also was the most expensive of Oregon's historic courthouses. The Portland Building is visible on the left. *Credit: Alan Viewig*

Multnomah County

County Seat:	Portland
Courthouse Address:	1021 S.W. Fifth Avenue
Year Completed:	1914
Architectural Firm:	Whidden & Lewis
Date of County Formation:	December 22, 1859

> *"The days of [courthouses as] marble palaces are gone, anyway, as far as I'm concerned."*
>
> —Paul C. Northrop, County Roadmaster,
> quoted in the *Oregonian*, December 20th, 1958

Portland, Oregon, has a split personality. It can't quite make up its mind whether to be a swashbuckling industrial giant . . . or a landed squire pruning rosebushes and meditatively watching salmon ascend to their mountain spawning grounds unhindered by dams, piers, sewage and other impediments of industry." Although this aptly describes Portland's current situation, the words were written more than fifty years ago by Richard Neuberger in the March 1, 1947 *Saturday Evening Post.* The early boosters sought to attract industry and population, but in recent times the definition of progress includes liveability. Although a concern for the entire state, this question is particularly important in Portland.

Few lived in the area in 1843 when William Overton claimed 640 acres on the west bank of the Willamette River, nine miles south of the Columbia River. Overton could not afford the fee to file his claim, and so to finance it, he sold one half of his claim to Asa Lovejoy. Overton soon sold his remaining land to Francis Pettygrove.

At that time, Oregon City was the leading town, but Lovejoy and Pettygrove thought their site had potential; it had firm ground extending down to the water, and the river was deep enough that sea-going vessels could dock there. The two soon laid out a sixteen-block town, two blocks wide, which paralleled the river bank. Lovejoy wanted to call the town Boston, after his native home, but lost the flip of a coin, so Pettygrove chose to name it after his home town.

Others soon settled near the townsite. One of the most influential was Captain John Couch, who claimed land to the north of Pettygrove and Lovejoy. Couch's choice of Portland as the terminus of his shipping line was significant; his reputation as a knowledgeable shipper was well known and his judgment was respected. Following his example, other captains began to dock in Portland.

Boosters in rival communities such as Milwaukee, Linnton, and St. Helens were eager to have their town be the metropolis, but Portland's backers were determined and united. So that farmers would have easier access to their wharves, Portland citizens constructed the Great Plank Road to the Tualatin Valley. When a San Francisco steamship line replaced Portland with St. Helens its northern terminus, Portland settlers purchased their own steamer, and then eventually persuaded the San Francisco line to dock again in their town. Although some competitors were defeated because of their locational attributes, Portland's leaders, according to Fred Lockley in *The Columbia River to the Sea*, showed "the courage, the initiative and the energy."

Portland grew as the trans-shipment point for eastern Oregon and Washington, as well as the Willamette Valley. In 1868, eastside and westside railroads, running on either side of the Willamette River, began construction south towards California. At stake were federal government land grants. The eastside line, through the maneuvering of Ben Holladay, was the winner, and the line ran through such towns as Oregon City, Salem and Eugene. When it reached Roseburg in 1872, however, Holladay's company was out of funds.

German investors sent Henry Villard to investigate, and Villard responded by forming a transportation conglomerate that included the eastside line and the westside line (which had reached St. Joseph, a town along the Yamhill River near McMinnville). Villard was instrumental in connecting Portland with the transcontinental railroad in 1883. Although he, too, ultimately ran into financial trouble, the transcontinental line gave Portland a major economic boost and aided its urban expansion.

Portland gained both national and international attention when it hosted the Lewis and Clark Exposition in 1905 at Guild Lake. Ostensibly, the fair commemorated "the Centennial of the exploration of the Oregon Territory," according to a souvenir book published at the time. However, according to the January 5, 1997 *Oregonian*, one member of the organizing board said it was to "celebrate the past and exploit the future." More than a million people attended the financially successful summer-long event.

During World War I, Portland shipyards and related industries, such as foundries and machine shops, expanded employment. The city experienced another economic boom during World War II when the Kaiser Company began making ships at the St. Johns, Swan Island, and Vancouver yards. Thousands poured into Portland for employment, and the local housing authority was forced to construct Vanport, billed as the world's largest war housing city.

Portland's growth in the past fifty years has stretched to encompass other neighboring towns such as Beaverton and Oregon City, now considered part of the Portland metropolitan area. Statisticians include not just Multnomah County but five other counties—Clackamas, Columbia, Washington, Yamhill, and Clark (in Washington State)—when studying employment in the metropolitan area. Approximately half of Oregon's residents now live in the Portland metropolitan area. With a diverse economy, the region is the manufacturing, trade, and services center for the state.

Visiting the Seat of Multnomah County Government

PORTLAND'S DOWNTOWN IS NOT ALONG a single street, but encompasses an area so large that the city divides it into districts. The courthouse is located in the government district, a three-block by three-block grid bounded by S.W. Second, Fifth, Salmon, and Jefferson streets. Coincidentally, S.W. Main Street, usually the principal commercial street in smaller towns, runs west from the river through the government district.

Located in the center of the government district is a row of three park blocks. Terry Schrunk Plaza on the south was built over a parking structure in the mid-1970s when the Federal Building was constructed across S.W. Third Avenue. The northern two parks, Lownsdale and Chapman squares, have a much older history. Although they were to be donated when the area was platted, the city never received title to them, and instead was forced to purchase them in 1870.

Called the Plaza Blocks, both squares have been a center of protests and celebrations over the years. The 1861 Fourth of July celebration ended with fireworks in the plaza; in 1886 torchlight demonstrations against the city's Chinese population were held on the blocks. In response to the number of unsavory single men, the city council passed an ordinance in 1924 that reserved Chapman Square for use by women, children, and their escorts. In Lownsdale Square, a monument to veterans of the Spanish American War stands at the junction of the walkways. The pedestal under the statue of a soldier states that the monument is erected to the Second Oregon United States Volunteer Infantry. The date displayed, 1904, does not relate to the end of the War (1898) nor when the statue was ultimately dedicated (1906). Eugene Snyder in *Portland Potpourri: Art, Fountains, and Old Friends*, suggests one possibility is that the date reflects when the citizens thought they would dedicate it.

On the north and south side of the monument rest two howitzer cannons used at Fort Sumter. Colonel Henry E. Dosch was in charge of the Oregon exhibit at the 1901 exposition in Charleston, South Carolina. When he visited the fort, Dosch found the cannons buried in the sand, exposed only at low tide, and brought them back to Portland. To appease Northern and Southern sympathizers, Dosch noted that both Union and Confederate soldiers (who had captured the fort) had fired the cannons.

In the middle of Main Street, separating Lownsdale and Chapman squares, is the Elk Fountain, presented to the city in 1900 by David Thompson to use for watering horses. Spouts in the form of animal faces provide water for the troughs, and at the top of the pedestal stands a bronze elk figure by sculptor Roland H. Perry. An elk was chosen reportedly because one once grazed in the area, but when the fountain was to be dedicated, the fraternal group Exalted Order of the Elks refused to participate because they found the statue distasteful. Over the years, the fountain often is used to represent Portland, though it also has been criticized. In 1936, a concerned citizen wrote to the city council stating that "in size it is colossal, and in effect (when beheld suddenly) frightful, dangerous." Another citizen wrote in 1937 that "the stag should be lighted up at least, as it's a hazard to congestion."

The parks offer an excellent place to view the nearby government buildings constructed over the past one hundred years. The oldest, completed in 1895, is the City Hall in the southwest corner of the district. It has an official address along Fifth Avenue, but the Fourth Avenue side, now a parking lot, was once a courtyard and the official entrance for greeting dignitaries. The building, designed by the same architectural firm as the courthouse, displays along Fourth Avenue pink granite and sandstone columns supporting a rotunda. Stone ornaments stood at the corners of the roof, which the November 21, 1993 *Oregonian* stated symbolized "the urns of fate from which destiny flows."

Although the City Hall today is an integral part of Portland's history, like many other structures it has not always been so highly regarded. According to an undated *Oregon Journal* clipping, a movement started in the early 1930s for a new city hall, in part aided by an employee who discovered that fifteen rooms violated the city's own building code. The East Side Commercial Club, seeing an opportunity, soon demanded that a new city hall be built on their side of the river, which was "the center of population." A solution to the dilemma was to increase office space by removing the 250 cases of zoological specimens.

Fifth Avenue is also the official entrance of the 1982 Portland Building, leaving fire exits and a parking garage to face the Plaza Blocks. The lack of a pedestrian entrance from Fourth Avenue was just one of the many controversies surrounding this building; others included its color, shape, and ornamentation. From the *New York Times* to *Seattle Times*, from *Progressive Architecture* to *Architectural Record*, critics voiced their opinions about the building, which was designed by Michael Graves. Cynthia Saltzman in the May 1, 1981 *Wall Street Journal* wrote, "The richly toned design, with its allusions to ziggurats and Art Deco, makes visible Mr. Graves' program for a new decorative way of building." Wolf Von Eckardt in the August 23, 1982 *Time* stated, "The trouble is that Graves' zeal to overcome glass-box monotony has led him into the increasingly popular, mystic fantasy world. . . . It is a world that is almost beyond beauty or ugliness: almost, because the Portland Building is ugly."

As the March 16, 1980 *Oregonian* noted, "There is more in Graves' design than can be identified and consumed in a single glance." The structure is rich with meaning, although it may not be easily identifiable to the average person. The colors of the building, according to a description by Michael Graves in a 1982 pamphlet, depict the "natural and built landscape as we know it." The blue-green base is likened to a garden. The terra cotta strips on the front and back are to be understood as columns, and support a similarly colored keystone which is analogous to the earth. The terra cotta strips on the building's sides, described as a colonnade, represent the passage from commerce along Fifth Avenue to the park blocks beyond Fourth Avenue. The city council vetoed Graves' idea of flowing metallic garlands due to concerns about pigeons, but they did approve the flattened, stylized garlands which symbolize nature and are, according to the architect, "traditionally understood as a welcoming gesture." The "Portlandia" statue above the Fifth Avenue entrance, the second-largest copper sculpture in the U.S., is an adaptation of the figure in the city seal and symbolizes commerce.

Considerably less controversial was the 1983 Justice Center on the block directly east from Chapman Square and the Portland Building. The architectural firm Zimmer Gunsul Frasca had the difficult task of satisfying the three government levels—city, county, and state—which were to occupy the building, as well as the federal government, which funded the building. Included in the complicated design was the county jail, which occupies floors four through eight. The October 16, 1983 *Oregonian* related that workers from the Portland Building "may note with sorrow that their office views compare unfavorably to those available to prisoners two blocks away."

Budget constraints and the building computer system initially caused problems when the structure opened. Prisoners could activate the smoke alarm system from their cells, which would send all elevators to the first floor as a safety precaution. According to the January 29, 1984 *Oregonian*, there were more than two hundred such "alarms" the prior December. The Portland police, occupants of the top six floors, originally had an "open door" office policy, only because their doors were left off to save money. The "officers had to 'steal' a door from a public area so they could secure an otherwise open utility room that holds their weapons and other equipment."

The building literally speaks about justice in two quotes on the front. One by George Washington states, "The due administration of justice is the firmest pillar of good government," while the other by Martin Luther King reads, "Injustice anywhere is a threat to justice everywhere." Two Turkish yellow travertine columns flanking the front entrance convey a more subtle message. The sculptor disclosed in the September 20, 1983 *Oregonian* that the columns vary slightly because "they are like justice; they arrive at the same conclusion by different paths."

Directly south of the Justice Center stands the Federal Building, a nondescript concrete and glass structure completed in 1976. More daring is the last building in the government district, the federal courthouse on the northeast block of the district. The structure, according to the July 6, 1993 *Oregonian*, was "the most expensive building ever built in Oregon." With architectural excellence stated as one of its objectives, the structure represented a shift toward more distinctive federal courthouses. The sixteen-story building stands taller than the other structures in the district, but the eight-story high "sidecar" was designed to match the height of the Justice Center's concave glass window and the roof of the Multnomah County courthouse.

A History of the Courthouse

THE LEGISLATURE CREATED MULTNOMAH County out of Washington and Clackamas counties in 1854, naming it after a Northwest Indian name for the Willamette River. Portland was named the county seat, and officials initially met at a rented building on Front Avenue near the Madison Street bridge (now the Hawthorne Bridge.) For the first courthouse, commissioners purchased the present-day courthouse block in 1863, which then was located on the edge of town and was the site of a house and an orchard.

Set back from the sidewalk by an expanse of grass, the former Multnomah County court-house seems to have been more congenial to passersby than the current one, which was built right to the sidewalk. Author's collection

The first courthouse, a brick and stone building, was not without controversy. The keystone over the main doorway was fashioned in the likeness of Abraham Lincoln, and according to the September 17, 1911 *Oregon Journal*, "the blood of southern sympathizers boiled" when seeing this. The cupola undoubtedly invoked a more pleasant response, as its base contained a three-foot wide promenade from which the surrounding countryside could be viewed.

Public hangings occurred in the courtyard to the east of the courthouse. At one double

hanging, according to the November 5, 1911 newspaper, the men sang songs in order to make their "departure as pleasant an affair as possible." One prisoner, when asked for his last words, gave a one-hour twenty-minute-long speech from the scaffold, as he believed that if he talked past the hour of his planned execution, he would not be hung. He was wrong.

The county expanded the courthouse toward the north in 1885, and toward the south four years later, but by the early 1890s the commissioners were contemplating larger quarters. The 1893 depression halted this idea, and instead repairs were made to the courthouse. The need for space became apparent in 1908, when three juries from separate trials retired to deliver a verdict. One occupied the jury room, another the judge's chambers, and the third the attic.

The July 18, 1909 *Oregonian* reported that plans for a new courthouse were completed. In order to house employees while the courthouse was constructed, the commissioners ingeniously planned to build one section of the new courthouse in the courtyard of the old building on the eastern portion of the block. When this section was completed, county employees would move into this structure, the old courthouse would be demolished, and the rest of the building would be completed.

The county accepted construction bids in July 1909. Almost a year and a half later, an editorial in the December 12, 1910 *Oregon Journal* asked when the courthouse would be finished, as the Spalding office building already had been started and completed. Nearly two years after construction had started, the old courthouse finally was razed in order to construct the western section of the new building. Not until March 1912 was scaffolding removed so that, according to the March 24, 1912 *Oregonian*, it could be the "subject of

On December 12, 1910, the editor of the *Oregon Journal* wrote lyrically about the courthouse delay: "All over the city the same order of progress obtains, save on the courthouse lot. There the spring and summer come and pass, there the autumn leaves turn and fall, and there the winds and rains of winter revel through the incompleted stories that are rising heavenward with the speed of a century."

admiration by thousands of people." In January 1914, almost four and a half years since construction began, the county finally issued certificates of completion to the contractors.

Although the building was completed, the controversy was not. The county settled on penalties with several of the contractors who had delayed their work on the east wing, one for up to three months. The Taxpayers and Non-Partisan League began investigating the costs associated with the courthouse, including a $3,000 intercom system that had been ordered by the county judge and then removed. Wondering why the architects seemed to be overpaid by $6,000, the league asked for a copy of the plans and specifications from one of the architects. The architect declined to provide them. The August 14, 1914 *Oregonian* reported that one of the commissioners displayed his acute knowledge of county procedures by stating, "Maybe there is something in their contract we don't know that gives them authority not to give out these plans even if we do demand them."

The Courthouse Today

THE COURTHOUSE DISPLAYS AN AMERICAN Renaissance style, which includes such characteristics as monumental proportions, smooth dressed exterior stone, and rectangular windows. The design of the courthouse, however, connotes "power" rather than "justice." The building crowds the sidewalk. Passersby can look through windows on only about half the building, leaving the remainder of the base at pedestrian height a blank granite wall which suggests a fortress. Above, between the third and sixth floors, towering Ionic columns lord over the street. With such a design, the county apparently believed that everyone would recognize it as the courthouse. In 1939, twenty-five years after the building was completed, the commissioners had to add a copper sign reading "Multnomah County Courthouse" near the front doors so that citizens would stop entering the building and riding the elevators looking for the city health department or water bureau.

The first phase of the building on the eastern portion of the site extended just over fifty-eight feet from the front of the

courthouse. The plans instructed that "all stone of west wing must be thoroughly bonded and tied to stone work of present east wing." With such workmanship, today it is difficult to see where the two sections were joined. No tell-tale cracks on the east or west face show through the Indiana limestone blocks; no breaks are evident in the terra cotta entablature. Despite this, a 1996 study noted concerns that during an earthquake the two sections might move separately and "repeatedly collide into each other."

Set back from the roof, the seventh and eighth floors are commonly believed to be a later addition, but this is part of the original structure. A jail was—and still is—located in this section. Originally it was hidden from the street by almost ten-foot high parapet walls, which later were removed due to structural weaknesses. Jails built

Because the Multnomah County courthouse is so busy, it is generally difficult to have an unobstructed view of the lobby. *Credit: author* in outlying locations eventually forced the sheriff to transport prisoners to the courthouse by a specially secured bus. Shackled together, inmates had to cross the sometimes pedestrian-laden Fifth Avenue sidewalk to the building. In 1958, a double-jointed prisoner slipped out of his handcuffs, broke from the chain gang, and dashed down Fifth Avenue. Deputies, with shotguns poised, immediately lined the rest of the inmates against the wall, but an unaware pedestrian blithely walked between the shotguns and the prisoners. Fortunately, nothing happened.

Concerns over possible escapes ultimately led to a novel solution. Today, Justice Center inmates board a bus, ride three blocks to the Fifth Avenue side of the courthouse, and disembark directly into a metal enclosure that frames a stairway to the basement. When not in use, the contraption slides down flush with the sidewalk, showing only a metal plate. Initially, a tunnel was proposed to transport prisoners from the Justice Center to the courthouse, but it was deemed too expensive.

To create another needed courtroom, the county blocked the central Fifth Avenue entrance, which once led to the second floor. Until recently, two side entrances on this street were still open, but these accessed only a portion of the first floor due to security concerns. For the best introduction to the building, one must enter at the formal Fourth Avenue entrance.

Evidence of the courthouse's apparently lavish $1.6 million budget is visible in the foyer, where the marble pilasters display chiseled fluting and the marble walls show an incised fret design. However, practicality now supersedes beauty. Mats cover the marble floor design; "weapons prohibited" signs now screen the bronze lamp bases. Discoloration is visible on the upper section of the marble walls, indicating just where the custodians cleaned and where they did not. Too many janitors was the problem in 1921, likely because "Nat" Wagner did the hiring. According to the May 4, 1921 *Oregon Journal*, a commissioner speculated, "Whenever anyone of importance had a man he wanted to get a job for I guess he went to 'Nat' and Nat good naturedly put him on."

To enter the lobby today, one must pass through a metal detector. Once inside, one can glimpse further reasons why the March 24, 1912 *Oregonian* called this building the "finest

Even without knowing the amount, elements such as the marble newel post suggest the size of the courthouse budget. *Credit: author*

courthouse on [the] Pacific coast." Plaster cornices exhibit a continuous wave-like pattern. Marble brackets supporting a hood distinguish office doors, and the marble statuary newel post is intricately carved with a garland. However, times have changed since the courthouse was built. The necessary security system and information desk, manned by the sheriff, intrude into the lobby. Attorneys and clients and witnesses bustle through the space, intent on judicial matters. So much traffic passes through the courthouse, according to one employee, that the elevators often break down because they were not designed to be used so frequently.

The windows above the main stairway landing reveal a 1951 addition built in the central courtyard. Originally, the courtyard allowed every office to have natural light, but during Prohibition it served another use when the sheriff poured confiscated alcohol down the courtyard drain. Scandal hit the courthouse in 1918 when it was discovered that employees had built a secret

The courthouse initially was equipped with the very latest technical advances, including a mechanical system that supplied the building with forced air and radiant heating, an on-site electrical generator for emergencies, and a built-in central vacuuming system with outlets for hose attachments located throughout.

tap in the drainpipe to siphon the drained alcohol. The courtyard also was the scene of an escape attempt in 1958 when a prisoner, having unlocked his handcuffs with a hidden key, scrambled onto a first-floor ledge and refused to come down. After a deputy's gunfire hit the prisoner's right index finger, he changed his mind.

The upper floors of the courthouse reflect "modern" refurbishing. The October 15, 1956 *Oregonian*, discussing proposed alterations, noted that the county planned to lower ceilings and add lighting to "eliminate some of its gloominess." In order to expand office space, hallway walls were to extend out into the "overly wide corridors." The marble, too, has not been preserved. In 1958, a story circulated through the courthouse that some marble intended for a sixth-floor courtroom had been inadvertently sold for junk and was displayed in a tavern somewhere in Portland. While the story was discounted by the auditor's office, they admitted that marble deemed unsuitable for the remodeling was sold.

While judicial functions occupy the upper floors, the courthouse once housed tenants such as the University of Oregon, the Oregon Parent-Teacher Association, and the state auto licensing department. Various veterans associations also had offices in the courthouse, but they were among the most objectionable. According to the March 29, 1925 *Oregon Journal*, the women's auxiliaries groups, in the course of cooking lunches and breakfasts, caused "all manner of odors" to permeate the hallways.

Only a few courtrooms have escaped the county's refurbishing. Room No. 544, with an original two-story-high ceiling, remains furnished in such an historical manner that it seems out of the past. A riot of colors catches the eye: tomato-red marble wainscot,

The March 24, 1912 *Oregonian* related, "Particularly attractive are the Circuit Court rooms in the building. Eleven have been provided, which will be adequate to care for the growth of Portland for an almost indefinite period. Each room is two stories in height. The floors and the stationary fittings and pillars are of marble. The judges' benches are marble with carved tops. The windows are high and are screened by heavy dull brass ornamentation."

avocado-green hanging tapestries, and green-black pilasters and columns. Both the pilasters and columns have elaborate plaster capitals; the shafts of pilasters are marble, but the shafts of the columns are scagliola (plaster work imitating marble).

Only six spectator benches are provided, but the matching wooden bar provides seating for extra plaintiffs or defendants. Although marble judges' benches are located in other courtrooms, this room has a wooden judge's bench similar in design to the other furnishings. The fluorescent lights hide the original splendor of the ceiling, but they do help to conceal a peephole drilled into the ceiling in 1990 for security during a volatile court case.

The March 24, 1912 *Oregonian* called the courthouse the largest building in Portland, and it was then undoubtedly also the largest building in the state, except for perhaps the state capital. Today from the high courtroom windows of Room 544, the neighboring twenty-eight-floor Standard Insurance building, erected almost six decades later, towers over the courthouse. Unlike small county seats, commerce clearly dominates in Portland.

The courthouse has been the scene of many
community events, such as in 1902 when merchant
W.C. Brown, who had lost a bet on the price of hops,
threw 2,000 nickels to scrambling schoolchildren.
Credit: author

Polk County

County Seat:	Dallas
Courthouse Address:	850 Main Street
Year Completed:	1900
Architect:	Delos D. Neer
Date of County Formation:	December 22, 1845

*To me, our courthouse would compete with any
(other building), including the cathedral at Notre
Dame."*

—Former Senator Mark Hatfield,
quoted in the *Itemizer-Observer*, May 3, 1989

Rickreall Creek is almost hidden from automobiles crossing the Main Street bridge that leads toward downtown Dallas. Though inconspicuous, the creek was instrumental in advancing Dallas's development from a crossroads trading center to a thriving small town; even today, it still shapes Dallas life. Logs no longer float down its banks to a Dallas sawmill, but a historic tannery still draws water from the creek to soak its hides. An electrical generating plant on its bank no longer illuminates city street lights, but Dallas children still cavort in the local swimming hole. Water, one of life's necessities, was critical in the life of Dallas.

Pioneers began farming in the early 1840s on the north side of Rickreall Creek. As population increased, James Nesmith, a local grist mill owner and state legislator, persuaded the legislature in 1845 to create a new county. Named after then U.S. President James Polk, the county initially covered all of southern Oregon west of the Cascade Mountains.

The first courthouse was completed in 1851, and business people soon established a nearby hotel and a general store. The hamlet initially was called Cynthia Ann (occasionally spelled Cynthian), after either a town in Kentucky or Mrs. Jesse Applegate, whose first name was Cynthia Ann. However, the townspeople fittingly renamed the community after George M. Dallas, the U.S. Vice President serving under President Polk.

In those days, a community that could not boast a college or another school of higher learning was considered less cultured by its more enlightened neighbors. In 1846, the Jefferson Institute was established in the town of Rickreall, four miles east of present-day Dallas, but in 1855, the school's first instructor, John Lyle, and other citizens met at the courthouse to discuss establishing a learning institution in Dallas. Three adjoining landowners south of the creek offered to donate acreage to the school, allowing it to occupy a small site and finance itself by selling the excess land.

The next year, an eighteen-block town was platted, with the largest block reserved for the school. Academy trustees initially sold lots for $100, but found few buyers. They then reduced the prices to fifty dollars for corner lots and thirty dollars for all others, provided that the purchaser built on the lot within a year. The residents of "old Dallas," believing that the north side of the creek had a limited supply of well water, gradually moved south.

In the *Polk County Centennial Souvenir Booklet*, a reprint of James Nesmith's 1875 speech to the Oregon Pioneer Association revealed his tactics in creating Polk County. A businessman "had constructed a ten-pin alley where some of my fellow members were in the habit of resorting to seek relaxation and refreshments from their legislative toils. I had a bill then pending to . . . establish the county of Polk, which measure had violent opposition in the body. One morning while most of my opponents were amusing themselves at horse billiards in Lee's ten pin alley, I called up my bill...I got a vote before the return of the horse billiard players and Polk county has a legal existence today."

In the late 1850s, John Waymire dug a mill race that took water from the creek near the present-day Hunter and Washington Streets, then ran east along Oak Street before veering south to empty back into the creek. The mill race powered Waymire's flour mill and eventually a foundry, woolen mill, and saw mill. The April 21, 1899 *Polk County Observer* reprinted an *Oregonian* article about Dallas that stated, "there are five moderate manufacturing establishments. . . . The result is that business is good in Dallas, houses all occupied and well kept-up. . . . The town enjoys no special advantages in the way of transportation; it in not on navigable water; it has no pull of any kind. It simply attends to its own business and depends on itself, wasting none of its forces in ambitions and longings for the unattainable."

The LaCreole Academy did give the town an advantage over less "educated" communities, if only in the minds of the townspeople. The August 5, 1898 *Polk County Observer* noted, "It is a well recognized fact that towns that have schools of higher learning are better socially, morally and intellectually. . . . We are somewhat in advance of many other towns because we have a school that offers better educational advantages." Despite the town's sophistication, the city council voted in 1898 to allow cows to run through the town, to which the December 9, 1898 newspaper printed an observation from a Klamath newspaper, "The city council of Dallas must be a body of mutton heads."

In an era of farming, the vast timber resources west of Dallas were a hindrance, but after the turn of the century, this liability became an asset. In 1906, Louis Gerlinger began operating a mill that employed sixty workers. The Gerlinger family eventually purchased the Dallas foundry to build locomotives to pull the logs out of their extensive timberland.

Today the lumber mill, the cornerstone of Willamette Industries, is the second-largest industrial employer in Dallas. The largest is a circuit board manufacturing plant, started by a former logger. Although Dallas has its own industrial base, the town has grown in part due to its close proximity to the state capital, Salem.

Visiting the Seat of Polk County Government

IN THE MORNING, AS SALEM-BOUND CARS make their way east along Ellendale Road, they pass the old Cynthia Ann site. Since the town grew on the south side of the creek, the north side had ample land to accommodate auto-dependent enterprises such as a modern shopping center and a national discount store. Any sense of Cynthia Ann is gone, but a marble marker on a triangular parcel between Main Street and Ellendale Road denotes the approximate site of the old courthouse. Down the hill on Main Street, one block north of the original Academy Square, stands the 1935 Academy building, a descendant of the early school.

An 1882 map shows that many Dallas merchants located their businesses between Oak and Mill streets, hedging their bets as to which institution, the school or the courthouse, would draw more business. The courthouse won. Commercial structures eventually grew on all four sides of the courthouse square, although the land directly opposite the front of the courthouse became the most prized. Fire, a frequent leveler of wooden structures, cleared this block in the late 1880s, and merchants took the opportunity to erect two-story, brick structures.

Today, three exuberantly decorated Victorian buildings collectively suggest a turn-of-the-century downtown block in a prosperous town. Although its facades appear the same, the mid-block building at 857-865 Main Street is really two buildings constructed to resemble each other—which undoubtedly saved time and money on the architectural design. The builder of the structure at 811 Main Street perhaps believed that his neighbor would do the same, as the elaborate pediment on the north side appears asymmetrical.

A central location must have been important to members of the Masonic lodge, who added a third story to their building at 831 Main Street after the turn of the century. Access to the upper floors was by way of a common stairway shared with the Odd Fellows, another fraternal group, who met in the second floor of the building directly south. For several years, the Odd Fellows met at 904 Main Street, which is lavishly decorated with cast iron made by the local Biddle foundry. The Odd

Fellows had personalized the pilasters, which today still display "IOOF" (International Order of the Odd Fellows.) At the bottom of the pilasters, perhaps for free advertising, Edward Biddle added his last name, the name of the foundry, and the date, 1890.

Biddle was not as aggressive in his advertising a year earlier, as the cast-iron pediments still remaining on Victorian buildings west of the courthouse show only the foundry name and the date, 1889. The *Polk County Observer* inspected Biddle's facilities and reported in their February 15, 1889 edition that the source of his metal was "old machinery that has been accumulating for more than a generation; this supply, however, is being exhausted and Oswego pig iron [from the town that was to become Lake Oswego] will soon be shipped here."

A History of the Courthouse

IN 1858, TWO YEARS AFTER THE NEW PLAT of Dallas was surveyed, the county constructed a second courthouse, while the lumber from the first located on the north side of the creek was unceremoniously used in building a saloon. The new courthouse exhibited a porch with two-story columns supporting a pediment. A wooden fence, reportedly to keep wandering cows off the grass, encircled the square.

In 1880, the citizens of Independence, located about ten miles southeast of Dallas, believed that Independence should be the county seat, and the issue was put to a vote in the June 1880 election. In the weeks preceeding the election, blusterous writers, extolling the merits of one location or another, wrote long letters to the *Polk County Itemizer*. To advance their cause, leading Dallas citizens promised that no new courthouse would be built in ten years if their town won, thereby suggesting that taxes would not be raised.

To further help their chances, Dallas citizens subscribed money to extend the Oregon Railway Company to their town. Although the March 26, 1880 *Polk County Itemizer* reported that "the people of this vicinity have agreed to pay the company $3,000 to complete the road to this point," other sources relate that Dallas citizens raised $17,000. Nevertheless, with exquisite timing, the first train arrived in Dallas just three days before the election. (The westside line of the railroad eventually ran from Fulquartz Landing, on the Willamette River near Dundee, to Airlie, southwest of Monmouth.) The June 11, 1880 newspaper reported that after Dallas's election victory, a bonfire was lit on the courthouse lot and "crowds of citizens thronged the streets."

According to Sidney Newton in *Early History of Independence, Oregon*, a petition to move the county seat to Independence circulated in 1889, but was defeated in the legislature. In 1890, a town called Talmadge, located between Independence and Monmouth, had eight full lots set aside for a public park. These lots were considered by Independence county seat advocates to be the ideal place for the courthouse. Mildred Stafrin, in the February 25, 1976 *Sun-Enterprise*, related that while cruising between Monmouth and Dallas in the family's automobile in 1911, she and her sister could still identify the trees that had been planted for the courthouse square.

Despite those efforts, the courthouse remained in Dallas. The question arose again in 1898 when Dallas citizens awoke early on the morning of June 10 to find their courthouse in flames. From the entrance hallway, the fire quickly spread to the rest of the building. A June 10, 1898 special edition of the *Polk County Observer* announced, "A sorry day for Polk County—untold trouble will follow" and that "the indications are that coal oil had been spread throughout the house."

Among the crowd watching the courthouse burning were the county clerk and sheriff, but perhaps these two were not feeling sentimental. The June 1, 1898 newspaper, after reporting that rumors were circulating over suspected arson, chastised the citizenry for unfounded speculation. Leaving the rumors forever in Polk County history, the newspaper then stated, "This week, slanderous reports have been . . . broadcast against Sheriff Plummer and Clerk Hayter in regard to the court house fire that have no foundation whatever." No one was ever indicted for the crime.

The Dallas newspaper mounted a campaign to build another courthouse immediately, undoubtedly to forestall any

questions about the county seat location. "Unanimous for a Court House" screamed a June 17, 1898 *Polk County Observer* headline, followed by quotes from citizens saying, "Build a court house." While a commissioner from Independence wanted to put the county seat question to popular vote, a commissioner from Dallas and the county judge overruled him. The county court wasted no time. By July 15, they had advertised for architects to submit plans; by July 22, the county judge had traveled to Salem to measure the dimensions of the Marion County courthouse.

An early view of the courthouse, when compared with its surroundings, suggests how grand it must have initially appeared. *Author's collection*

Perhaps haste caused the court to accept the nearly identical plans of the Lane County courthouse, then under construction in Eugene. The architect, Delos Neer, and several assistants had spent more than five months designing the Lane courthouse, but the plans for Polk County's courthouse were conveniently available within a month. Just over two months after the old courthouse had burned, the county let the first contracts on the new building.

The September 30, 1898 newspaper noted the rewards of Dallas being the county seat. "Already our little city is beginning to see the good resulting from the erection of the new county buildings. Times are better than they have been in Dallas for the past ten years." On October 21, 1898, the newspaper predicted, "The coming season will see in Dallas a new court house finished, water works in operation and all her manufacturing plants in motion. What more does Dallas want?"

On September 29, 1899, the *Polk County Observer* touted that "no building of a like character on the Pacific coast has been put up for such a small sum of money." Economy was an issue in Polk County. Lane County had paid more than $75,000 for their courthouse, while the Polk County building, which was dedicated in June 1900, cost under $40,000. For over half a century, nearly identical courthouses, one of brick and the other of stone, stood just seventy miles apart in the two county seats until the Lane courthouse was demolished in the late 1950s.

The Courthouse Today

EVEN IF ITS COURTHOUSE WAS ESSENTIALLY a copy, Polk County slowly personalized its courthouse square with its memorabilia, a practice that continues today. Near the southern side of the courthouse, the county placed the four-foot diameter mill stones from a grist mill constructed for the Northwest Indians on the Grande Rond reservation.

However, the meaning in some of the mementos has changed. The Gerlinger foundry donated an elegant fountain for the southeast corner of the square, but the complicated mechanisms continually broke and it now serves as a reminder to bygone "modern" technology. In front of the courthouse, flanked by a pair of threatening cannons, two displays each bearing the words "Military Honor Roll" exhibited tourist information.

Today, the annual courthouse Christmas tree lighting ceremony attracts many Dallas citizens to the square, and it has served historically as a place of social gathering. Residents watched a daring aerialist slide down a cable from the courthouse tower to the ground via a ring held in his teeth.

Another time, a balloonist landed amid a milling crowd. Prominent merchant W. C. Brown, who had lost a bet on the 1902 price of hops, threw 2,000 nickels into the air over the heads of 400 children.

For many years, a "hanging tree" stood on the southern lawn. The actual date of this tree's demise is disputed, but so many other trees have been called the "hanging tree" that it is a source of amusement for local historians. Today, the square has fewer likely imposters, as workers have removed several trees in order to maintain a clear view of the courthouse from the street. As Commissioner Mike Propes related in the October 17, 1990 *Itemizer Observer*, "We've got the prettiest courthouse in Oregon, and we can't let it be blocked by trees."

The February 3, 1966 *Itemizer Observer* recounts another event at the courthouse. "Fireman Walter Syron high dived head first from the top window of the courthouse tower and from the roof of the high school into a life net. . . . 'The dive was a perfect swan with a quick flip just before he lit in the net,' the [fire] chief said."

In the early days of the courthouse, Polk County's jail was a separate structure that stood across the street where the city hall stands now, and prisoners were led across the square to attend court. In the late 1920s, the county erected a pink-colored jail on the square, which the locals named the "Pink Pokey." When a new jail and expanded office facilities were needed in the mid-1960s, the county discussed razing the 1900 courthouse. Instead, they constructed an "annex," which has more than four times the square footage of the 1900 building. The annex, forming a "U" around the courthouse, provides a stark contrast of architectural styles separated by just sixty-five years.

The original building displays the Richardsonian Romanesque architectural style with its massive, heavy appearance. To help achieve this weightiness, the exterior exhibits blocks of rock-faced sandstone extracted from a local quarry. Although the *Polk County Observer* predicted in 1899 that a number of substantial buildings would be constructed with this material, the courthouse is the only major structure in Dallas that displays such an extravagance of stone. Near the northeast corner of the building, now hidden behind a fence, one block displays a fossil of a prehistoric fish.

Fortunately, Polk County constructed an annex instead of replacing its courthouse with an entirely modern building.
Credit: author

The arched second-story windows and porch openings represent another characteristic of Richardsonian Romanesque architecture, as does the asymmetrically placed tower. In contrast to the heaviness of the style, a pressed metal frieze displays delicate garlands that suggest a wedding cake decoration. On the front of the courthouse, a plaque displays "1899" and a hand holding a set of scales. Although traditionally cornerstones are laid on the northeast corner, the Polk County Courthouse cornerstone is located on the northwest corner, perhaps because the usual location would place the stone at the rear of the building.

The Polk County courthouse has two front entrances, but Neer designated the main entrance by placing it under a tower and making the porch entry four and a half feet wider than the southern entrance. Over the original double swinging doors, a leaded glass window mimics the arch in the porch opening. With a pressed metal ceiling, fir wainscot, and tile floor, the foyer suggests the interior finish of the rest of the building.

Although Neer designed a graceful building, the entrance is awkwardly positioned. Without turning from the foyer into the lobby, one would run directly into the side of the stairway, which also blocks any grand view of this public area. Perhaps Neer realized the problem with the Lane County courthouse,

but the rushed courthouse plans for Polk did not allow time for any changes. For the Baker County courthouse nine years later, Neer would place the stairway against the far wall, away from the foyer.

The lobby seems unchanged since the courthouse was built in 1899. Even after almost a hundred years, the ocher and periwinkle floor tiles still have vibrant colors. *Credit: Alan Viewig*

The subtle transition from the foyer, a room of minor importance, to the lobby, a space of major importance, is signified by the change in the design and color of the tile. Although both rooms have a floor border, tile in the foyer is only white, while that in the lobby is in the rich colors of ochre and periwinkle. Because the building has settled over the years, visitors with sensitive feet will be able to detect unevenness in the tiles.

In the Benton County courthouse, Neer graced the arched doorways with feminine faces, but in the Polk County courthouse, he used masks, faces that grimace and bare their teeth. According to the December 29, 1961 *Capital Journal*, local tradition is that these fierce faces, believed to be Vikings, were placed to frighten crooked politicians into honest ways. Others, according to the article, stated that the Vikings were to "discourage meddlesome reporters from entering [the courthouse]."

Polk County citizens added their own decorations over the years. On one wall, a framed article glorifies the 1908–09 Oregon basketball team, which included some students from the Academy. Miniature portraits of stern-faced pioneers aged seventy to ninety hang on the opposite wall over the words, "This is what Sparkling Mountain Water and Pure Air does for us in Polk County." The benevolent merchant and nickle-tosser, W.C. Brown, is shown, as is his wife, Martha Brown, who herself appears to be wearing a photograph of a couple on her broach. Those with sullied reputations were not excluded. Lawyer and politician Benjamin Hayden is shown, a man whose contemporaries called "Dirty Ben."

At the top of the stairs, an unusual statue standing of a woman stands in a niche clutching her robes to her breast. The circuit court judge's office has enclosed part of the hallway, and a feeling of expansiveness that must have existed once is no longer there. The wainscot, newel post, and doorway surround reflect less expense than seen on the first floor, even though the path to the courtroom would be well traveled.

As in the lobby, somber wood tones are prevalent throughout the courtroom. The formality of the room is offset by the flamboyant pink, white, and gold pressed-metal ceiling. Darrell Williams, a former judge, once called the courtroom the "Sistine Chapel of Polk County," but another judge reported that some say it reminds them of a "turn-of-the-century cat house."

The courtroom is wide enough to fit three rows of benches, but the length of the courtroom has been diminished by adding a back wall, which created two extra jury rooms now located just outside the courtroom doors. However, the original size of this commodious courtroom seems too large for Polk County. It is likely that the 500-seat courtroom designed for Lane County, whose population was twice the size of Polk's, was used in this courthouse simply because a change in the plans would have delayed construction.

At the head of the room, a tall wooden panel, another Neer trademark, stands more than thirteen feet high and towers over the judge's bench, which is only four feet high. The original jury chairs have been replaced, and the second row stands farther back from the footrest than the first row. Small wooden boxes, covered in avocado green or kelly green carpet, provide a footrest for shorter jurors.

From the judge's office, a stairway winds up to the tower. From the landing just under the clock, one can see the Victorian buildings on Main Street. These buildings and the courthouse give a sense of a turn-of-the-century town and create a unique place in Dallas. Although the Polk County courthouse was not as expensive as the Lane courthouse, the county kept it from being destroyed. From cutting the trees on the square to displaying a drawing of the courthouse on county signs, Polk citizens show their pride in their courthouse.

Although the symmetry of the front might have alluded to the kind of treatment a citizen could expect, the equal entrances at the Tillamook County courthouse give no clue as to which one leads to the offices and which one leads to the courtroom. While the exterior is devoid of ornamentation, the rising steps and the colossal columns were masterfully designed. *Credit: author*

Tillamook County

County Seat:	Tillamook
Courthouse Address:	201 Laurel Avenue
Year Completed:	1933
Architectural Firm:	Lawrence, Holford, Allyn and Bean
Date of County Formation:	December 15, 1853

"In the editorial printed alongside this letter, in which you advocate immediate construction [of the courthouse], you call all those opposed to such construction now 'obstructionists' and 'malcontents.'"

—J. L. Steinback in *Tillamook Herald*, June 9, 1932

To many people, Tillamook County and cheddar cheese are synonymous. Along Highway 101, the Tillamook County Creamery Association factory makes about forty million pounds a year of "yellow gold" under the curious eyes of thousands of visitors. The creamery's old feed mill tower is one of the landmarks in the county seat. The students on the local high school team are not cougars or bears but Cheesemakers. The county, which devotes the entire month of June to "Dairy Month," has more milk cows than human residents.

Dairy farming **was years** away when Joseph Champion sailed into Tillamook Bay in 1851, intending to stay a few months and trade with the local Northwest Indians. Before building a cabin, he lived in a hollow spruce tree trunk which he called his castle. He later wrote that "the Indians seemed pleased with the prospect of having the whites settle among them (Poor Fools)." As Champion was preparing to try his luck in the California gold fields, others moved into the area to settle.

More arrived within the next two years. At that time, Tillamook was part of Yamhill County, but McMinnville, the county seat, was over a day away by horse. Furthermore, the settlers believed their region had all the promising economic advantages for prosperity. Just two years after Champion's visit, the settlers petitioned the legislature to create a new county, even though they had only twenty-nine signatures. The legislature named the county after the local Northwest Indian tribe that had provided trail guides and assisted in cattle drives.

Despite the early settlers' expectations, Tillamook's geography, with mountains on three sides and the ocean on the fourth, kept it isolated. Although the county has three bays, treacherous bars had to be carefully navigated, and ship after ship sank. For those willing to brave a landing in Tillamook Bay, waiting for a favorable high tide could take several days.

In 1860, Thomas Stillwell, a robust seventy-year-old ex-Northwest Indian fighter, purchased a donation land claim on the south side of the Hoquarten Slough, which flowed into Tillamook Bay and was accessible by ship. Stillwell started a general store catering to those who traveled by water or land. In 1861, he laid out a modest four-block plat, which lined the slough. He called his new town "Lincoln" after the then U.S. president.

In 1872, three local landowners filed a new, more ambitious "Town of Lincoln," which added eleven blocks to Stillwell's original four. At the time, county officials who previously had met in different towns were contemplating a permanent location for the county seat. The recently filed plat, recorded just before the upcoming election, solidified Lincoln as a legitimate town and helped it win the position over the competing communities of Garibaldi and Concordia (no longer a town).

Initially, the citizens informally called Lincoln by several other names, including "Hoquarton" (believed to be a Northwest Indian name for the area), "the Landing," and "Tillamook Landing." When the townspeople applied for a post office to be registered in the town of Lincoln, postal officials refused. Local lore states that another town of Lincoln already existed in Oregon, but Lewis McArthur in *Oregon Geographic Names* disputes this.

The town gradually grew along the Hoquarten Slough. One store owned by George Fear nside was constructed on a scow so that when business was slow he could float it to another town. A more permanent mercantile was designed with its back over the water so that it could serve boat traffic. Tillamook stores were dependent for supplies on steamships whose schedules were erratic; storekeepers frequently would say, "I am sorry, we are just out, but we expect it in on the next boat."

As the forests were cleared, farmers found that the clover and grass which grew in its place were well-suited for dairying. Many produced butter which they then exported by boat or pack train to Portland and other towns in the Willamette Valley. However, winter storms in the Coast Range and the treacherous Tillamook Bay bar often delayed the transportation of the butter, which then deteriorated in quality due to the lack of refrigeration. A more adaptable product with a stronger constitution was needed.

In the late 1880s, dairy farmers began experimenting with cheese making but had little success. Peter McIntosh, a Canadian, then started several factories in the county, and his cheddar recipe restored the idea that the Tillamook cows were aptly suited for cheese making. Small factories, farmer-owned cooperatives, sprang up. In 1909, some of the cheese factories banded together to market their product, and the Tillamook County Creamery Association was born.

Contemporary literature from the association states that it began as a "quality control organization," but the December 1, 1932 *Tillamook Herald* gives an additional reason: "More and more farmers have discovered that cooperation is the eventual solution for suicidal prices and chaotic agricultural conditions. . . . The more unorganized farmers there are the longer that success will be in coming." By the early 1930s, the association had years of experience in inspection, production, and marketing. During the Depression, the citizens were to do their civic duty; the June 2, 1932 newspaper ran an advertisement stating that during "Buy Tillamook Cheese Week," one person in each of the 3,025 families in the county should send at least one loaf to a friend outside the county in order to increase sales.

Cheese was not Tillamook's only industry. Forests covered the Coast Range and a thriving timber industry had begun in the 1890s. In 1933, a devastating fire, the first of several that collectively were called the Tillamook Burn, destroyed more than 285,000 acres of forest land, most of which was in Tillamook County. A modern sign along Highway 6 calls it "one of the nation's worst forest fires." Subsequent fires in 1939 and 1945 burned young trees and destroyed sources for reseeding. Today, the replanted trees are just beginning to be harvested.

While a lumber company is now the second-largest private employer in the city of Tillamook, the creamery is still by far the largest. Occasionally the odor of cows drifts through the town, providing a pleasant sensory experience of the local economy.

Visiting the Seat of Tillamook County Government

FARMING AND TIMBER ARE NOT ENOUGH to create a boom economy, and Tillamook's transition to more expensive fireproof structures in its business district was slow. As late as 1933 a landlord was still replacing a wood-frame building in the business district. The April 6, 1933 *Tillamook Herald* labeled the old structure an "eye-sore" and praised its concrete replacement as the "most artistic store building in Tillamook county." This structure, still standing at 2011 Third Street, once displayed an Art Deco style with fluted pilasters jutting above the roof and zigzags projecting along the facade. The newspaper reported that the structure, called the "K" Building, was "modernistic in design"; contemporary "modernization" has removed its once lavish ornamentation.

One of the few multi-storied downtown structures where the landlord has not shrouded the upper floors with aluminum siding is the Beals Building, standing at the southwest corner of Main and Third Streets. Arthur Beals once reminisced that he and his brother acquired this site and adjoining acreage when it was still a cow pasture and a rodeo site. The downtown then was concentrated near the slough, but with the approval of the Post Master, Beals and others planned to relocate the post office to some of their property on Main Street, then called "Uptown." They moved it secretly in the middle of the night, and the next day the "downtowners" were in an uproar.

Civic improvements such as electricity, telephones and street paving are taken for granted today, but their presence once was a symbol of a city's progressiveness. The 1912 *Oregon Almanac*, published by the state for "the information of homeseekers, settlers and investors" listed Tillamook as having "hard surface" streets. The city had just begun paving its streets that year. The Pacific Railway & Navigational Company's railroad line finally connected Tillamook with Portland, and the citizens believed that they now were a modern town and needed to show it.

The 1912 *Oregon Almanac* also listed Tillamook as the head of tidewater and navigation on the Hoquarten Slough. The railroad gradually replaced the slough as the main mode of transportation, and the waterway was no longer dredged. Where today's Highway 101 crosses the slough, a 1905 Sanborn map shows a narrow bridge. West of Highway 101, old piling standing along the Hoquarten once supported such businesses as "Lamb's Wharf and Freight House" and "I. F. Long's Sawmill and Box Factory." At the corner of First Avenue and Stillwell Street, amid the modern-day industrial buildings and far from the downtown, Claude Thayer's stone building still has the word "Bank" over its doorway.

The Tillamook Creamery Association's feed store at 4 Ivy Street, one block from the slough,

The October 12, 1911 *Tillamook Headlight* reported on the arrival of the first train. "The Tillamook mist did not dampen the peoples' interest in this long looked for event. Business houses closed and the people flocked to the depot to welcome the train and the railroad officials. As the train approached the city whistles were kept blowing, and on reaching the depot the band played and the crowd cheered and notwithstanding that it was an unofficial visit of the railroad officials, Tillamook City gave them such a rousing reception that it surprised them."

Although cars have replaced trains as a primary means of transportation, older railroad stations still stand in many Oregon towns. *Credit: author*

sells products for the "cow part" of the cheese-making process. Visitors drive through the downtown on their way to see the transformation of milk into cheese at the creamery association's factory further north on Highway 101. The complex, located there since the late 1940s, once allowed tourists to stroll through the aisles, peering over the workers' shoulders; today, for sanitation reasons, they stand behind a glass window in a second-floor viewing area to see the pumpkin-colored bricks being made.

A History of the Courthouse

THOUGH TILLAMOOK HAD BEEN DESIGNATED the county seat since 1872, officials met in a general store for the next sixteen years. When the commissioners began to discuss finally building a courthouse, William Stillwell, the son of the merchant who had platted the first "Town of Lincoln," donated a block for the courthouse. The county accepted his gift, and began the foundation. However, Claude Thayer, a shrewd banker, immediately platted four blocks of his land on the east side of town. Although construction was already a month along, for some now unknown reason county officers accepted a block from Thayer for the courthouse, halted construction on Stillwell's former property, and began building on the Thayer block. Stillwell protested, arguing that the courthouse would be too far away from the town, but even his subsequent lawsuit lost in court.

Tillamook's first courthouse, a two-story wooden structure with a hipped roof, burned in a 1903 fire. The November 19, 1903 *Tillamook Headlight* reported, "A great many rumors gained currency that the court house had been fired because the county officials' books were being experted [checked]. . . . It is true that a week or so previous it was reported around town that the court house would be burned down." While the cause of the fire remains unsolved, two months later the sheriff, found to have embezzled county funds, killed himself.

The Tillamook County *Inventory of the County Archives of Oregon* described the county's first jail. "This structure, built by T. C. Quick for $236, was a one-room building, entrance into which was effected through the roof. The inconvenience of this arrangement was apparently not officially recognized until 1880; but on January 7 of that year the county court ordered the sheriff 'to repair the jail of Tillamook County by placing a door in the building'."

For Tillamook's second courthouse, the commissioners hired architect Charles Burggraf, who had designed the Sherman and Wheeler County courthouses. The new courthouse was constructed of fire-proof concrete with a tower which rose sixty feet. A place on the tower was reserved for a clock, but the mechanism was never installed.

By the early 1930s, the second courthouse was in need of repair, though it was only thirty years old. The county had saved more than $100,000 to repair the structure, but after hearing quotes that a new building would cost only $160,000, they decided to construct a new facility. After visiting courthouses around the state and reviewing the applications of almost forty architects, the county court hired Lawrence, Holford, Allyn and Bean, a firm the February 4th, 1932 *Tillamook Herald* called "one of the best in the state." When the plans were completed, the June 2, 1932 newspaper referred to the building's style as a "modified classic design."

One local firm bid for the general contract, but to the dismay of many citizens, the low bidder was a Portland firm.

The hiring of local labor was particularly important because of the Depression, and the contractor promised to hire as many county residents as possible. To the satisfaction of many taxpayers, the final bids came in at approximately $145,000, about $15,000 less than initially anticipated. Even as the courthouse was under construction, officials and taxpayers were conferring about eliminating or consolidating some county positions.

The July 29, 1932 *Tillamook Headlight* happily reported that of sixty men on the courthouse job, "all . . . except a few foremen are Tillamook county people." Not only workers but much of the building material came from the county, including the sand and gravel for the concrete. Garibali and Tillamook companies furnished the lumber; the Tillamook lumber was sawn at the mill located just two blocks away from the courthouse site.

As the courthouse was nearing completion in January 1933, rumors spread that the construction quality was inferior, and the Chamber of Commerce requested that the county court withhold acceptance of the building until a disinterested party examine the structure. Officials hired a structural engineer, but even though the report would be completed in ten days, the delay was a concern because it would cost the county "considerable expense," according to the January 12, 1933 *Tillamook Herald*. When the structural engineer reported that the building was being constructed according to specifications, county officials began packing their effects in anticipation. By the middle of February, all officials had moved into their new quarters.

Depression worries continued. The June 15, 1933 newspaper, writing about the courthouse square, stated, "It will depend entirely upon financial conditions whether or not concrete sidewalks leading into the two entrances of the building will be constructed, or whether the old board walks will again be replaced temporarily." During that same month, taxpayers asked county officials to take a salary cut, and at least one—the treasurer—agreed.

The Courthouse Today

THE TWO TILLAMOOK COURTHOUSES STILL STAND within one block of each other, but the older building is now the Pioneer Museum. Scattered in the books published by the Pioneer Society are stories of trials once held in that older hall of justice. In one case, when the editor of the *Tillamook Herald* wrote that the editor of *The Independent* could drink enough to float a steamship, the editor of *The Independent* printed that he would see him in court. The maligned editor was awarded one dollar in damages.

Tillamook citizens also were in court during Prohibition. In 1925, a "movie company" came to town to film "Daughters of the Sea." Local crowds were hired as extras, accommodations for forty actors and actresses were reserved at nearby hotels, and a grand party was planned. Such a gala event needed liquor, even if it was illegal, and local distillers were contacted to drop off shipments a few days before the event at the film company's temporary headquarters. When the first bootlegger arrived, he found to his chagrin that the "film producer" was a representative of the state prohibition department. The sheriff arrested the man and led him to the back of the building while a deputy drove the lawbreaker's car to a hiding place. Thus, the setting was cleared to trap the next bootlegger. The local justice of the peace later fined each distiller $500 plus $250 for the return of his or her car.

Although Tillamook is one of the few county seats where the old courthouse is adjacent to the newer quarters, several alterations have drastically changed the older building's appearance. The clock tower is gone, and the principal entrance has been moved to the rear. Inside, the former county quarters are full of items from Tillamook's past, including a replica of Joseph Champion's first tree house. Somewhere in the building is the spade that turned the dirt for the construction of both the 1905 building and the 1933 building.

Thayer, the donor of the first courthouse block, lived for several years in a house on the site of the current courthouse. Thayer undoubtedly could see from his front window the fruits of his persuasive tactics, the county's first courthouse. His own home stood on a lot almost one and a half times the size of a typical city block. Years after he had moved, a miniature golf course occupied part of the block before the courthouse was built.

Community mementos such as an anchor from a British ship found in the Tillamook Bay are displayed on the museum grounds. However, the courthouse square contains only a cruciform-shaped concrete walkway with a plaque near its head commemorating those "who made the supreme sacrifice." Except for a smattering of trees, the landscaping is kept to large stretches of grass. This apparently is attractive to dog owners; on the grounds are four "No Pets" signs.

The Tillamook County courthouse was done in a Half-Modern style, reflecting a period when architectural tastes shifted from classical embellishment toward simplified exteriors. While the main design element of the barbell-shaped building is red brick, at each end projections extend slightly higher than the roof line and each encases two massive twenty-two-foot high concrete columns framing entry doors. Even though the facade is austere, the courthouse's substantial length (211 feet) and imposing height (40 feet) connote importance.

The exterior of the building remains relatively unchanged except for two obvious alterations. On the south side, a small brick extension served as an entrance to the basement in case of a nuclear attack. This does not detract from the building's

Using only a few elements such as the stairs and the columns, the architect conveyed the grandeur of the building. *Credit: author*

formal style as much as the prisoners' cyclone-fenced exercise area—an unsightly necessity—installed on top of the roof.

The June 2, 1932 *Tillamook Herald* related that the architect envisioned one entrance to serve the administrative offices and the other for judicial functions. However, since the two projections are identical, they cause confusion as to which leads where. Flanking the sides of the northern doors are two plaques, one commemorating the architect and builder of the 1905 courthouse, and the other, the architect and builder of the 1933 facility. This entrance opens to a one-story anteroom that adjoins the county clerk's office in the main section of the building. In the hallway, much of the original character of the courthouse interior has been preserved, including Douglas-fir doors and marble flooring.

Along the central hallway, black-and-white photographs depict different aspects of Tillamook County. Several show the blimps at the former Tillamook naval air station, where the largest wooden free-span structure in the world still stands. Earlier residents likely remembered the air base for a different reason. When the government assumed ownership of the property, it included a graveyard, and those wishing to visit the dead required a military escort.

Unlike other Oregon courthouses, the circuit courtroom is located on the first floor, just off the lobby by the southern entry doors. Gracing the wall above the courtroom doors is a fresco painted by Lucia Wiley. The Tillamook native, who later became Sister Lucia, had painted "Captain Gray's First Visit to the Oregon Coast" in the Tillamook post office (now the city hall). She was then commissioned to paint a fresco in the courthouse, and here created "The Building of 'The Morning Star'," showing Tillamook pioneers and local Northwest Indians working together to build their first ship. A pamphlet states, "Towards dusk in the half-darkened room, this painting can still be seen as if it had a light shining through it." To entice visitors to look closely, it notes, "This painting was made in 33 sections. How many can you find?"

Like the exterior, the windowless, two-story courtroom shows a minimalist approach. Dark brown fir paneling extends more than three-quarters up the walls, adding to the somber feeling. At the top of the paneling, a faded stenciled design in green and blue could be trees against the sky, perhaps tying the design to one part of Tillamook's motto, "cheese, trees and ocean breeze."

The judge's bench and the railing match the wainscot, but the blond wooden spectators' benches, looking like church pews, do not match the other furnishings. A staircase through a door on the right allows the sheriff to move prisoners between the second floor jail and the courtroom. Visitors, however, have to take the main staircase to the second story. When the building opened, the janitor also served as the night jailer and lived with his family on the second floor of the courthouse. One of his duties was to cook food for the prisoners—a job that replaced, according to the February 16, 1933 *Tillamook Herald*, "having to carry it from some of the local eating houses."

Another official county office on the second floor was that of the 4-H club leader, who promoted agricultural and home economics for Tillamook boys and girls. According to an early Chamber of Commerce pamphlet, one of the goals of the clubs was to "keep young people interested in the farm and the farm home." The clubs apparently were successful, as many dairy farms in Tillamook are handed down from generation to generation. Tillamook County has other industries besides cheese, but the marketing of its dairy products is so successful that cheese and Tillamook are inextricably linked. Despite that relationship, the symbol of Tillamook City is not a cow; it is a chicken.

Trees obscure a clear view of the entire Washington
County courthouse, but they do allow a vista of the
front pavilion, where the building's decoration is
concentrated. Although the courthouse looks like it was
all built at the same time, it actually was constructed in
1912 and 1928. *Credit: author*

Washington County

County Seat: Hillsboro
Courthouse Address: 145 N.E. Second Avenue
Year Completed: 1928
Architect: Orlo R. W. Hossack
Date of County Formation: July 5, 1843

> *"Maybe I've taken it [the courthouse] for granted.
> Maybe I have become a little bit indifferent to the
> present, and thereby utterly reckless of the future."*
>
> —Henry Hagg, quoted in the *Hillsboro Argus*,
> October 28, 1968

Traces of Hillsboro's farming past remain in the southern part of town along First Street, where the old Carnation Company condensed milk plant and the Imperial Feed and Grain storage facility stand. To the north of Hillsboro, acres of yesterday's prime farmlands have attracted sophisticated high-tech companies with sprawling buildings protected by expansive grass borders. This new wave of industry, economically now much stronger than farming, has fueled Hillsboro's growth in the past few decades. Today, Hillsboro is a town of two faces: one old, one new.

One of the first settlers in the area did not prefer farming. After reportedly telling the chief factor of the Hudson's Bay Company that he was trying to avoid work, Joseph Meek, a former mountain man and fur-trapper, settled near the present-day North Plains. The influx of other former fur-trappers into the region raised the question of whether to break with the Hudson's Bay Company's rule and establish a local government. At a May 2, 1843 meeting in Champoeg, when participants were about to vote, Joseph Meek reportedly shouted out, "Who's for the divide? All for . . . an organization, follow me!" The measure passed.

The settlers formed a provisional government, which divided the Oregon County into four districts: Clackamas, Tuality, Yamhill, and Champoeg. (Later, the government would call these districts counties.) Tuality, where Meek lived, extended south of the Columbia River, west of the Willamette River, north of the Yamhill River, and east of the Pacific Ocean. Tuality district men took part in the new government, as Meek was elected sheriff, and David Hill served in the three-man tribunal until the position of governor was established.

David Hill had settled in the Tualatin Plains on a claim in the southern part of present-day Hillsboro. Hill apparently was adept in political matters; besides being a member of the tribunal, he became postmaster of the settlement of Columbia, later named Hillsboro to honor him. In 1849, he sold forty acres to the county government, which in exchange promised to pay him $200 from the proceeds of the lot sales. The county, which changed its name to Washington to honor the first president, also acquired land north of Hill's property. In 1850, a surveyor platted twenty-four full blocks, seventeen fractional blocks, and a central public square.

Hillsboro began to grow in 1871 when the Oregon Central railroad connected the town to Portland. The initial relationship between Hillsboro and the railroad was tenuous. City leaders reportedly refused to give Ben Holladay, the owner of the railroad, free land within the town for his depot. To spite them, he constructed his line considerably south of the initial settlement.

While the railroad transformed Hillsboro from a hamlet to a market center, the interurban railways changed it to a suburban community. In 1909, the Oregon Electric Railway linked Hillsboro to other towns in the Willamette Valley through a network of lines, although Portland was the most prized connection. Promotional literature designed by the Hillsboro Commercial Club advertised the town as "Just Fifty Electric Minutes From Portland." In the same literature, the commercial club attempted to lure Portland workers by promising that "the business section is taking on a metropolitan air." Despite its urban "sophistication," the town still had farm-based industries. The Pacific Coast Condensed Milk Company, later the Carnation Company, operated a large plant along First Street. In 1920, a cannery began on Baseline Road, and it eventually became a Birds Eye frozen-food plant, one of the first facilities in the United States to package frozen food. Although the plant reportedly made the town smell like broccoli, at its peak it employed 900 workers.

With the cannery demanding fruits and vegetables, many farmers switched to row crops, which were more labor intensive than dairy farming or cereal fodder crops. A labor shortage during World War II attracted the first wave of migrant workers to the area. The war also solidified the town as a "bedroom community" when burgeoning employment at the Portland shipyards during World War II pushed home seekers further west into Washington County.

Suburbanization continued in the second part of the century. In the 1980s, several high-tech companies began locating in the Hillsboro area and other parts of eastern Washington County. For a few years during the 1980s, Washington added more people that any other Oregon county, and Hillsboro, which gained about 10,000 people over that decade, shared in that growth. Even though Hillsboro has a traditional main street with a courthouse square, the surrounding region has become so heavily populated that Hillsboro's role is less of a traditional county seat and more of a bedroom community in the Portland Metropolitan area.

Visiting the Seat of Washington County Government

Hillsboro still possesses a downtown along Main Street. Once the sole commercial district, it attracted residents by its stores and movie theaters. About 1910, Hillsboro citizens were introduced to silent movies during a Fourth of July showing in Shute Park by Orange Phelps, a local businessman. He eventually changed the face of the downtown by building several theaters in Hillsboro, including the still standing Town Theater west of 257 E. Main Street and the former Hill Theater at 127 E. Third Street. Movie theaters, providing escape into an imaginary world, had to have fanciful architecture. While the Town Theater displays a Spanish influence with a red tile mansard roof, the Hill has an Art Deco style with a stepped parapet.

In Hillsboro, as in other towns, the rise of shopping centers along major arterials has diminished the number and type of downtown tenants. A 1930s photograph shows numerous shops along Second Street south of Main Street. Some of the merchandise, such as furniture, meat, and pharmaceutical drugs, now are sold by major stores that have scant interest in the limited parking and small buildings in Hillsboro's downtown.

While shopping centers offer convenience, their architecture generally lacks character, unlike the downtown 1911 Shute Bank Building at 276 E. Main, which exhibits terra cotta lions on the cornice. At 205 E. Main, the Morgan and Baily Building, constructed between 1888 and 1892, has arched windows with stained glass. As new structures gradually replace the old, these vintage buildings become distinctive and acquire a personality.

A History of the Courthouse

Long before the development of Main Street, county officials began convening in several places including Presbyterian and Methodist meetinghouses before moving to a log cabin on the land purchased from David Hill. In 1852, the county commissioned a two-story cedar and pine courthouse to be built on the public square designated in the original plat of Hillsboro, now the site of the present-day courthouse. In 1871, officials proposed a new building, but about ten percent of the population, perhaps fearing higher taxes, petitioned against it. Despite their effort, the county completed a brick structure in 1873 that featured arched windows and a cupola. However, a letter to the editor in the May 28, 1880 *Polk County Itemizer* stated that the Washington County courthouse "was so badly constructed that in a short time it was necessary to put in hog-chains and braces to keep it from falling to pieces."

In 1891, Delos Neer designed an addition that incorporated the 1871 structure. The new front entrance of the courthouse featured a clock tower, but the county could not afford the mechanism and the clock faces remained empty. In 1909, two residents approached officials about purchasing a clock, and were told that the county would donate $100 if they could raise $1,000. They apparently were not successful.

In 1912, the red brick courthouse again was expanded, this time with a buff-colored brick addition. With rectangular windows instead of arched, and an entablature instead of bracketed eaves, the addition made no attempt to look like the old. The addition also reflected advances in construction technology. The June 6, 1912 *Hillsboro Argus* reported that the reinforced concrete floor was durable and strong enough to "last as long as the pyramids of Egypt."

Washington County still has its old 1853 wooden jail, now standing at the fairgrounds. According to the February 27, 1986 *Hillsboro Argus*, the jail is thought to be the state's oldest surviving log building, and believed to have housed a famous historical figure for one night. Lore is that while in charge of the Vancouver Barracks, Ulysses S. Grant ordered supplies from a San Francisco store, but because of transportation and communication difficulties, did not pay the bill. The sheriff waited in Portland for Grant, arrested him, and took him to Hillsboro for trial. He later was acquitted.

In 1928, citing a shortage of space and high cost of repairs, the county called for bids on yet another addition to replace the 1873 and 1891 portions of the courthouse. The March 29, 1928 newspaper sentimentally lamented that "the old court has seen everything in trials from murders to petty larceny and booze cases; it has know sadness and gladness." The liquor from those "booze cases" remained a part of the old structure until its destruction, when a "spilling party" poured 600 gallons of evidence down the bathtub drain in the old jail.

The Courthouse Today

THE COUNTY WAS NOT FINISHED EXPANDING on the courthouse square, although subsequent structures were not considered to be part of the courthouse. In the 1970s, the county constructed two supplemental buildings on the square. By the early 1990s, the county had outgrown its space in the courthouse and additions, and a new three-story Administrative Building was erected one block west on First Street. The movement of county offices toward the concentration of buildings along First Street and away from the once main entrance of the courthouse has effectively left the courthouse square as a "back yard."

While additions have come and gone, the sequoia trees on the square, now more than 100 years old, have endured. The profusion of other trees and bushes, though not as old, has changed the square from the usual grassy expanse to a secluded park. Protected by the landscaping, one can still almost hide from the bustle of county government in the nearby buildings.

The square has become a repository of tokens from the past. The weathered cornerstone from the 1891 addition is placed on the southwestern corner of the square. A marker located by the flagpole commemorates all veterans "who honorably served" in past wars. Fittingly, the square served as the site for the July 4, 1918 celebration for local boys heading to Europe. Perhaps it was part of their stamina training, for the ceremonies lasted from 10:00 a.m. to

In 1968, just weeks before an election in which voters were to decide on expenditures for expanding the courthouse and jail facilities, the *Hillsboro Argus* ran articles about how the crowded the facilities were. To get to the Department of Records and Elections, a visitor had to walk down a steep and poorly lighted stairway to the basement, and anyone over six feet would have had to stoop to avoid banging his or her head on overhead heating pipes when conducting business at the counter. At the jail, the kitchen was not large enough to prepare meals for all the prisoners, so TV dinners were served for lunch and dinner. Doubtless, that would have made any prisoner contemplate a law-abiding life.

7:15 p.m. Today, a farmer's market lines the periphery of the square on summer and fall Saturdays.

The amount of decoration concentrated on the front pavilion distinguishes it from the rest of the courthouse. *Credit: author*

Initially, the 1912 northern structure and the 1928 southern addition seem to have been built at the same time. Since the architect apparently had not been commissioned to alter the 1912 section, the 1928 addition was designed to match it. With this constraint, the architect lavished the decoration on the entrance pavilion, providing a great contrast between this section and the rest of the building.

Accordingly, Greek motifs are concentrated on the entrance pavilion. Terra cotta, a clay easily molded into intricate shapes, was lavishly used. On the entablature, eighteen lions with sharply pointed ears gaze down on Washington County citizens. The central decorating theme, however, is the palmette, a common Greek ornament derived from the palm leaf. Palmettes are well represented in such places as on the roof line, the capitals on the Ionic columns, and the stained glass lanterns hanging above each of the three entries.

Inside, a metal detector is now necessary for this "big-city" courthouse. Modernization efforts have obliterated any separate sense of either the 1912 or the 1928 buildings. Perhaps because each section was itself an enlargement, the interior finishes likely were unremarkable even when new.

Unlike other counties in Oregon, Washington County never had one grand courthouse. Since 1891, the buildings that served this function were additions, some of which blended with the earlier structures and some of which did not. Without big boom periods, farmers tend to be cautious, and the modern economic expansion by the computer industry is years too late to build a magnificent courthouse. Community attitudes and fiscal policies have changed.

Southwestern Counties

The 1929 courthouse was expanded on both sides by two additions constructed in 1956. While the additions were plainer in design, they did match the height and window spacing of the original building. A Justice Center was constructed later behind the courthouse, but county officials thoughtfully had the building designed so as not to loom over the courthouse.
Credit: author

Douglas County

County Seat:	Roseburg
Courthouse Address:	1036 S.E. Douglas Street
Year Completed:	1929
Architect:	John Tourtellotte
Date of County Formation:	January 7, 1852

> *"In the evening [of the courthouse dedication]. . . .*
> *The local machine gun company will give a*
> *demonstration of machine gun use."*
>
> —*Roseburg News-Review,* October 17, 1929

The presence of a large proportion of the timber resources of Douglas county in a national forest guarantees for all time a steady flow of raw material," wrote the supervisor of the Umpqua National Forest in the October 17, 1929 *Roseburg News-Review.* In the years following World War II, Douglas County became one of the leading timber-producing counties in the state, and Roseburg even billed itself as the "Timber Capital of the Nation." Although lumber brought prosperity, it also penalized the county with cycles of unemployment at levels higher than the state average. Roseburg people today, with wisdom gained by experience, have encountered a scenario different from what the forest supervisor forecasted in 1929. While lumber is still important, the town is trying to build a more diverse economic base.

Forests were an untapped resource when Aaron Rose purchased the squatters' rights to a donation land claim near the confluence of the Umpqua River and Deer Creek in 1851. Surrounded by hills on the east and Mt. Nebo on the west, the land lay near the Applegate Trail, a route running from

California to present-day Oregon. In addition to farming, Rose built a general store and eventually a tavern, a butcher shop, and an inn.

The area's increasing population led the legislature to create Douglas County in January 1852, and they named it after Stephen Douglas, a fiery Illinois senator who was fighting for Oregon's statehood. The temporary county seat designation went to Winchester, a town located approximately five miles north of Roseburg. In the fight for the permanent county seat position, Winchester was joined by Roseburg and Lookingglass, a community about nine miles southwest of Roseburg. Rose thoughtfully offered $1,000 and three acres of land for the courthouse if his town won. According to the October 17, 1929 *Roseburg News-Review*, he also invited Lookingglass voters to come for a large dinner and "he was such a perfect host" that Lookinglass citizens showed their appreciation by casting their ballots for Roseburg.

Roseburg also benefitted when the Northern Battalion of the Oregon Volunteers, fighting the Northwest Indians on the Rogue River in 1855–1856, made the town its base. To compete, Winchester secured the federal land grant office, and built a two-story building to show off its accomplishment. Rose then donated the land and $1,400 for a three-story schoolhouse of "grander proportions." Finally, in 1859, Winchester citizens conceded defeat and bodily moved the land office, two stores, and several residences to Roseburg.

In 1872, the Oregon & California railroad, which originated in Portland, reached Roseburg and ran out of funds. For nine years, Roseburg enjoyed its position as the southern terminus of the railroad. Townspeople built warehouses and granaries, and after these became too small, they constructed larger facilities. When the railroad company began building south, Roseburg was predicted to suffer a great hardship. Instead, the railroad made the town a division point. The railroad eventually employed so many people that a whole neighborhood, today called Mill-Pine, grew east of the tracks so that employees could walk to work.

After the railroad constructed a new main line through the Siskiyou Mountains in 1927, the division point was moved to Eugene. When the Veterans Administration began searching for a hospital site in the Northwest in the late 1920s, town leaders saw their chance for another big employer with steady, secure jobs. Since Roseburg already had the Oregon State Soldiers' Home constructed to house non-Indian soldiers who had fought in the Rogue River War, leaders considered their town a logical choice. After considerable politicking, the town was named the site, and after Roseburg citizens heard in September 1931 that the Veterans Hospital was finally theirs, a thousand citizens paraded through the streets, dressed in what the September 19, 1931 *Roseburg News-Review* called "prosperity garb."

The demand for plywood soared after World War II, and the county boomed due to its vast acreage of Douglas-fir trees. According to statistics published in the 1959 *Population Trends in Roseburg*, fifty-four mills operated in the county in the 1940s, but 134

The relatively mild Roseburg climate influenced a seventy-six-year old Minnesota man to walk 2,100 miles across the country in 1931. With a push cart for his belongings, he spent about seventy dollars on the trip, which took him a year and a half to complete. Once in Roseburg, he planned to support himself with a wood-cutting job. Ironically, the day before he arrived in Roseburg, the September 3, 1931 *Roseburg News-Review* published that the Chamber of Commerce, concerned about the effects of the Depression, was stating, "We suggest that each Roseburg citizen definitely discourage new people from coming among us unless they have the available cash to see them through the next twelve months. Roseburg and Douglas County have their own unemployment problems and our valley cannot be made a mecca for the distressed of other localities."

mills were running in 1950. With an abundance of well-paying jobs, Roseburg's population grew from 4,924 in 1940 to 8,390 in 1950, an increase of seventy percent.

In the midst of this prosperity, disaster occurred early in the morning of August 7, 1959. A trash can fire located three blocks west of the downtown ignited a nearby parked truck laden with two tons of dynamite and four-and-a-half tons of ammonium nitrate carbonitrate. The resulting fireball created a crater 15 feet deep and 45 feet wide; the tremor was heard as far away as fourteen miles. Whole city blocks were flattened, and further away, windows burst and roofs collapsed. Fourteen people eventually died, and 125 were seriously wounded.

The blast drew national and international attention with calls offering assistance from New York and London. One resident later wrote an article for the *Saturday Evening Post* succinctly titled, "The Night Our Town Blew Up." According to the August 7, 1960 *Oregonian*, town promoters set up signs along the major roads into Roseburg, stating, "34 city blocks BLASTED . . . Tour The Area, See a City Rebuild."

Roseburg did rebuild, and went on to endure several difficult economic periods reflecting its timber-based industry. In the 1980s and 1990s, concerned over the long-term timber supply, mills began reducing employment. Although lumber remains an important part of the economy, today significantly fewer people are employed in this industry than in 1970. Roseburg and Douglas County are trying to diversify by attracting other employers. The Veterans Hospital, an old provider of "steady, secure jobs," has helped attract retirees to the area, who are playing a larger part in the Roseburg economy.

Visiting the Seat of Douglas County Government

MAIN STREET IS NOT THE PRINCIPAL commercial street in Roseburg, although it did begin as such. An 1873 survey shows the Deer Creek bridge at the foot of Jackson Street, which likely contributed to its rise as the predominant downtown street. For a now unknown reason, the surveyor of the initial plat made the blocks separating Jackson and Main Streets south of the courthouse square only one lot deep, instead of the usual two, and thus today some stores have back entrances on Main Street.

Downtown structures usually face the main route of commerce, but the drug store at the corner of Jackson and Washington Streets presents its back toward the central business street. The drug store is part of a shopping center straddling Rose Street, one block west, which replaced a junior high school and commercial building both damaged in the

1959 blast. Other modern changes resulting from the blast are not as obvious. At least two downtown buildings, at 506 and 539 S.E. Jackson Street, had the second story removed because of damages to the upper floor, and many landlords covered other second-floor damage with new facades. The August 4, 1960 *News-Review*, under the headline "A Sparkling New City Is Rising From Ruins," boasted that "Along the Jackson-Cass business area . . . there is little evidence that a blast ever occurred. . . . Most of them [the structures] have new, modern fronts." While some buildings have been historically renovated, other structures still reflect Roseburg's past when the blast was recent and lumber was king.

Like the Grand, hotels once clustered within blocks of a railroad station to provide lodging for train passengers. Credit: *author*

Unlike Grants Pass or Medford, Roseburg already was established when the railroad was constructed, and so the tracks ran west of the downtown. From Jackson Street, one can see the depot built directly at the end of Cass Street, four blocks west.

So strong was the railroad as a generator of commerce that Roseburg landlords also constructed buildings along Cass Street to be closer to the railroad. During the 1950s, Roseburg workers ate at the appropriately named Timber Room and Timber Grille in the five-story Grand Hotel at 732 S.E. Cass Street, while lumber companies and labor unions occupied offices at the four-story Perkins Building across the street. Today, the structure is called the Pacific Building, but it still has an employee operating the elevator, an anomaly in a small town.

On the west side of Pine Street between Oak and Washington Avenues, just one-and-a-half blocks from the railroad station, lies the site of the parked explosive truck. Originally, several plans were discussed for the rebuilding of Roseburg. According to the September 8, 1959 *News-Review*, the National Lumber Manufacturers Association suggested asking nationally known architect Richard Neutra to design a "showplace for the lumber industry" which, according to the city manager, "'would have far-reaching influence on the entire city of Roseburg.'" Today, only an eight- by ten-inch bronze plaque affixed on a boulder commemorates the blast. A wooden "Parts" sign from the adjacent auto dealership now stands over the boulder, making the marker even more obscure.

Based on its exterior design, it is easy to imagine the 1898 courthouse having many interesting interior spaces.
Author's collection

A History of the Courthouse

LIKE ROSEBURG'S EARLY COMMERCIAL buildings, the first courthouse was a two-story wood frame building with a porch and a false front which stood on Main Street. The structure cost the county just $200; Rose donated the ground on which the present-day courthouse stands, contributed $1,000 for building materials, and bestowed and an almost equal amount in free labor. The first courthouse later was used as a store after the county commissioned a two-story brick and wood courthouse with a cupola to be built in 1868. Twenty-three years later, according to the October 17, 1929 *Roseburg News-Review*, the county expanded the building and added a tower in the center of the roof. Not just county workers occupied the courthouse, however, as attorneys conveniently rented offices there until the commissioners ordered them to move in late 1896. After a fire in 1898, the exterior walls of the devastated structure were used in rebuilding a larger courthouse that featured elaborate brickwork and an asymmetrically placed tower.

Anticipating the need for yet another courthouse, the court set aside $50,000 in 1917. Earlier practices by the Oregon & California railroad inadvertently produced the rest of the funding for the courthouse. As an incentive to lay track, the federal government authorized land grants to the railroad in 1869 under several conditions, including that they sell the land to settlers at a certain price. After the railroad failed to fulfill the terms of the grant, the federal government took back the unsold land in 1916. The affected counties, eighteen in all, then argued that they had been deprived of property taxes they could have collected had those lands been under private ownership. In 1927, Douglas County received a check from the federal government representing eleven years of back taxes, adding

The December 10, 1886 *Plaindealer* reported, "The average expense of our circuit court amounts to about 5 cents a minute. So every minute the lawyers dispute with each other over trivial affairs, raising technical questions and arguing frivolous questions or asking witnesses questions that are irrelevant … costs the taxpayers."

$200,000 to the courthouse fund which by then had grown to $75,000.

In February 1928, the court commissioned construction; eleven months later, the local newspaper reported that the finishing work was in progress. However, the front of the new courthouse could not yet be constructed because the new building had been placed so close to the old one. After the older structure was demolished, its building material was recycled to construct a county machinery shed.

The celebration of the courthouse completion was scheduled for October 19, 1929, and citizens from all parts of Douglas County were involved in the planning. The slogan, "County-Wide Day of Pride," was printed on windshield stickers and distributed to drivers through local service stations. Other decorations for the opening day included flags and buntings placed on storefronts and across Roseburg streets. In the spirit of the celebration, the October 17, 1929 newspaper printed in the Poem for the Day column a verse titled "Douglas County's Jubilee":

> Hear Mother Douglas shout her call!
> Hear Roseburg's echo—one and all!
> From Gardiner, Gunter, clear to Glide,
> Oh, come, behold the county's pride!

Believing that the granges represented the entire county more than any other group, the court selected them to perform the dedication ceremony. Afterward, Governor I. L. Patterson gave a speech remarking that the courthouse "will favorably impress all who visit your county seat with the progressive, prosperous, forward-moving character of your community." This undoubtedly pleased county leaders, who had at that time already begun campaigning for the new Veterans Administration hospital.

The opening day was not all speeches. Out-of-town visitors could attend a football game or a movie matinee. In the early evening, when the streets were lit by red flares and searchlights, games such as an old-fashioned hoop-rolling contest and a bicycle obstacle race were held in front of the courthouse. A dance was held at the armory. Citizens throughout the county celebrated the opening of the courthouse. Ten days later, investors throughout the nation would experience another, less-welcome event: the crash of the stock market.

The Courthouse Today

A WIDE EXPANSE OF GRASS EXTENDS the length of the building, separating the Douglas County courthouse from the street also named Douglas. The courthouse square displays no community mementos, but the county created a separate place east of the main walkway honoring Douglas County veterans. Here, the relatively flat ground rises to encircle a bowl-shaped space containing a curved bench and plaques commemorating those who died in the two World Wars, Korea, Vietnam, and the Persian Gulf.

The building visible from the front of the square is really the 1929 building plus two wings added in 1956 that altered the courthouse's shape from a breadbox to a barbell. The wings have considerably less embellishment, reflecting both the then-prevalent architectural trends and the usual county economizing. Unlike additions to other courthouses, this one blends with the building through the close matching of height and window size.

When the 1929 courthouse was constructed, the April 1, 1929 *Roseburg News-Review* boasted that it "will be heralded throughout the architectural world as a new achievement in concrete construction." Concrete buildings themselves were not new, but the Douglas County courthouse supposedly was the first major building not to need stuccoing or plastering on the exterior after the concrete was poured. The concrete was poured into forms designed to give the impression that the building had been constructed of stone blocks, and to further this illusion, workers dusted the exterior with granite. In the October 17, 1929 newspaper, John Tourtellotte, the architect, called this "con-stone," a method of "creating a stone building in appearance and structural integrity [which] is the equal and in many respects superior to the older methods of construction."

The height of these two-story columns adds to the stateliness of the courthouse.
Credit: author

Tourtellotte said that he intended to design a temple of justice so that citizens "may recognize this building and its purpose at a glance." To do this, he employed Greek ornamentation on the concrete building, including a row of six two-story columns across the front. Without a pediment and with the length rather than the width of the building facing the street, this "temple of justice" resembles the side of a Greek temple rather than the front.

Other Greek-style embellishments include the cornice above the columns which feature large dentils, and the balustrade on the roof. According to the architect, the balustrade was designed to hide the barred windows of the jail that once was located on the roof. Tourtellotte said that the jail "has the appearance of an art gallery and breaks the skyline with a graceful and pleasing contour." One of the reasons for the jail's location was so that there would be "no danger of friends passing files or saws through the bars." Although the high location prevented the passing of files or saws, inmates once exercised on the roof and, according to one county employee, occasionally escaped by shimmying down the branches of a huge neighboring elm tree.

Although stairs run across more than half the frontage on the 1929 building, they lead to only two entry doors located near the middle of the structure. Inside, hallway walls display stone-like blocks in a range of gold tones, but like the exterior, these too are concrete. Set in one of the walls is a plaque about the 1929 courthouse, while on the other is a plaque about the 1956 addition. The latter plaque features a rendition of Aaron Rose, and is fittingly rose-colored. The terrazzo floor border exhibits another shade of rose.

Details such as the terrazzo floor, gold paint, and ceiling beams adorned with dentils end abruptly at the start of the 1956 wings, which, like their exterior, have a plainer finish. By the time the county had constructed the wings, it had experienced almost a decade of the lumber boom. In the late 1970s, the county built the four-story Justice Center north of the courthouse. Upon its completion, all judicial functions and the jail moved to the Justice Center, leaving the 1929 courthouse with only administrative offices. The former circuit courtroom, called by the October 17, 1929 newspaper "one of the beauty spots of the building" with its walls designed to look like stone blocks and a "heavy-beamed ceiling with its attractive ornamental plaster," now serves as an office.

Tall and monolithic, the exterior of the Jackson County courthouse gives few clues to the Art Deco splendor inside. When it was built, the courthouse was designed to house not only county offices, but a community theater and clinic. *Credit: author*

Jackson County

County Seat:	Medford
Courthouse Address:	10 S. Oakdale Avenue
Year Completed:	1932
Architect:	John Link
Date of County Formation:	January 12, 1852

> *"A tourist to see it [the courthouse] will have to drive about nine blocks off his course, going north or south. So nobody will ever know what the tourists think about it, and what they really think does not matter."*

> —Arthur Perry, *Medford Mail Tribune*, September 1, 1932

Jacksonville already had reigned as southern Oregon's leading town for almost thirty years when Medford was established near the railroad line, about five miles west. Medford grew as a distribution point, but it boomed after its commercial club promoted the town as the center of bountiful orchard land. Jacksonville faded in prominence, and its buildings now appear so arrested in time that the town is a National Historic Landmark District. Medford landlords were prosperous enough to update their structures, and today many original facades hide behind 1950s and 1960s remodeling. The fifth-largest city in Oregon, Medford is seeing urban sprawl and traffic jams, the price of its economic vitality.

Southern Oregon was relatively unsettled until the winter of 1851–52, when gold discoveries along Jackson Creek caused prospectors to rush to the area. Jacksonville began as a makeshift mining camp, but soon became a flourishing trade center. Gamblers and prostitutes came to the town, as did settlers, who began farming wheat along creek bottomlands. The early years, however, were not a quiet existence, for the newcomers had several skirmishes with the Rogue River Indians.

With the population influx, the legislature created Jackson County in January 1852, naming it after President Andrew Jackson. State officials, however, were uncertain as to where the southern border of their jurisdiction lay, and ordered a survey to see whether the present town of Yreka, California was located in the Oregon territory. Jacksonville, the only settlement of any size, eventually was named the county seat.

The Oregon & California railroad, which had stopped in Roseburg in 1872 due to financial insolvency, resumed construction in 1881. Jacksonville residents were dismayed to learn that the railroad was planning to bypass their town unless they secured a right-of-way and donated an additional $25,000. The townspeople were divided over the matter, but ultimately reasoned that Jacksonville had been the leading town in southern Oregon for years and could thrive without the railroad.

The railroad began staking a route in the middle of the Bear Creek Valley. Four settlers there offered to donate land to the company in return for the railroad building a depot and establishing a town. J. S. Howard, a surveyor, platted an eighty-two-block plat with the railroad track positioned in the center. Fittingly, it was a railroad engineer who named the town Medford as a shortened version of "middle ford," a reference to nearby Bear Creek.

Even before the first passenger train came to the town, merchants started erecting wooden buildings paralleling the railroad tracks, and by the winter of 1883–84, Medford had almost forty buildings. J. S. Howard, the surveyor, also owned a store and operated the first post office. A cigar box initially held the incoming mail, but as the town grew, it was replaced by a soapbox with nine compartments, and then a case with thirty compartments. Jacksonville citizens disparagingly referred to the rival town as "Mudville," "Rabbitville," and "Chaparral City."

After Joseph Stewart, an early orchardist, started shipping fruit by train in 1890, others soon followed. In 1905, the Medford Commercial Club constructed a building by the railroad depot which exhibited apples, cherries, figs, and other produce indigenous to the county. The display was to entice outsiders to invest in the community, and trains stopped for ten minutes so that every passenger would have the opportunity to view the exhibit.

The club was phenomenally successful in luring outside money into the area. Fueled by astounding prices paid for Rogue Valley fruit, a land boom began. The valley became known nationwide as a place where nearly anyone could plant fruit and make money—a notion promoted by club brochures that promised one's investment would return a thousand-fold within ten years.

As the center of the orchard boom, Medford's 1,791 people in 1900 mushroomed to 8,840 people in 1910. Wealthy Easterners, coming in droves, created an "upper class" in Medford. Local residents disparagingly called some "remittance men," referring to the monthly check many received from their parents back East to stay away. This outside money, according to Catherine A. Noah in *Land in Common*, helped Medford in 1910 to boast the highest number of cars per capita in the world.

However, not all the land speculators were wealthy; many spent their life savings to purchase land. Taking advantage of those who were ignorant of orchard practices, one advertisement touted that large rocks, heated by the sun in the day,

Commercial clubs, the predecessors of chambers of commerce, frequently were the source of "information" booklets that spoke in flowery language about the opportunities and livability of the area they were promoting. Long on generalities and short on facts, their goal was to entice settlers to move to and invest in their area. With the influence of the Easterners, Medford was well known for its sophisticated taste in art. The Medford Commercial Club published a booklet in 1910 that addressed Medford's love of the theater. "Medford is known among theatrical folks as the best 'one-night stand' west of the Rocky Mountains, when population is considered."

kept the trees warm at night. Wealthy and poor alike lost their investment when international markets closed during World War I, while blight and poor irrigation decreased the yield. Although a number of irrigation canals were constructed after World War I, the Depression years were another time of hardship.

With the local and national demand for lumber after World War II, the county's timber industry grew. Today, the timber industry is less important to Medford. One of the town's largest employers, a mail-order company selling fruit and other specialty foods, is the largest employer during the peak season.

Visiting the Seat of Jackson County Government

WITH TRUCKS NOW THE PRIMARY FRUIT shipper, the former railroad station, which once had an address of "0 Front Street," no longer is the symbolic center of Medford. According to the October 19, 1910 *Medford Mail Tribune,* visiting railroad magnate Edward H. Harriman had reportedly turned to the station's general manager and said, "Build these people a depot and give them the best there is." Although Harriman died shortly thereafter, the structure that was built was "said to be the most handsome in the state of Oregon with the exception of the one in Portland." After cars became more important than the train, the city laid Sixth and Eighth streets across the railroad's property. Today, the red brick building with a hipped tile roof endures as a commercial structure.

When the railroad was still the primary source of fruit transportation, packing structures and storage houses lined the track. While many of these buildings have been destroyed by fire, the former Pinnacle Packing Plant No. 3 still stands opposite the former railroad station as a testimony to that time. This utilitarian structure retains its large open docks for unloading and loading fruit from trucks to freight cars. The wall facing the track, though faded, still advertises "Pinnacle" and a later name, "Medford Feed & Seed."

The commercial center is no longer concentrated along the railroad tracks, but has spread out primarily along Main Street and Central Street. Modern facades, sometimes updated two or three times, hide the ages of the older buildings. A dry goods store once occupied the circa 1886 brick-fronted building at 120 E. Main Street, but by 1912, a bank completely remodeled the front with two-story Ionic columns and a marble facade. After the bank moved in 1954, the owners updated the structure with a sheet metal facade that featured fourteen-inch disks that look like suction cups. Locals refer to the structure as the "Bathmat Building," speculating that if the facade fell onto the street, it would be impossible to move because of the suction.

The few structures in downtown Medford that are unremodeled suggest the wealth of the town by their exuberant embellishment. When the local economy boomed after World War II, J. C. Penney erected a building at 106 N. Central Street which still features a curved two-story front, exemplifying the style popular at the time. In the mid-1980s, J. C. Penney relocated to a shopping center on the fringe of Medford, but the Southern Oregon Historical Society has preserved the earlier building as its museum.

Very few downtown buildings remain that were home to the wealthy Easterners during Medford's first orchard boom. The 1910 Hotel Medford, which stood at the northwest corner of Main and Ivy Streets, served as one of the leading hotels. Medford's elite would meet at the restaurant for Sunday dinner. At one time, the exclusive Colony Club, formed to help orchardists' wives socialize while their husbands attended to business, rented two rooms. The change in lifestyles over the years made this tall hotel obsolete for the wealthy. Ironically, the hotel was being converted to low-income housing when it burned in 1988. In an attempt to keep the past, the new building was rebuilt to the almost exact appearance of the old.

A History of the Courthouse

JACKSONVILLE, AS THE ONLY SIGNIFICANTLY populated town in the county, was the first county seat in 1852, but its accommodations were primitive. In 1854, the judge held court in a structure next to a saloon. According to the *History of Southern Oregon*, "The bench was a dry-goods box, covered with a blue blanket, and it is quite probable that the uncomfortable seat occupied by the judge was so irksome that it had something to do with his rapid dispensation of justice."

After meeting in various buildings, county officials occupied the first floor of a Masonic lodge, and then eventually took over the entire structure when the Masons moved. In the early 1880s, after a commissioner favoring new quarters was elected by a large majority, the county began building a two-story brick courthouse with a bell tower. To celebrate its completion, Jacksonville residents organized a ball, with dancing held in the courtroom and supper provided in several offices.

As county government grew, space in the courthouse became scarce and the official records had to be stored in a wood shed on the square. According to the August 31, 1932 *Medford Mail Tribune*, a fire in the late 1910s started by a smoking jail employee fetching wood prompted civic organizations to call for a new courthouse. This movement brought up the question of moving the county seat, since Jacksonville was no longer the leading town, but the measure failed. However, rather than constructing a new building, the county instead enlarged the courthouse by adding a vault and jury room to the rear.

In mid-1926, with eight county offices located in rented quarters outside the courthouse (and six of these in Medford), the court decided that the old building was no longer acceptable. Before the court made a decision, the Medford and Ashland chambers of commerce asked that the location issue again be put to a vote. To help their chances of winning the county seat, the Medford city council then thoughtfully offered to construct a fireproof "city hall" which would be available free to the county for five years.

Days before the election, the October 27, 1926 *Medford Mail Tribune* related that by having the

Helen Colvig Cook in the November 28, 1926 *Medford Mail Tribune* noted the courthouse "was used in the past for all the large social and civic gatherings which the town and county had. It has been the scene of famous Fourth of July celebrations and those wonderful pioneer reunions, community Christmas trees, grand balls, and even formal weddings."

courthouse and the sheriff in Jacksonville, it was "encouraging crime in Jackson County." The Pacific Highway was the center of crime in the county, and since the sheriff had to drive four to five miles just to get to the road, it gave criminals the advantage. Other persuasive tactics also were employed. The County Seat Removal Committee ran an advertisement in the October 30, 1926 newspaper displaying a small picture of the Jacksonville courthouse, obscured by trees, next to a larger, clearer picture of the Grants Pass courthouse with the caption, "Why This Antiquated Structure—When Jackson County Needs a Modern Building Like Grants Pass Court House Shown Above." (At the time, that building was already ten years old.) Calling the Jacksonville courthouse a "fire trap," the committee reminded the public that there are no banks in Jacksonville and county officials must risk holdups by transporting money to Medford.

The October 30, 1926 newspaper further rallied their readers by stating, "It is now or never with the courthouse. Failure this time means failure forever. But if Medford does her duty the victory is won." With a winning vote of 4,761 to 1,836, Medford did her duty. The old courthouse eventually became a museum.

By early 1930, with the lease of the "city hall" soon to expire, officials chose the Washington Grade School block as the site for the new courthouse. Citizens, citing the central location, availability of parking, and the attractive setting, approved the choice. Jacob Crane, a nationally known planning engineer in town to develop a planning survey for Medford, told the local Kiwanis Club that he also favored the site, but that the courthouse should face Oakdale Avenue because it could not

The November 28, 1926 *Medford Mail Tribune* printed Helen Colvig Cook's article lamenting the decline of Jacksonville's eminence. "First Jacksonville was robbed of her gold and deserted by those who ravished her; later the railroad snubbed her and cut her off from the main thoroughfare of progress. She has seen her younger generations depart, seeking success in far away places, and finally in her old age the upstart town of Medford, like an ungrateful stepchild, has stolen her court house from her."

be "advantageously placed to provide a view of the building from Main Street."

By June of 1930, officials were conferring with five different architects and visiting other courthouses around the state. The county court was involved in all aspects of the courthouse planning. In January, 1932, shortly before work began, County Judge Alex Sparrow was in Klamath Falls inspecting the heating system in the courthouse there, with the prospect of installing a similar system in the new courthouse. During the tour, he accidentally fell into the furnace pit and suffered head injuries. He died four days later.

Mrs. Sparrow was among the guests of honor at the dedication ceremonies on September 1, 1932. Billed by the *Medford Mail Tribune* as the finest ever staged in southern Oregon, the ceremonies started with a parade, which included a woman carrying a fan that had been used at the opening ball for the Jacksonville courthouse. On the steps of the new building, noted speakers praised the $265,000 courthouse (Arthur Perry in the September 1, 1932 *Medford Mail Tribune* commented that there "was no dearth of oratory"). After the flag ceremony, the estimated crowd of nearly six thousand dispersed, many to attend the afternoon baseball game or the evening boxing match and dance.

Like many courthouses, early pictures before the landscaping is mature allow a better view of the whole building. *Credit: Southern Oregon Historical Society*

The Courthouse Today

THE COURTHOUSE SQUARE STILL BEARS TRACES from its past as a school site. On the northwest side of the site, a sundial honors a beloved teacher, reading "I count none but sunny hours." The gnomon, however, is now missing. Children must have played under the grandiflora magnolia tree planted sometime between 1910 and 1920 near the southeast corner of the site. To refresh both children and adults, a drinking fountain was added later near the front of the courthouse. It and a matching bench feature samples of petrified wood.

The courthouse, rising three stories with a four-story central pavilion, appears to be a monolithic concrete building from a distance. Closer, the exterior of Indiana limestone blocks shows subtle differences in shades of buff. According to Arthur Perry in the September 1, 1932 newspaper, "The limestone is the covering for concrete walls, which rest upon a firm foundation of bedrock. A fool notion can butt the courthouse and not shake Jackson County to its very foundation."

The December 3, 1930 newspaper reported that county officials had wanted to "eradicate all 'gingerbread' effects and have straight lines predominate in the lines of the courthouse." The style that satisfied their needs was Art Deco, which included among its characteristics a vertical emphasis, ornaments in low relief, and windows with metal sashes. According to Rosalind Clark in *Architecture Oregon Style*, so many 1930s buildings featured this style that the public began to call it "Depression Modern."

The most identifiable low-relief ornamentation is near the roof, where twin eagles are exhibited beak to beak. Eagles, like government, are not to be shown resting, and those on the courthouse, with their wings ready for flight and action, are no exception. Another decoration with less apparent ties to the courthouse includes fleur-de-lis in heraldic shields on the entrance pavilion. Between the front door openings, five-petaled flowers decorate the top of fluted columns. These "implied columns" and the cornice above were to represent "Roman and Grecian ideas," noted the August 31, 1932 newspaper.

The attention given to the smallest details on the eagles suggests the importance of the courthouse.
Credit: author

Near the southeast corner, a secondary doorway with the word "Auditorium" incised in terra cotta over the entrance was described by the August 31, 1932 newspaper as "smaller and less decorative, but equally attractive." The architectural blueprints show the auditorium, now used by county commissioners for official meetings, as a community theater with a stage, small dressing rooms, and a checkroom near the entry doors. The entrance on the north side labeled "Court House" is now for employees only. This entrance once led to a children's clinic in the basement. On the rear of the building, another entrance is left blank, but according to the newspaper, it was to be marked "Museum." A 1957 addition and the parking lot were built in the rear of the courthouse and the basement entrance today serves as the main entry.

Burglars entered a rear window in February 1933, while a political rally for an insurgent group called the Good Government Congress was being held at the auditorium. The thieves stole election ballots to prevent a recount that might have overturned the victory of their Good Government candidate for sheriff. The break-in resulted in the death of a deputy as he came to arrest one of their leaders. These events are an enduring chapter of the county's tumultuous political history; the now sealed rear window, the sixth window south of the back entrance, still symbolizes this past.

Ironically, the Good Government Congress alleged that several local officials were corrupt, and many small orchardists and farmers, suffering from the Depression and looking for solutions, were among those attracted to the group. During that time of economic hardship, use of local materials in the courthouse was both symbolically and economically important. All lumber, cement, and granite were Jackson County products, including the granite from the Ashland area that forms the wide steps leading to the original aluminum-clad main doors.

Foyers, which serve as transitions from the outside of the building to the inside, generally receive very little attention because people pass through them quickly. In the Jackson County courthouse, the foyer is one of the most elegant spaces. The architect carefully designed a light and airy room with Alaskan marble walls rising up to a white ceiling, which is graced with intricate molding. Even the foyer doors harmonize with the rectangular design displayed on the exterior doors.

Unlike many courthouses, the Jackson County building exhibits a sophistication in its design. Stairs rise to the lobby, and then another stairway ascends to a landing bright with natural light. Marble bands on the floor denote the transition from the central area to the side hallways. Sometimes designed features are not entirely successful, such as the balcony, directly over the foyer, which faces the main stairway. Originally, the county judge's office was located off the balcony, and possibly public addresses were to be made to the citizens who gathered on the stairs. Now accessed through a labyrinth of offices, the balcony provides a convenient storage space.

Despite the Depression, the interior of the Jackson County courthouse speaks of opulence. Black, oval-shaped drinking fountains, not the standard white, were specially ordered to complement the Alaskan marble-covered walls, which are a light gray with dark trim. Speaking for those suffering during the Depression, Arthur Perry observed in the September 1,

1932 newspaper that the "marble wainscoting . . . does not harmonize with the faded blue overalls of the victim of economic strife."

Slat benches from the train station, a visible reminder of the role the railroad played in developing Medford, are located throughout the halls. However, a less apparent tie between the railroad and the courthouse exists. As an incentive to lay track, the federal government authorized land grants to the Oregon & California railroad in 1869 under several conditions, including that they sell the land to settlers at a certain price. After the railroad failed to fulfill the terms of the grant, the federal government took back the unsold land in 1916. The affected counties, eighteen in all, argued that they had been deprived of property taxes had those lands been under private ownership. When several years of accrued funds finally were allocated to Jackson, the county had enough money to build the courthouse. The benches are a legacy from the railroad, but so are the floors, walls, and ceilings.

Women's lavatories in turn-of-the-century Kansas courthouses once were outfitted with furniture to serve as a true "rest room" for farm women while their husbands conducted business. The women's restrooms in the Medford courthouse exhibit both old and new concepts.

In the Jacksonville courthouse, a separate restroom for women is believed not to have been constructed until 1921. By the 1930s, women held a variety of county jobs, and the regular appearance of women's restrooms in the Medford courthouse is subtle recognition of their presence in the workplace. Unlike the men's restrooms, the women's were designed with anterooms, which on every floor except the first hold a couch.

In the late 1970s, the judicial department had grown too large for the 1930s facilities and moved to a separate building one block south of the courthouse. The old courtroom still provides a glimpse of what was called "the grandest of the courtrooms in southern Oregon." The August 31, 1931 newspaper, noting the mahogany paneling that extended almost from floor to ceiling, related that it gives the courtroom an "aristocratic appearance characteristic of the English courts."

Behind the mahogany railing protecting the jury, plush leather-bound armchairs served as jury seating.

From the back of the courtroom and up a narrow winding staircase is the upper jury room, one of the courthouse's hidden places. The former jail—now replaced by the 911-emergency center—also was on an upper floor, and was an island unto itself with its own fingerprint lab and kitchen. The location near the roof, however, was intended to be a disadvantage for the prisoners. Arthur Perry in the September 1, 1932 *Medford Mail Tribune* observed, "The jail is on the roof, and is supposed to be very difficult to get out of, without a good lawyer. In the summer it will be quite hot for the inmates, but it is their own fault, as most of them caught themselves. They knew where the jail was located."

The maintenance department, usually crammed into a small space next to the basement boiler, has the loftiest facilities: a penthouse that once served as the jailer's apartment. On this level, the upper section of the roof is accessible through a door on the stairway. For those who have reached the top level of this Art Deco palace, the reward is a closer look at the eagles. The June 11, 1930 newspaper reported that when officials were contemplating the courthouse's design, they wanted "architectural beauty, along with perfect detail." Although the eagles would be viewed primarily from the ground, at a close distance one can see that workers even added a pupil to the eagles' eyes and defined the skin on their talons.

The Josephine County courthouse can appear plain
from the street, but it was constructed when traffic
moved at a slower pace and people could better
observe its subtle design. *Credit: author*

Josephine County

County Seat:	Grants Pass
Courthouse Address:	500 N.W. Sixth Street
Year Completed:	1917
Architect:	E. E. McClaren
Date of County Formation:	January 22, 1856

"With an on-going game of 'musical offices' taking place in the old courthouse, even old-timers find it difficult to zero in on the department they're seeking."

—Wally Burke in the *Daily Courier*, July 27, 1976

The wilderness in Josephine County begins just outside its population centers. The county has just two incorporated towns, Grants Pass and Cave Junction, where about thirty percent of its population lives. Grants Pass boomed as a tourist area in the early 1920s, aided by nearby natural attractions such as the magnificent Oregon Caves and the legendary Rogue River. At Grants Pass, the Interstate 5 freeway turns southeast toward Jackson County's urbanization, and the Redwood Highway runs southwest toward great unpopulated spaces.

In 1851, a group of miners discovered gold in a remote creek flowing into the Illinois River. Although prospectors raced to the area after hearing the news, their efforts were daunted by the uprising of the Rogue River Indians. Later that year, some Willamette Valley farmers and others came to locate their fortune but were unsuccessful, according to the *History of Southern Oregon*, because of their "lack of skill and almost total lack of mining tools." In succeeding months, other prospectors were luckier farther south near the Oregon-California state line or east in present-day Jackson County.

Early in 1852, some "sea-faring" men struck gold in the headwaters of the Illinois River, and the area gradually became known as "Sailors' Diggins." In the next few years, a town with several stores, saloons, and hotels grew between the west and east fork of the Illinois River. As a testimony to the area's remoteness and the vagueness of early surveying, the town was named Waldo after California's governor because the miners believed it was situated in that state. Some miners even voted in the California election. Regardless of which state they believed they were in, many paid taxes to neither.

At that time, the roads to Jacksonville, the county seat of Jackson County, were only trails, making the recording of mining claims and other government matters a long and arduous journey. In January 1856, the legislature organized Josephine County, naming it after Josephine Rollins, the first white woman in the area and the daughter of a miner. Waldo, near the mining strikes, became the county seat.

Near the location of present-day Caveman Bridge, Joel Perkins started a ferry to carry miners across the Rogue River. Although Perkins moved after skirmishes with the Rogue River Indians, an early settlement called Perkinsville grew on the river banks and the California Stage Company began stopping there in the 1860s. Popular lore is that when the stage road was undergoing improvements along the present-day Sexton Pass, the workers heard of General Grant's triumph at Vicksburg and called the surrounding area Grants Pass. The stage stop gradually assumed that name.

The Oregon & California railroad, after terminating in Roseburg in 1872 due to financial difficulties, resumed laying track southward in 1881, and all of southern Oregon speculated where the route would go. Towns thrived or died depending on the railroad, and fortunes were made guessing correctly where the depot would be located. While it appeared that the railroad would pass near the stage stop, the exact location was uncertain. The winner of the depot site was Jonathan Bourne, a Portland attorney who had various holdings around the state and who had only recently purchased several local donation land claims.

The town of Grants Pass, with eighty-nine blocks in the initial plat, showed Bourne's confidence in its future growth. To ensure that no other additions were annexed to his plat, an undedicated 100-foot buffer zone bounded the entire townsite, which prevented others from connecting to his streets. In the center of his townsite lay a 400-foot long railroad right-of-way, dedicated as the Oregon & California Railroad Depot Grounds. The first passenger train arrived in Grants Pass in December 1883. According to the December 8, 1883 *Douglas Independent* newspaper, "quite a concourse of people were collected to receive the train, many of whom had never seen a railroad."

Weather hampered the continuation of the line for the winter, and so for a short time Grants Pass enjoyed its status as the terminus for all railroad trade. It was still an undeveloped town with muddy thoroughfares, and trees and stumps dotted the area. A few months before the arrival of the train, John Howard, a merchant, had set up a tent near the present corner of G and Sixth streets. In friendly rivalry over who would construct the first building, he hurriedly erected a structure. According to his wife in the April 3, 1935 *Daily Courier*, "So close was the race, it really must have been the first nail that counted for we have an old battered hammer on the handle of which is the inscription: 'This hammer drove the first nail in the first building in Grants Pass, OR.'"

Another business person constructed a general store on the northwest corner of Sixth and G streets, and gradually merchants, hotel operators, and saloon owners erected a row of buildings on G Street opposite the train depot. Both Sixth and G streets developed as the main commercial area, filling with hotels, saloons, livery stables, a box factory, and dry goods stores. Commercial development north of the tracks was stymied, principally because the railroad had located its depot within the Sixth Street right-of-way. It was not until the 1890s that the railroad finally moved out of the street and built another station just west of Sixth and G streets.

Gold and silver mining continued to play an important role in the area's economy. Members of the commercial club, however, believed that the area's mines would not be productive forever and sought to emphasize the region's agricultural resources by holding an Irrigation Convention and Industrial Fair in 1907 along the downtown streets. They also erected arched signs proclaiming "Orchards and Vineyards" and "Mines and Timber" over Sixth Street, prominently visible to those on the train. Grants Pass became known as the "little town in the Rogue Valley with the big street arches."

In 1922, one of the most successful efforts of town boosterism was the creation of the "Oregon Cavemen," a group of residents who dressed in animal skins and wielded clubs. Over the years, they performed at a variety of events, such as helping to inaugurate the Jackson County courthouse, blocking traffic in Reno, and appearing at the San Francisco World's Fair. As a tribute to their enduring efforts, many Grants Pass businesses today include "Caveman" in their name. A giant rendition of a caveman stands in a small triangular-shaped park south of Morgan Lane, visible to travelers coming off the Interstate 5 freeway. One former resident reported that when she was in high school, a common prank was to diaper the Caveman statue.

In the 1920s, the town became a gateway to tourist attractions as the Redwood Highway linked Grants Pass to Crescent City, and the road from that highway to the Oregon Caves was completed. The Rogue River became a playground for several famous figures, including Clark Gable. After World War II, the community developed a thriving lumber industry, although the diminishing timber supply has significantly reduced the number of forest product jobs in the county. Retirees, tourists, and government employees now contribute significantly to the local economy.

Visiting the Seat of Josephine County Government

TODAY, THE FORMER REDWOOD HOTEL, a six-story 1920s building at 306 N.W. Sixth Street, marks the start of the downtown. The hotel once had a well-known banquet room called the Caves Grotto that featured stalactites and stalagmites in subdued lighting to imitate the Oregon Caves. The hotel's rooms are now apartments and offices, and a commercial tenant occupies the former restaurant quarters. The advertisement

"W. G. Wright Assayer" remains in the sidewalk in front of the hotel, a link to Grant's Pass's mining history. At the turn of the century, buildings once crowded the blocks opposite the Redwood Hotel, but now parking lots surround the modern buildings, leaving little sense of the structures that once stood shoulder to shoulder.

Across the former Southern Pacific mainline railroad tracks and beyond the "It's the Climate" sign (a city slogan), the downtown buildings become more concentrated. During the prosperity of the 1950s and 1960s, many landlords along Sixth Street added modern facades effecting masks to the upper stories of their buildings. A structure's real age sometimes still shows in the weathered brick on the sides.

The four-story 1949 Wing Building at 201 S.E. Sixth Street was designed in the International Style. This design, amid the buildings along a small town main street, looks out of place, and indeed it is. The owner, Charles Wing, was in southern California when he spotted a building he liked, and he asked a Long Beach architect to design a similar one for Grants Pass.

For ten years the passenger depot, situated between G and F streets, jutted into Sixth Street. Later, the station was located where the 1960s Caveman Shopping Center Plaza is now. Early in the morning, before the parking lot becomes full of cars, one can stand under the building overhang by one of the arches that suggest a cave opening and get a glimpse of S.W. G Street's brick buildings as they might have looked from the train.

Many of these brick buildings on S.W. G Street were constructed after a devastating 1894 fire. Several painted signs add to the historical flavor, including "Dixon Dry Goods" on the side of the building at 125 S.W. G Street. On the west wall of the building at 128 S.W. H Street, another sign advertises Bull Durham tobacco on one half and Owl Cigars on the other. One sign was painted over the other, and a later building protected the bottom half from the sun until fire destroyed this structure and the advertisement again was exposed. Because they age and weather, these advertisements commonly are called "ghost signs." Although the buildings on S.W. G Street could have become ghosts as well, restoration efforts have helped preserve these buildings.

History of the Courthouse

A LOG CABIN IN WALDO PURCHASED FROM the sheriff served as the first courthouse in 1856, but the county was without a jail. When one culprit was apprehended after breaking into a store, the justice of the peace ordered him to be held for trial in a higher court. With no jail and the accused without money, the justice made him sign a note for fifty dollars to secure his appearance at the proper time.

When mining strikes fueled the start of the town of Kerbyville (sometimes called Kerby), citizens voted in 1857 to move the county seat there. Although officials initially considered building a courthouse, they instead rented various buildings. Kerbyville was known to be "extremely lively." Its citizens were obviously conscious of past international events. For a short time the town was named after the French emperor, reportedly because "Josephine (County) should have her Napoleon."

After miners deserted the spent mines in the early 1860s, property values plummeted. According to the April 3, 1935 *Daily Courier*, when the sheriff turned in his resignation, he sarcastically addressed the commissioners of what he called the "fast decaying county of Josephine." In 1870, the legislature voted to remit the state's share of the county's property tax in order to keep Josephine solvent. A large number of pessimistic citizens petitioned the legislature to dissolve the county, but their request was disregarded.

In 1885, with no railroad stop scheduled to be located in Josephine County, wily officials petitioned state legislators to expand the county's eastern boundary to include Grants Pass. Four months after this was granted, a county seat election was held, and not surprisingly, Grants Pass won fifty-eight percent of the vote.

Solomon Abraham, an enterprising businessman who had acquired the Railroad Addition to Grants Pass, then made the county a generous offer to donate $500 and a block for the courthouse, half of the lands in the addition, and half the proceeds from his remaining property. The county accepted and began planning for a courthouse on the block south of the railroad tracks bounded by Dimmick, Clarke, Foundry, and Isham streets.

Jonathan Bourne, fearing that his town's future might be in jeopardy, filed a lawsuit stating that the voters had selected the townsite of Grants Pass for the county seat position, not some nearby addition. Bourne supporters used all available tools to press their case, including racial slurs in the style of the time. Although the defense argued that one-half the population in the immediate area lived in the addition, the county court agreed to construct a courthouse in Bourne's plat along what is now Sixth Street on the site of the present-day courthouse.

The county immediately solicited bids for a courthouse and in 1886 awarded the job for $2,400. The first courthouse in Grants Pass, like many wooden courthouses, had the jail as a separate structure in the back. A picket fence with a gate at the center walkway enclosed the courthouse square.

Almost thirty years later, the court accepted plans for a new courthouse and in 1914 imposed the first of a four-year levy to fund the project. In November 1916, the county had enough funds to start construction and awarded the job to a Portland firm for $76,443. In October 1917, the court sold the old courthouse for $100, with the provision that the building and debris be cleared by January 1, 1918.

The Courthouse Today

WHEN THE COURTHOUSE WAS CONSTRUCTED in 1917, traffic—by car, horse, or foot—moved at a slower speed. Today cars go past the courthouse at twenty-five miles per hour, making it harder to appreciate the building's subtle ornamentation. Raised surfaces, principally on the panels between the first- and second-story windows and the quoins on the corners, create shadows to give the exterior texture. Both egg-and-dart molding and dentils grace the finely detailed cornice.

Terra cotta, a clay that could easily form the subtle ornamentation on the cornice, clads the exterior of the courthouse. Though terra cotta was available in a wide range of colors, the courthouse is white, distinguishing it from other Grants Pass buildings. The architect, E. E. McClaren, practiced in Portland and possibly was influenced by the number of light

While the architect could have left the central pediment to loom over a visitor, he added a balcony to make it more on a human scale. *Credit: author*

terra cotta-clad buildings constructed there. These reportedly provided contrast to Portland's frequently cloudy weather, while Grants Pass and the rest of southern Oregon is well known for its relatively large percentage of sunny days.

The Josephine County courthouse also exhibits Greek embellishment such as the central pediment. A balcony on the second floor divides the pediment and creates a more human scale on the courthouse face. Although the balcony conjures images of old-time politicians giving speeches to the populace, local residents could not recall any such addresses except during the dedication. According to one former county employee, it was a convenient place to take her daughter to watch parades.

The classically styled cornice and pediment give visual clues that the building is a courthouse, but to ensure that visitors were not confused, "Courthouse" was etched in the pediment frieze. Officials apparently were concerned that visitors might be bewildered as to the county in which it stood, for "Josephine County" subsequently was painted in gold letters on the parapet.

The columns and pilasters display reeding, the reverse of the usual fluting, which in the Greco-Roman tradition symbolizes harmony. The nearby cast-iron light fixtures also show reeding. Here, with simulated leather straps, the reeding suggests the handle of a fasces, a bundle of rods bound around an axe with a projecting blade, a symbol of political authority in ancient Rome. The lion's paw at the base perhaps not only represents courage and fairness, but also the light fixture's ability to grip the terra cotta.

A brick retaining wall now divides the square from the sidewalk, and plants and bushes have crowded the once relatively bare square. However, the greatest change to the square has been the spread of county buildings. The courthouse has expanded on both the north and south sides

Even light fixtures were carefully selected so that they blended with a courthouse's architectural style. Credit: author

Some decisions made long ago, such as the amount of marble to use in the lobby, has a significant impact on what we see today. *Credit: author*

with brick additions. Visitors may note that the brick color is not uniform, because a part of the additions were built at a later time. The county also built a Justice Center with the jail onto the back of the 1917 building, repeating the turn-of-the-century arrangement when the jail was relegated to the back of the courthouse.

While many counties spent a lot of their construction budget on their courthouse's exterior to display the best possible face, Josephine County officials and others also were concerned with the interior of the building. Glazed three-quarter-inch square tiles cover the floor, but instead of being entirely utilitarian white (as usually is seen in restrooms), a whimsical pattern in green and gray occurs at regular intervals. More remarkable is the amount of marble, rising seven-and-a-half feet high on the walls and comprising the main stairway and railing.

The offices have changed over the years. One employee related that they have been remodeled and then remodeled on top of the remodeling. The sheriff, now in the Justice Center, originally had an office on the courthouse's main floor. During the late 1930s, county financing was so limited that one sheriff, A. Donley Barnes, had to furnish his own gun and patrol car. His past training as a jeweler aided him in fashioning a badge.

The present-day election-night gathering at the courthouse of proponents and opponents awaiting the results is a holdover from the past. The clerk's office, besides its election-time duties, once was responsible for the payment of bounties for bobcats. Hunters occasionally carried smelly bobcat carcasses into the courthouse and down the hallway for the requisite ear clipping, which prevented the pelt from being presented again for bounty. The clerk's office continues to handle the filing of mining claims, and so-called scavengers—people searching for expired claims let go by careless miners—still riffle through the books.

Josephine County's mining tradition is remembered in the painting hanging over the main stairway landing. Different forms of mining are interwoven into the scene, including techniques such as panning and stamping. Hydraulic mining, now considered ecologically harmful, is depicted prominently in the center.

When the courthouse was constructed, it featured the latest conveniences of the time. Almost every office had a private sink. In the judge's office on the second floor, the court stenographer had a dumbwaiter to alleviate the lugging of heavy books up and down the nearby internal stairway. Not all of these luxurious touches have survived, as some sinks have been removed, and the dumbwaiter now serves as a storage closet. Even the internal stairway is gone.

Sheriff work was different in the days when A. Donley Barnes held the position. According to an interview with him in the July 10, 1986 *Daily Courier*, "In those days, Barnes notes, a man's word was his bond. If a man promised to be at the Courthouse on Monday morning after running afoul of the law, that appointment was kept. He knew damn well that if he didn't show up, you'd come and get him and that wouldn't be no fun."

The original courtroom on the second floor, called Courtroom No. 1, now is darker with the addition of wooden wall paneling and the building's extension blocking one wall of windows. These changes and other remodeling make it difficult to determine whether the original courtroom was once plain or grand. Only strips of marble on the floor base, balustrade, and judge's bench suggest that this room might have had careful attention to its appearance.

At the foot of the courtroom hangs a picture of Matthew Deady, a territorial supreme court justice assigned to the southern Oregon counties who in 1853 was temporarily removed because his appointment erroneously read "Mordecai Deady." A photograph of Orval Millard, the first circuit court judge exclusively for Josephine County, hangs at the head of the room. The judge, believing that to wear a robe while presiding was not necessary, is shown in his typical court attire, a suit.

A stairway from the second floor leads to the roof. From this vantage point one can see the development of Grants Pass; the proposed courthouse site in the Railroad Addition is now obscured by buildings. Today, people squabble over the location of government buildings just as they did in 1885. The stories of yesterday and today are generally the same.

An undated newspaper clipping from a Grants Pass resident indicates that the county assessor's life is not always easy. The article relates that Deputy Assessor Merle Griffin stopped to assess a house and heard a woman yelling inside. After being hampered by two barking dogs, he found that the woman was screaming because a two-foot-long bull snake was in her bird cage. "A plan of action was quickly formulated, and Griffin went outside to get a stick. But the canary was not saved at once, for the assessor found two goats prancing proudly atop his car. After removing the goats, Griffin killed the snake and saved the bird. Incidently, he [then] assessed the property."

Eastern Counties

"There will be no better building on the Pacific coast,"
forecast the architect when trying to sell the design of
the Baker County courthouse to the commissioners.
Credit: author

Baker County

County Seat:	Baker City
Courthouse Address:	1995 Third Street
Year Completed:	1909
Architect:	Delos D. Neer
Date of County Formation:	September 22, 1862

> *"The court house will not be a cheap, bargain counter affair . . . "*
>
> —*Baker City Herald* , December 24, 1907

Baker City's past is filled with hardy homesteaders and townspeople who dreamed that their hamlet would become a metropolis. Baker City also had other figures: wealthy mine owners, down-on-their-luck prospectors, and leading citizens who formed an "upper-crust" society. Once called the "Queen City of the Inland Empire," this town formerly ruled as the center of the wealthiest gold strikes in the state. Today, its past makes a saleable heritage for tourists visiting the town.

In the fall of 1861, a number of miners, after hearing tales of fabulous gold reserves, left Portland for eastern Oregon. Wandering for days and arguing among themselves, the prospectors divided into two factions. One group traveled northwest to retrace their path, while the other headed northeast to return on the Oregon Trail. The latter party prospected as they traversed the region and after making camp one night on the eastern slopes of the Elkhorn Mountains, they discovered gold in a small stream that emptied into the Powder River.

Other prospectors, hearing of the discovery, rushed to the area. The mining soon led to disputes such as claim jumping, theft, and murder, but since the region was part of Wasco County, the nearest sheriff was stationed more than two hundred miles away in The Dalles. The miners called statewide attention to their plight by sending their June 1862 ballots to the legislature as "the election results of Baker County." Four months later, the legislature granted their wish by creating Baker County, naming it after Oregon Senator Edward Baker, who was the only member of Congress to die fighting in the Civil War. The county seat honor went to Auburn, the sole town.

Not all the inhabitants of Auburn and the surrounding area were miners. Settlers, some of whom had bypassed the area en route to the Willamette Valley, trailed the prospectors back to eastern Oregon. The miners needed sources of food, and the homesteaders sold them vegetables and meat at handsome prices. Others, providing drink and female companionship, also followed.

Of the gold strikes discovered in the region, one of the richest was to be the Virtue mine. The owners, Colonel J. S. Ruckel and his partners, needed a stamp mill that would pound the rock and break out the gold. Because no source of water power was nearby, they located the mill eight miles west along the Powder River. Nearby, Royal Agustus (sic) Pierce, an attorney, platted a seventeen-block "Town of Baker" in the spring of 1865.

The first commercial structure—a saloon—soon was erected, followed by a boarding house, a hotel, and a blacksmith shop. The townspeople had their priorities: a race track was started before the first church was finished. Soon the stage line began running to Baker City, carrying passengers, U.S. mail, and the Wells Fargo & Co. Express.

The first big mining boom in Baker County occurred in the 1870s, and Baker City's central location was critical to its prosperity. *An Illustrated History of Baker, Grant, Malheur and Harney Counties* related that Baker City "was the depot of supplies for a large section of country and goods from its mercantile houses found their way into mining camps fifty to seventy-five miles distant."

The boom died by 1880, but in the fall of 1884 the Oregon Railway & Navigation railroad, running through Baker City, linked it with the rest of the nation and opened up new markets for the county's cattle and lumber products. A second mining boom began in the 1890s. In 1895 alone the mines near Baker City shipped $1.3 million worth of gold and employed 1,000 workers. The town in 1899 boasted more than forty brick and stone buildings. Scores of new mercantile and industrial establishments started: a smelter, two planing mills, two cigar factories, two wholesale grocers, two wholesale liquor and tobacco houses, and a steam laundry employing thirty-two people. At the turn of the century, Baker City's population was about 6,600, making it the third-largest city in Oregon.

Despite his legal training, Pierce was preempted by J. M. Boyd, who applied for the same property in 1868. For an unknown reason, Pierce's request had not been processed, and, in later legal battles, the U.S. government affirmed Boyd as the true owner, awarding him the remaining unplatted portion of Pierce's original claim. The General Land Office retained ownership of the unsold lots in the "Town of Baker." Apparently Boyd was not as civic minded, for the public square was lopped off.

Gold output in the county declined after 1910, but it resurged during the Depression when the U.S. Treasury increased the price of gold. Many unemployed workers began toiling in the mines until the federal government ordered miners to assist in the war effort. Although many Baker City residents are employed in logging, trade, or civil service, weekend prospectors still dream of striking it rich.

Visiting the Seat of Baker County Government

THE SUBSTANTIAL DOWNTOWN BUILDINGS standing today were constructed largely between 1890 and 1910, during the prosperity of the second gold boom. Those built before the turn of the century generally exhibit intricate brickwork near the roofline or elaborate cast iron pilasters and pediment, but after the turn of the century, stone buildings came into vogue. The gray volcanic tuff, extracted from a nearby quarry, was easily shaped into blocks that hardened with exposure to air. Although a few of these buildings are on Main Street, by the time they were in fashion much of the downtown was already developed and so many of these structures stand on nearby streets. One of the first of these buildings, at 1998 Valley Street, was built by stonemason John Jett, and the building still displays an elaborate tuff inscription, "J. H. Jett, Marble Works 1901," which both identified the structure and advertised his skill.

Not all of the downtown was "respectable." On the southern part of Main Street and on the neighboring Resort Street (so named because of its available pleasures), bawdy houses, saloons, and gambling establishments once flourished. Even today, some residents still remember their parents admonishing them not to walk on the east side of Main Street. As late as the mid-1980s, the Alfred Building at 1806 Main Street still had a second floor left intact with peepholes and reinforced doors to forestall raids by authorities. Today from the sidewalk, the only visible reminder of the bawdy houses is the figures of women painted on upper story windows for the annual Miner's Jubilee celebration, while the more respectable figures of miners, homesteaders, and their wives are depicted at the street level.

The more refined had their own cultural amusements. They sponsored and attended a four-story opera house that stood on the northeast corner of Main and Church streets. (A bank now occupies the site and has an extravagant display of gold nuggets found in the local area.) They attended dinners at the Geiser Grand Hotel, which still proudly stands at 1932 Main Street. Constructed in 1889 with the very latest conveniences including hot and cold running water, it featured a balcony for the ladies to overlook the lobby and a dining room that could seat 200 people. Even its meals were sophisticated. The menu for the 1905 Christmas dinner, among other fine selections, featured "Boiled English Pheasant" and "Saddle of Antelope with Grape Jelly."

Hoping to replicate the Geiser Grand's eminent position in Baker City in the twentieth century, some three hundred local citizens pooled their money to construct the nine-story Hotel Baker, a landmark at 1705 Main Street. Extravagantly described by the April 24, 1929 *Baker Democrat Herald* as the "finest anywhere," its grand opening was held just two months before the 1929 stock market crash. The hotel, still the tallest building in Oregon east of the Cascade Mountains, was the last grandiose architectural statement on the main street. After the Depression and World War II, building construction shifted to the town's outlying areas, which had more land to accommodate the increasing use of cars.

While the gold discoveries helped to fund prosperous-looking buildings, it was another even earlier historical event, the Oregon Trail, which helped revive the town. The opening of the interpretive center next to the Trail in the early 1990s brought swarms of tourists to the town. Like the proverbial miner in town after a strike, tourists happily relinquish their gold in their search for recreation.

A History of the Courthouse

WITH ITS GOLD STRIKES WANING, AUBURN did not remain the county seat for long. By 1868, Baker City had enough residents who voted to move the county seat position to their town. But the act providing the change said nothing about how the transition would occur should Baker City win, and Auburn residents refused to give up the records. Early one morning, Baker City citizens rode to Auburn, where they loaded their wagon with the records and swiftly made their way back to Baker City before Auburn residents could stop them.

Officials in 1869 initially considered constructing a courthouse and separate jail of stone and brick, but decided upon inexpensive wood. Sixteen years later, a fire burned the jail, killing five of the six prisoners and nearly burning down the courthouse. The next year, the officials erected a sturdier brick building, crowned with a decorative battlement that suggested a castle. In its shadow on the courthouse square, women played tennis and the first public whipping in the state, for wife beating, took place.

Even though the courthouse was only fifteen years old, by the turn of the century bricks began dropping from the battlement, causing the surrounding courthouse grounds to be wryly referred to as "a brickyard." Officials soon began considering a new courthouse, a move supported by the local newspaper. The February 15, 1908 *Baker City Herald* declared that "Baker county will not have to suffer ridicule from visitors, who, after looking over the city, cast their eyes on the county court house with a look of surprise and disgust."

After attending a convention in Portland, the commissioners toured several courthouses, but were most impressed with the one in Lane County. The commissioners quickly engaged the architect, Delos Neer, who sent the plans just one month later. Neer then traveled to Baker City to persuade them to build the structure. "There will be no better county building on the Pacific coast," he prophesied.

The county court warned Neer that there would be no graft in courthouse budget. Such profiteering was apparently routine, as the January 13, 1908 newspaper reported that "heretofore graft has marked so many . . . county affairs." This time, officials made an extra effort by requesting that members of leading business groups appoint inspectors to monitor the courthouse budget and construction. The local newspaper observed that "the people are pleased with the change. They are no longer treated as England treated the colonists in colonial days."

Beginning from the initial clearing of the site, the newspaper followed the progress of the construction. When the electric elevator arrived, the newspaper noted that it could carry any load except political aspirations. When promoting the town, the June 9, 1909 *Baker City Herald* specifically noted that the courthouse cost $125,000. By mid-July, county workers, temporarily housed in the city hall, were too impatient to wait for the courthouse furniture to arrive and began moving in three weeks early. Several wagons were running back and forth from the city hall to the courthouse, and the July 12, 1909 newspaper, mindful of male-female relationships, thoughtfully warned that "if there is anything that tests a man's temper, it is moving day and it might be a little risky for ladies to venture around the scene of activity today without due warning."

The Courthouse Today

AS THE BUILDING HAS AGED, THE COURTHOUSE square has evolved. Blue spruce trees, planted to enhance the structure's appearance from the street, have grown to obstruct its view. On the northeast corner, a set of nine-and-a-half-foot high logging wheels rests after years of service hauling trees. A cannon, one of the two war memorials, faces out from the square. The cannon is sealed, doubtless because mischievous children once filled the former cannon with nails and chains and then fired it at a neighboring boarding house. A gas-fueled "eternal flame" commemorates Baker County veterans from World War I through the Vietnam War. However, budget cuts have extinguished it.

The courthouse possesses the architectural characteristics of the Richardsonian Romanesque style, which uses materials such as stone to create a massive-looking building. Like other structures in Baker City, the cut stone blocks fit together like a jigsaw puzzle, but the greater amount of embellishment on the courthouse required more cost and expertise. Blocks below the water table, the encircling band of smooth stone between the basement and first-floor windows, feature more refined workings with a surrounding band of chiseled points commonly called a draft line. The blocks supporting the arched porch opening required even greater skill.

The intricacy of Baker County courthouse stonework distinguishes it from the other stone buildings in Baker City.
Credit: author

Before the addition, the courthouse had an expansive porch area. Serving as an introduction to the building, entrances can convey the lavish decor found in the interior. *Credit: Baker City Oregon Trail Regional Museum*

The arched windows and porch openings are another trait of the Richardsonian Romanesque style, as is the soaring clock tower. Under its copper roof now weathered to a patina, the tower displays reddish brown stone highlighting the quarter hours on the clock. With such thoughtful details, it seems unusual that the smooth stone over the main porch entrance, which normally would proclaim the building as the Baker County Courthouse, was left strangely bare.

Originally, the main entrance was far grander, with two stairways placed at a right angle leading to a larger porch. However, in the 1960s, the county removed one of the stairways and diminished the porch size to construct a concrete block addition. Now, the stripped-down main entry, instead of being the focal point of a building, seems more like the side entrances on the north and west sides of the courthouse.

Only the front entrance displays two swinging doors under a semicircular window with sashes forming a sunrise pattern. Inside, four-foot high marble wainscot covers the hallway walls. Dark green and white hexagonal tile, with a Greek fret design outlying the edge, covers the floor. Near the ceiling emergency light on the west side, one white tile mysteriously exhibits the numbers "20/133," written in an old-fashioned hand. Another set of numbers appears on a tile in the west side hallway, but the significance of both these markings remains a puzzle.

Another mystery in the hallway concerns the "boy with a leaky boot," a metal statue that once stood in the fountain on the square before the county moved it inside to prevent vandalism. Although several legends exist, an often-told tale is that the statue represents a boy who served water to wounded soldiers during the Civil War. One hopes the boy was a Unionist, because the tombstone of Senator Edward Baker, a personal friend of Abraham Lincoln and the county's namesake, stands against a far wall. Although Baker's body lies in the Presidio in San Francisco, the gravestone curiously was found in a pet cemetery near Colma, California before being moved to Baker County in 1979.

Despite the refined appearance of the hallway, signs once hung here proclaiming, "This Building belongs to the People of Baker County. Do Not Deface It! Do Not Mark the Walls! Do Not Spit on the Floors or the Walls!" More permanent embellishment to the hallway includes the decorative scroll-shaped brackets with hanging garlands on the piers. Faces in the keystones, one of the architect's signature pieces, show their horror at embellishing only the hallway leading to the back entrance.

Under the gaze of these unhappy faces, county employees transform the hallway into a dining room the Friday before Christmas by serving a huge buffet with turkey and accompanying dishes. The courthouse remains open, and the citizen who comes to file a last-minute document will find over one hundred people feasting at tables in the hallway. After the meal, attorneys and others are welcome to the leftovers.

In past years when mining claims had to be renewed, lines of prospectors sometimes trailed into the hallway from the clerk's office. Besides the monotonous filing of paperwork, the courthouse has been the site of mining drama. According to the maintenance man, occasionally a miner has come charging into the courthouse hallway, taken a quick look around, breathed a sigh of relief, and then scurried into the clerk's office. A few minutes later, a competitor has run in, made a quick survey, and then bolted into the clerk's office.

Baker's mining heritage is portrayed in the Virtue Mine photograph hanging in the county court room across the hall from the clerk's office. The county court once held meetings at a remarkable three-person desk, which they have since moved to offices in the basement. Under the 1995 photograph of the replacement Geiser Grand Hotel tower being towed past the courthouse (the soaring courthouse tower is clearly seen in the background, insinuating a taunt of "mine is bigger than yours"), the wood wainscot still displays the marks of a past official—since ousted—who tipped his chair back and dozed during meetings.

The men's restroom in the basement harks back to an earlier day. Two black-painted arched swinging doors open to a working display of an old lavatory. Porcelain urinals, described by the custodian as "bathtubs leaned up against the wall," line one side of the room. Toilets, one with an old oak seat, are operated by a chain hanging down from a high overhead tank.

In 1909, the jail was located in the courthouse's third floor, but from the early 1960s to the mid 1970s, the jail occupied part of the basement. Because the jail now is located outside of town, the old basement cells, accessible through the commissioners' office, protect only dead files, broken chairs, and surplus computers. The eight- by ten-foot cells once held up to four people, creating a feeling of claustrophobia that should have deterred anyone from crime. On the wall, the decades-old painted words still warn that "cigarette butts/ ashes on the floor will result in loss of smoking privileges!"

On the second floor, the courtroom shows "modernization" such as the yellow plastic chairs for spectators and jury (the original swivel chairs for the jury are now at the Brass Parrott restaurant at 2150 Main Street). Neer's architectural skill in creating a visually integrated room is still evident. The pattern of the wood wainscot is repeated on the judge's bench and the looming judge's panel. The panel, itself a typical Neer feature, displays columns echoed in the door and window millwork.

When workers removed part of the railing to allow the sheriff access to the bench from the side door, a railing post was altered. One judge, Milo Pope, was fanatical about maintaining the historic atmosphere of the courtroom, and offered to pay the additional cost himself to keep the post looking authentic.

However, the tools were no longer commonplace, and the bill of $400 for seven pieces of wood included the labor and materials to create the shaper knives.

Pope believed he simply needed a "pencil, paper, robe and desk" to operate as a judge. Even his gavel was relegated to a desk drawer. In the several years he presided, he used the gavel only once to silence two attorneys talking in the back of the room. "It was so loud," he noted, "it surprised everyone, including myself, and I laughed!" Another item stored in the desk drawer used more frequently was the jury's "oogah" horn, used to summon the bailiff.

Some of the cases heard, such as claim jumping and cattle rustling, are indigenous to the region. Although an average cow is worth less than $1,000, cattle rustling in Oregon is considered so serious a crime that it is classified a felony. A retired judge explained that "it's considered a crime against a way of life." In his years in the legal profession, the judge encountered some cattlemen who are fervent about prosecuting rustlers the old-fashioned way. He noted, "they just want to take 'em out and hang 'em."

A door on the third floor above the courtroom allows access to the fourth floor attic, where in the mid-1960s Civil Defense foodstuffs and water were stored in the event of a nuclear attack. The attic still contains empty water buckets and full tins of candy and crackers, which, according to the labels, fortunately were made with preservatives. Occasionally, a maintenance person has opened one of the forty-pound candy containers and brought the decades-old sweets to one of the offices, where it has been happily consumed.

In another part of the third floor is the stairway to the clock tower, now littered with dust and pigeon droppings. The clock no longer operates, a victim of age and tight budgets. When it did work, it played "Westminster Chimes" on every quarter hour, and the July 12, 1909 *Baker City Herald* touted that when the clock was installed, "It is doubtful if any city the size of Baker on the Pacific coast can boast of having such beautiful chimes." Although the chimes are now silent and the years have seen changes, the grandeur of the Baker County courthouse remains.

Virginia creeper covers the front of the Crook County courthouse, providing a hiding place for birds, which chirp during courtroom proceedings. The architect apparently was so confident that everyone would recognize this building as a courthouse that the only official sign is the Oregon state seal in the central pediment. *Credit: Alan Viewig*

Crook County

County Seat:	Prineville
Courthouse Address:	300 E. Third Street
Year Completed:	1909
Architect:	W. G. Pugh
Date of County Formation:	October 24, 1882

> *"The whole game has been shown in its true light, a game to build an expensive court house for Prineville's glory at the expense of the taxpayer."*
>
> —*The Bend Bulletin,* June 15, 1906

Crook County's history, with stories of vigilantes and range wars between cattlemen and sheepmen, could serve as a script for a Western movie. Prineville itself had such establishments as the Bucket-O-Blood Saloon and Glaze's Opera House. Today, businesses with more common names occupy buildings that are more functional than flamboyant. One exception is the courthouse. Planned in the days when the mainline railroad might still be built to Prineville, and when "westsiders" in today's Jefferson and Deschutes counties might still be persuaded not to separate, the courthouse remains a modern monument to the county's past hopes.

In 1866, three Willamette Valley farmers, looking for rangeland, explored the Ochoco Valley and became impressed with the waist-high meadow grass. Undaunted by the hostile Northwest Indians who burned their small cabin that winter, they returned to the area with their families the following spring. More settlers came the following years, including Barney Prine, who in 1868 settled in the meadow where the Ochoco Creek flowed into the Crooked River. According to a report in *An Illustrated History of Central Oregon*, "During that summer Barney Prine started Prineville by building a dwelling house, store, blacksmith shop, hotel and saloon. I think he was all of one day building them." In addition to these improvements, Prine later laid out a race track that ran along the banks of the Crooked River.

In the fall of 1870, Prine traded his rights to his land claim to a farmer named Monroe Hodges for a horse and twenty dollars. Hodges erected a hotel and later a stable and meat market. After receiving his land grant, Hodges filed a nineteen-block plat which lined the banks of Ochoco Creek. Hodges sold the lots for ten dollars, although as a marketing strategy, he shrewdly donated some lots to help the town grow.

Crime increased when the population grew, but the cost to transport an accused to The Dalles more than one hundred twenty-five miles away was onerous. According to *An Illustrated History of Central Oregon*, in 1880 a correspondent for *The Dalles Times-Mountaineer* wrote that because of the expense, "many offenses are allowed to shock the moral sense of the community without any attempt to visit punishment upon the heads of the offenders." The reporter also noted that many settlers felt "a new county of our own we should have, and that immediately!" Not until two years later, after Prineville resident Frank Nichols was elected senator, did the House of Representatives pass the bill creating a new county. However, it was tabled without discussion in the Senate because Nichols had refused to vote for a certain senatorial candidate (at that time, the legislature chose the state's U.S. Senators).

Classic political wrangling saved the Crook County bill. The chairman of the counties' committee also was the brother of the state treasurer, who desperately needed a bill passed that retroactively would approve of his payment out of the Oregon treasury to retire some state debt. With Nichols pledging to have that bill passed in the House, the Senate passed his bill, and a new county, honoring the general who had been instrumental in winning the Snake Indian wars, was created. Crook County at the time included present-day Deschutes and Jefferson counties and part of Wheeler County. Prineville was named the temporary county seat, and its position was finalized in a general election in 1884.

The region was desperately in need of local law enforcement. Several months before the county was created, ranchers A. H. Crooks and S. J. Jory were killed in a land dispute. Masked men later overpowered a deputy, shot the suspect, and then dragged the suspect's employee (who was somewhere else when the two ranchers were killed) by horse through town before hanging him from the Crooked River Bridge. A group calling themselves the "Vigilantes" began terrorizing the countryside, killing those who defied them. The slaying of two brothers finally started a reactionary group, who showed themselves to be a formidable enemy by riding down Prineville's Main Street fully armed and daring some Vigilantes in a saloon to face them on the street. Soon after, in the election of 1884, anti-Vigilante supporters were elected to office, and the intimidating group lost its rule.

Growth in Crook County led to another confrontation between cattle and sheep ranchers after the turn of the century. In the surrounding counties, cattle ranchers, claiming encroachment of their rights, had been terrorizing herders and killing hundreds of sheep. In 1904, horseback riders killed sixty-five sheep east of Prineville and others later killed a thousand sheep. An anonymous letter sent to the *Oregonian* from a group calling itself the Crook County Sheep-Shooters' Association reported that "we have slaughtered between 8,000 and 10,000 head during the last shooting season. . . . We have just received a shipment of ammunition that we think will be sufficient to meet any shortage." After the grim killing of more than two thousand sheep in Lake County, federal grazing rights were implemented, and the range wars finally ended.

At the turn of the century, Prineville lagged in the construction of durable brick or stone buildings, indicators of a prosperous town. *An Illustrated History of Central Oregon* printed a letter sent to a local paper which revealed that "the growth and development of Prineville has been slow. . . . The city does not present the beautiful picture of fine buildings and picturesque avenues. . . . Men by the score have gone to Prineville and engaged in business only to reap a golden harvest for their efforts and then move to the valley or some larger city, and the result is that some of the largest business houses in Oregon are transacting their business in wooden structures, some of them almost a makeshift."

Despite its appearance, according to *An Illustrated History of Central Oregon*, at the turn of the century Prineville had control of the largest trading area in the United States not traversed by a railroad. The title, however, was not a desired one, and although railroad companies and investors surveyed routes, a line was not laid. Finally, in 1909, when two railroads started building competing lines south along the Deschutes River to Bend, Prineville citizens were disappointed to learn the railroad would bypass their town.

Prineville residents would not be daunted. Various proposals were examined to construct a trunk line to the main line, but all failed until the city decided to build its own railroad in 1916. For years, the line ran at a loss until after World War II, when lumber mills, attracted to the stands of pine in the nearby Ochoco National Forest, came to the town. The lumber supply dwindled in the mid-1980s, but the wood products industry is still the largest employer in Prineville. A tire retreading and distribution center, with strong ties to Prineville, is the largest single employer.

Visiting the Seat of Crook County Government

AS TOURISTS MAKE THEIR WAY ALONG Highway 26, which serves as Third Street through Prineville, they cross the center of town at Main Street. At this intersection, three buildings clad in stone once proudly displayed some of the area's geological resources. On the northeast corner, the Hotel Prineville featured reddish stone blocks and reportedly the owner was so certain that the structure was fireproof that she did not carry insurance. It burned in 1922. The grand Spanish-styled Ochoco Inn, complete with bell tower and central courtyard, replaced the hotel, but it too was destroyed by fire in 1966. A highway motel, without such flamboyant architecture, now stands on part of the site.

The two stone buildings still standing on the southern corners of Third and Main streets were both once banks. The builder of the one-story building on the southwest corner was so sure it would always be a bank that they inscribed "First National Bank" on the parapet; a later owner turned the

building into a pharmacy and called it "Bank Drugs." On the opposite corner, the historical society's museum occupies the two-story building, and the teller cages and marble counters remain intact. When the building first opened, the June 13, 1912 *Crook County Journal* claimed

A newer Crook County building sports a western theme. *Credit: author*

that its interior equipment "is considered finer than anything in any city in the United States which is not on a railroad."

From 1892 until 1992, Crook County was a "bellweather" in presidential elections, and every four years journalists flocked to Prineville. Although some residents winced at being portrayed as inhabitants of a westernized version of a Norman Rockwell painting, in the July 12, 1992 *Oregonian* one resident still characterized Prineville as "a little cowboy town." The saloons and gambling establishments are long gone, but south on Main Street is a 32,000 square-foot indoor arena, the site of the Crook County Rodeo.

While the rodeo boosts the local economy, for years the City of Prineville railroad earned the town the title of "City without Taxes." One of the few municipally run railroads in the United States, it still operates north of town near Main and Tenth Streets. The city's three diesel engines pull rented box cars that sport big-city graffiti back and forth from Prineville to Prineville Junction, nineteen miles away. Ironically, in the mid-1990s when the Bend railroad station needed to be moved for highway expansion, the state granted the structure to Prineville. Prineville also acquired the old Redmond train station, Bend's duplicate, for Prineville Junction. Although neither station had been moved by 1997, Prineville was vindicated after losing the railroad to Bend so many years ago.

A History of the Courthouse

COUNTY OFFICIALS MET IN A STORE on Main Street before building a two-story courthouse with shiplap siding in 1885 on the block of the present-day courthouse. Prineville streets became busy when circuit court was in session—so much so that light attendance was remarkable. (The May 5, 1904 *Prineville Review* commented that "usually the town is crowded during court week, but in this instance no one would suspect court was in session.") When not officially used, the courthouse served other functions, such as a classroom while the first high school was being constructed. During the 1906 Fourth of July celebration, a resting place for women and children was provided at the courthouse, along with a matron to look after those coming from the country. Combs and brushes were provided.

Believing that the county records stored in the wood-frame building were unsafe, officials in 1905 commissioned Walter Pugh of Salem to draw up plans for a new courthouse, and advertised for bids in Portland newspapers. Bend

The Crook County courthouse initially had two side entrances that matched the grandeur of the front entry. They were removed in the early 1940s to create more office space.
Credit: Crook County Historical Society

citizens, however, did not look with favor upon a new courthouse, nor on how the officials were handling the matter. A January 11, 1907 *Bend Bulletin*, recounting the history of the courthouse, asserted that "the Prineville ring determined to stick the county for a big expensive court house. . . . Plans were secretly prepared and bids advertised for in an inconspicuous manner, in a Portland paper. No one outside of the ring knew what was going on until the scheme was discovered and exposed by the *Madras Pioneer*." The July 19, 1906 *Prineville Review* refuted the charges of subterfuge by sarcastically stating, "Don't publish advertisement in small papers like the *Oregonian* or *Portland Journal*. Give the job to the *Laidlaw Chronicle*, or maybe *The Bend Bulletin*, which are read all over the world and in some parts of Crook county."

Bend citizens asserted that the new building would raise taxes, which the June 15, 1906 *Bend Bulletin* decried would "glorify Prineville at the county's expense." Bend residents filed an injunction to prevent the county from borrowing money to fund the courthouse. The county scaled back the estimated cost of the courthouse, and Prineville citizens offered to donate $6,500 to help fund the building. The January 11, 1907 edition reported that the contractor offered to start construction and complete it when the county had the money.

After moving the old courthouse off to the side and building the basement and part of the new superstructure, the contractors defaulted. County officials then hired J. B. Shipp to finish the courthouse. The May 6, 1909 *Prineville Review*, under the headline BUILDING FINISHED, reported, "It is said to be the best county building in the state but one, that of Baker

Not long after the courthouse opened, the July 7, 1909 *Bend Bulletin* reported that the foundation walls were bulging due to improper construction. Prisoners in the jail, "fearing for their safety, made a great complaint and were removed." The July 21, 1909 *Bend Bulletin* then stated that after experts examined the walls, it was found that "the casing of one of the basement windows had sagged in, which caused the foundation to look as though it was bulging. The window was straightened, and now all is O.K."

county." The newspaper noted that Baker County had spent more than $100,000 on their courthouse, while Crook County had spent only $80,000. The May 26, 1909 *Bend Bulletin,* seemingly forgetting its anti-courthouse crusade, noted that "the contractors have done exceptionally good work," and conceded it was "one of the very best in the state."

The Courthouse Today

THE CRUMBLING CONCRETE FOUNTAIN on the courthouse square once stood in the courtyard of the ornate, Spanish-styled Ochoco Inn. The local garden club, which donated the fountain, added a plaque that bears plant-related wisdom: "The heritage of the past is the seed that brings forth the harvest of the future." Nearby, an "eternal" gas flame bestowed by the American Legion now stands unlit. A newer flagpole on the grounds replaced the original one constructed on top of the clock tower, undoubtedly to the relief of the maintenance person who would have to raise and lower the flag.

The height of this courthouse makes it unusual in Oregon. Instead of a two-story building with a half-basement, the courthouse rises a full three stories. Above the roof, a clock tower soars more than forty-seven feet. The stone exterior further distinguishes this building, as most of its contemporary structures in Prineville were made of brick. The commanding design, at a time when officials were trying to both entice the railroad to Prineville and quell Bend and Madras citizens who wanted their own county, suggests that Crook County was giving notice that Prineville, not anywhere else, was the center of the region.

Although the county eventually lost to both factions, the design choice made almost one hundred years ago left Prineville with an architectural legacy unique in central Oregon. Photographs of Prineville usually include the courthouse, and the building is even reproduced on wooden postcards made by a local company. County officials, mindful of the tourists traveling along Third Street, the main route through town, keep the courthouse brilliantly lit until midnight.

The courthouse exhibits the American Renaissance style with its monumental size, long flight of stairs and rectangular windows. Classical decorations, another element of the style, are frequent on the building exterior. While an abundance of dentils, columns, and pilasters generally suggest that the building is a courthouse, the only official designation is the state seal barely visible in the central pediment.

The courthouse was even grander before the county removed the side entrances, each of which had a long flight of stairs and porch similar to the front. The quest for more office space also forced the county to move the boiler out from the middle of the basement to a furnace room which now juts out from the back of the building. The workers thoughtfully used the excess stone from the stairs on the exterior of this addition.

A jail also was located on the ground floor, but now only a metal strip from the bars remains on one southeast corner window. Prison bars, however, were not always a factor in preventing escape. During Prohibition, Crook County Sheriff Stephen Yancey arrested several prominent bootleggers, but was puzzled why "moonshine" was still easily available. He later discovered that the bootleggers had whittled a wooden key out of a broom handle, and after everyone went home for the night, would let themselves out, then lock themselves up again early in the morning.

With Bend citizens decrying the cost of the new courthouse, econo- mizing on the interior was necessary, although some grand measures still were employed. The extravagant twin interior stairways have been replaced by a single stairway, although the thirteen-foot high ceilings remain. Wooden wainscot appears to be oak, but it is really pine. Minute black lines were painted on the wood to imitate oak grain.

Like the sounds of human joints, the court-house reveals its age through its noises. The front door squeals; the steps groan. With the high

Although the stone appears solid, an eighteen-year-old prisoner chiseled his way out of the jail in six hours with an iron bar. According to the August 6, 1936 *Wheeler County Chronicle*, "There's a big hole in the wall of the Crook county jail." The prisoner later was recaptured.

ceilings, the closing of an office door reverberates through the building, as do the footsteps of cowboy boots or work shoes across the linoleum tile floor. One sound no longer heard is the cow bell ringing at 10:00 a.m. and 3:00 p.m., that called all courthouse workers to break during the 1950s.

Miniature Corinthian-style columns make up the balustrade of the worn stairway leading to the second floor. Ex-church pews line the narrow hallway, and when court is in session, the space becomes crowded with attorneys conferring with clients, children waiting for parents, and witnesses speaking to friends. The voices spill into the adjacent offices off the hallway. In the course of a day, court officials and citizens intermingle in the narrow corridor, just like on the streets of any small town.

As on other floors, some doors feature frosted glass windows with old-fashioned, hand-painted signs. Some still retain ghost lettering: the deputy district attorney's sign still shows "Crook County Library," the district attorney's sign still evidences "County Superintendent." One door with an unaltered window painted with the word "Attorneys" leads to the judges' chambers, where the two judges share a large two-sided partners' desk—seemingly more appropriate in a detective movie.

While the judge's entrance to the courtroom remains the same, the public entrances once were on the side of the courtroom when the original stairways were intact. In addition to the sole entrance at the foot of the courtroom, other changes have been made. One of the jury boxes is gone, but a row of coat hooks on the wall—a practical and simple necessity—remains. The modern court reporter's desk is planted in the middle of the room, but the judge's bench, constructed with an exterior of simulated oak to match the wainscot, rises above it. Windows behind the bench form a backdrop, and when the windows are open, chirping birds nesting in the Virginia creeper augment the court proceedings. Sometimes sparrows make a mistake and think the courtroom is the route home.

Piers near the center of the room obstruct some of the spectator's view, but these are not original. A 1989 windstorm blew the clock tower above off its center, stressing the building so that it cracked walls and warped floors. After officials moved county employees to temporary quarters at the fairgrounds,

The clock tower in the Crook County courthouse is one of the most accessible in the state. *Credit: author*

they placed "unsafe to occupy" signs on the courthouse doors. Workers added reinforcing piers on all floors, including those in the courtroom which were then covered with matching wood wainscot.

Workers installed additional shoring in the attic. The attic is the route to the clock tower, which is the most accessible of Oregon's courthouses. Visitors can see on the top landing the central mechanism running the four clock faces, and the original wooden crate that protected the clock still lying off to the side. On the wall the instructions read, "Wind the clock at a uniform time, once a week." The clock's weight is simply a wooden box full of local rocks.

Pencils conveniently lie on a ledge by the central mechanism to encourage visitors to sign their names on the walls. Names with dates from 1912, 1932, and 1956 indicate that this has been a long-standing county tradition. An October 18, 1962 *Central Oregonian* reported that the tower walls include the signature of a woman from England, as well as the "Bend Bunch, 1910." The memories of Crook County citizens and their visitors remain on the clock tower walls through the changing times.

Although Deschutes County was created in 1916, it was slow to build a courthouse. The county constructed this building in 1940 after the school they were planning to use mysteriously burned. *Credit: Alan Viewig*

Deschutes County

County Seat:	Bend
Courthouse Address:	1164 N.W. Bond Street
Year Completed:	1940
Architect:	Truman E. Phillips
Date of County Formation:	December 13, 1916

"Various members of the two groups indicated they favored the construction . . . of the business building type, without costly frills so evident in many of the court houses of Oregon."

—*The Bend Bulletin*, March 24, 1937

After the turn of the century, Bend changed from a tiny hamlet to a prosperous town in just twenty years. The area's vast pine forests attracted two large lumber mills which employed thousands. Part of Bend's conversion, though, was due to one major land owner, The Bend Company, which tirelessly promoted the town. Today, the large mills are gone, and timber's role in the economy is slight. Year-round recreational uses such as skiing at nearby Mt. Bachelor or rafting in the Deschutes River now draw seasonal tourists and permanent residents. With national retailers crowding Highway 97, and million-dollar houses in the surrounding area, the former mill town has clearly followed a different path than other Oregon resource-based communities.

Its beginnings, however, were less remarkable. John Todd, a stockman, established a ranch in the late 1870s along a crook in the Deschutes River where the canyon walls dropped down, allowing wagons access to the water. Because his homestead was at the last bend in the river for those traveling northward, it gradually became known as Farewell Bend. Todd sold his ranch operations to John Sisemore, who also built a small hostelry and attempted to locate a post office there in 1886 under the name of "Farewell Bend." The postal authorities, who considered the name too long, granted him one under the name of Bend.

Over the next several years, the area attracted other cattle ranchers who also established homesteads. In 1900, Alexander Drake, a Midwest entrepreneur, and his wife were traveling in central Oregon scouting for arid land that could be irrigated and granted to them under the provisions of the 1894 Carey Desert Act. According to local lore, Drake unexpectedly met W. P. Vandevert, a local rancher who previously had worked for Drake as a guide, and he soon illuminated his former employer about the advantages of the area. Within six months, Drake had obtained land on the east side of the Deschutes. In May 1904, Pilot Butte Development, Drake's real estate company, filed the plat of Bend which included a total of thirty-three blocks.

The Bend Company purchased the townsite in 1911 in a deal that included 3,000 acres of timber land, 2,000 acres of agricultural land, 1,300 platted lots, a sawmill, a power and lighting plant, and the city water system. As large landholders, they were instrumental in promoting the town and providing land for community development. Over several years, they donated or sold at a reduced price the land for several churches, the Bend Amateur Athletic Club at 520 N.W. Wall Street, and Drake Park along the river west of the downtown. However, these transactions occurred later, after the railroad extended to Bend and started its economic boom.

In 1909, a bitter railroad conflict began when James J. Hill of the Great Northern Railway and his competitor, Edward H. Harriman of the Union Pacific Railroad, both commissioned their companies to construct a rail line south from the Columbia along the treacherous, steep slopes of the Deschutes River. The two companies, vying to finish first, swiftly built their rail lines down opposing sides of the canyon with the help of more than a thousand laborers. Crew members sometimes would sneak over to the opposite side in the night and detonate their competitor's powder. At another time, they fired bullets at each other across the river, but according to the diary of one worker quoted in *East of the Cascades* by Phil Brogan, "Fortunately, no one seems to be much of a shot." When the cliffs became so steep that only one rail line could be built, the companies finally consolidated their resources. The railroad reached Bend in October of 1911, and Bend citizens celebrated for two days. When James Hill addressed the crowd, a spectator called out, "I have known you since 1858 and you are the best man that ever lived, Mr. Hill."

The town was poised for growth. The May 5, 1912 *Bend Bulletin*, a tireless champion of the community, boasted that the area had "20,000,000,000 [board] feet of the finest yellow pine timber" and that "at least 250,000 horse-power [is] easily obtainable from the Deschutes at or near Bend." In 1915, two Minnesota-based firms, the Brooks-Scanlon Company and the Shevlin-Hixon Company, began building mills in Bend on the south side of town, divided only by the Deschutes River. With so many available jobs, Bend's population grew by one thousand percent in a decade, from 536 in 1910 to 5,415 by 1920. However, the timber supply did not last forever. By 1950, a timber-exhausted Shevlin-Hixon Company sold its assets to Brooks-Scanlon, and by 1994, the second big mill was gone.

The face of the town, however, already had begun to change. Skiing facilities built on Mount Bachelor in the 1960s augmented the area's summer tourist draws such as camping and fishing. With extensive recreational opportunities, central Oregon draws not only year-round tourists but residents from out of state who could afford upscale housing.

Visiting the Seat of Deschutes County Government

DOWNTOWN BEND ORIGINALLY BEGAN along Wall Street, so named because of the adjacent stone wall that enclosed Drake's residence. The commercial district quickly grew to encompass Bond Street, running parallel to the east. Many of the downtown buildings still standing were constructed in the expansionist times immediately after World War I, when many former soldiers returned to work in one of the two busy lumber mills. Today, the downtown's small shops, galleries, and restaurants reflect the prospering tourist industry.

Downtowns usually have several building cycles, beginning with wooden structures and moving to sturdier buildings after landlords become convinced the town will endure. One 1909 wooden-frame building, at 937 N .W. Wall Street, still stands from the earlier period. N. P. Smith, who helped survey the original Bend townsite for Drake, built this structure to sell hardware. Smith's family lived on the second floor above the store, a tradition that continued through the mid-1990s when Smith's daughter still lived in the "family home."

The time in the building cycle from wood to stone or brick was extremely short in Bend due to the advent of the railroad. The July 3, 1912 *Bend Bulletin* reported that in the previous year, the town possessed no permanent business structures, but now Bend had nine brick or stone business buildings. One of the first permanent structures in the downtown, the 1912 J. H. Bean Building at 855 N.W. Wall Street, exhibits Bend's native pink and gray tuff.

Several quarries west of Bend supplied the stone for the new buildings, but in 1912 a local brick plant was founded. The Bend Brick and Lumber Company was a frequent advertiser in the *Bend Bulletin*, which may be why the newspaper, when touting local building materials, usually would mention brick before stone. Extensive advertisements for brick undoubtedly influenced builders, and stone gradually fell to disuse. Unfortunately, while brick is used extensively in towns throughout Oregon, stone is more rare and could have created a more distinctive downtown.

A new type of construction—reinforced concrete—was introduced in the downtown in 1916 by Hugh O'Kane, whose numerous former professions included wrestling, sailing, mining, and stage coach driving. O'Kane's Bend Hotel had burned the previous year, and he flamboyantly decided to construct the largest building in the downtown at 115 N.W. Oregon Avenue. In his later years, the 300-pound O'Kane usually could be found sitting in a chair propped against his building, fast asleep. Large letters over the parapet still announce in a grand style the structure as the O'Kane Building, and in case this is missed, a large "O" with a "K" in the center is above the garland over the entry. Stained glass mezzanine windows displayed the word "Bend" within a circle, an emblem that once signified The Bend Company.

A History of the Courthouse

DISCUSSIONS OVER SEPARATING FROM Crook County had begun as early as 1907, after many Bend settlers began to consider their business affairs different from those of the ranchers who lived in the eastern part of the county. The January 18, 1907 *Bend Bulletin*, under the subheading "Many Good Reasons," noted that "the county court's recent bull-dozing tactics in foisting an extravagant court house upon the tax payers for the beautifying of Prineville . . . has created a determination to forever be rid of such treatment."

A bill for a separate county died in the legislature, but Bend residents bided their time. In 1914, discussion over the issue began again, to which the Prineville paper, as reported in the July 22, 1914 *Bend Bulletin*, retorted, "good riddance" and "a part of the southwest portion of this county has for several years been as a troublesome fester on the body politic."

In the 1914 election, the bill for Deschutes County was defeated by about fifty votes. In an editorial the day after the election, the November 4, 1914 *Bend Bulletin* responded to a

The *Bend Bulletin* was a strong supporter of a separate county. One of the first shots they fired at Prineville was an article dated January 18, 1907. It begins, "The rupture has come. The high-handed proceedings carried on by the county court have produced the inevitable result. The people of this section of the county are tired and disgusted with the idea of forever feeding the insatiable maw at Prineville—putting their hard-earned money into a fund that goes to the beautifying of the county seat while appeals for roads, bridges and kindred improvements go unheeded and not a cent is spent thereon; tired of being dictated to by a ring of political hucksters and grafters whose highest ambition seems to be to bleed this section to glorify their favorite city; tired of corruption and graft."

letter accusing the town of boosterism by modestly noting that "Bend has sprung from nothing to Crook county's leading town, with the largest population, by far the greatest investment in buildings, and a citizenship which wins recognition and praise from far and near." (Such editorials undoubtedly increased the irritation of Prineville residents.)

After the opening of the lumber mills attracted a larger populace, another vote on the county issue was held in 1916. Although the measure finally passed, some opponents decried the results at one of the precincts, where votes against the new county had been miscounted. The election results were contested in court but the creation of the new county was upheld, giving Deschutes the status of being the last county in Oregon to be created.

The county government, perhaps to be frugal, rented office space in several downtown buildings until the spring of 1935 when they leased a vacated school just north of the downtown. Two years later, the county began contemplating purchasing the building, effectively making a cast-off building its first courthouse. The night before a local representative was to seek legislative approval, a fire of unknown origin mysteriously erupted. Except for its brick exterior walls, the building was destroyed. The February 10, 1937 *Bend Bulletin* speculated that because the course of the fire was so rapid and "marked by explosions," it "could have resulted only from materials placed to hasten the destruction." The newspaper did not speculate that it was some "fire-bug" who believed that the county should have a proper courthouse. Rather, the state auditor had been in town inspecting the county's financial records, and according to the newspaper, "the cynical view taken around town today ties the fire and the prospective results of the general audit together." The cause of the fire remains unknown.

The county quickly moved back into its old quarters, many of which were still empty (even after two years, apparently due to the Depression). Although the county and the city began discussing a joint building, the local citizens rejected this at the polls. At a later election, voters, anticipating that a Public Works Administration grant would cover 45 percent of the funding, approved a levy to raise money for a new courthouse.

The grant, however, was not forthcoming, apparently because the county did not yet have all of its own funding. The county, having reduced the budget in order to finance the courthouse by themselves, received construction bids totalling $79,219. A Works Progress Administration grant did provide the laborers to clear the site, and work began, in a heavy flurry of February snow, almost two years after the fire.

As the building neared completion, the newspaper noted the use of local materials, such as the unstained natural pine in the courtroom. While most of the county offices had moved in by December 30, 1940, some details still were uncompleted. Not until May did venetian blinds replace the makeshift brown paper covering the windows. Also arriving that month were fourteen hat racks of native ponderosa pine, made by the advanced woodworking class at Bend High School.

The design features on the Deschutes County courthouse are concentrated in the central pavilion, where the front doors are located.
Credit: author

The Courthouse Today

THE COURTHOUSE STANDS ON A PROMONTORY above the street, facing west toward the Cascade Mountains. The only obvious use of local materials is the irregularly coursed volcanic stone, which forms a wall along the street and the main stairway. Other than a small memorial honoring war veterans at the base of the flag pole, no community memorabilia occupies the landscaped grounds surrounding the courthouse.

A futuristic-looking sky bridge connects the courthouse to the Justice Center. *Credit: author*

The courthouse, standing three stories high with a set-back fourth story originally used as the jail, was constructed at a time when architectural styles were shifting toward plain exteriors. Embellishment is chiefly limited to the stepped central pavilion, which encloses a tall, eighteen-

pane window over the entry doors. The few decorative elements, in an Art Deco style, include a chevron on the parapet and oblong light fixtures flanking the front doors. The building's gray unpainted concrete exterior, designed to simulate limestone, is devoid of any other color. With its height, austerity, and color, the structure appears to be a bastille rather than a courthouse.

When the neighboring Justice Center was constructed in the mid-1970s, legal-related offices moved out of the courthouse. Subsequent growth in the county forced expansion into other buildings. Newspaper articles when the courthouse was constructed are vague about whether its inside was plain or elaborate, but today, renovations have obliterated the 1940s finish. The interior also lacks a sense of the community, perhaps because many people now living in Deschutes County were born elsewhere. Instead, the courthouse presents a strictly businesslike face. For the Deschutes County courthouse, the workings of government are all.

A moderate budget, and architectural styles shifting away from lavish ornamentation, resulted in a courthouse with a plain exterior for Harney County. Despite these limitations, the county has personalized the interior. *Credit: author*

Harney County

County Seat:	Burns
Courthouse Address:	450 N. Buena Vista Avenue
Year Completed:	1942
Architectural Firm:	Roald and Schneider
Date of County Formation:	February 25, 1889

> *"Archie McGowan, Burns, urged that the court
> house be built only to meet the [basic]
> requirements as 'such things are overdone nearly
> every time'."*
>
> —*Burns Times-Herald,* April 12, 1940

arney County covers 10,180 square miles, but only about seven thousand people live within its boundaries. One can travel along a main highway for miles without seeing a house or fence, just an occasional road that leads seemingly nowhere. While communities such as Blitzen and Ragtown faded, Burns managed to endure and became "the biggest town in the biggest county in Oregon." With the exception of the later community of Hines to the south, Burns today stands alone, the only town within a seventy-five mile radius.

The discovery of gold in eastern Oregon in the early 1860s brought thousands of prospectors through the area, and their presence soon led to violent skirmishes with the Northwest Indians. To restore peace, the federal government established several military camps in the present-day Harney County before negotiating a treaty in 1869. Cattle ranchers, attracted by the vast amount of bunchgrass and the railroad available at Winnemucca, soon began moving their herds into the region.

While small, family-owned farms grew on the northern sections of the county, several vast cattle ranches, financed by out-of-state owners, developed on the southern end. For the next several decades, an uneasiness that sometimes erupted in violence brewed between the settlers and the cattle barons as each jockeyed for land ownership and water rights.

Burns consisted of a hotel, a saloon, and a barber shop in the early 1880s. George McGowan, a merchant from a rival settlement, soon moved to the town and started a general store with Peter Stenger. When establishing a post office, Stenger wanted to name the community after himself, but George Francis Brimlow in *Harney County, Oregon, and Its Range Land* wrote that McGowan discouraged this, observing that too many might call it "the Stenger town where they got stung." Instead, McGowan suggested the name of Burns, after Robert Burns, his favorite Scottish poet.

The Burns townsite was part of a land grant given the builders of the Willamette Valley and Cascade Mountain Wagon Road, which extended from Albany to the Washoe Ferry on the Snake River. Although the quality of the road in some locations was poor, the federal government awarded the land grants, the promised incentive. Subsequent owners of the military road land grant recorded a twenty-four-block plat called the "Town of Burns" in 1883. One early settler wrote that in the mid-1880s, "There was nothing attractive about Burns in those days; in fact it was as raw and crude a little burg as one can well imagine. There were two saloons, two small mercantile stores, a rough-and-tumble hotel, a blacksmith shop and a livery stable in the making." The saloons, by far the most popular businesses, attracted visiting cow-punchers and settlers, who made it their headquarters while they were in town.

While the cattle barons had access to larger cities such as San Francisco, Burns served the needs of the small homesteaders. In 1902, when *An Illustrated History of Baker, Grant, Malheur and Harney Counties* was published, the writer noted, "Were it not for the long freight trains [of horses] that are to be seen daily on the streets, the arrival and departure of stages and the conspicuous absence of the locomotive's sonorous whistle, one might easily forget that he was in a frontier town more than a hundred miles from the nearest railroad."

In 1916, the Oregon Short Line railroad extended as far as Crane, twenty-nine miles southeast of Burns, but it took the initiative of Burns residents to extend a railroad line to the town. In the early 1920s, the citizens pressured the federal government to make a deal involving the sale of Blue Mountain timberlands to the north in exchange for a lumber company extending the railroad to Burns and building a mill within five miles of the town. When the train finally arrived in 1924, approximately four thousand people attended the celebration.

A second firm, the Edward Hines Lumber Company, ultimately fulfilled the terms of the agreement when it constructed a mill in the newly developed town of Hines just south of Burns. Between 1920 and 1930, in response to the jobs at the mill, Burns's population grew from 1,022 to 2,599. The Hines company went bankrupt in the mid-1980s, and a subsequent lumber company ultimately failed in the mid-1990s. The large industrial site in Hines, for almost seventy years a lumber mill, then attracted a recreational vehicle manufacturer, but government and cattle still are economically important.

Visiting the Seat of Harney County Government

HEADING NORTH ALONG BROADWAY, the main street, a movie theater called the Desert reflects the area's semiarid conditions. The lack of rain hampered settlement, and in the early days the Ford dealership at 188 N. Broadway experienced unusual obstacles due to the town's isolated location. Barges carried the cars from Portland to The Dalles, and then hired help drove them over primitive, bumpy roads to Burns. Sometimes salesmen would spend up to five days at a far-flung ranch in the county, attempting to make a sale.

The first section of Broadway Street to be graveled was in front of the Ford dealership, reportedly so the salesmen could demonstrate their cars in front of their building. One of the dealership's associates, Harry Smith, was also a contractor who constructed the two-story building at 307 N. Broadway for Charles Voegtly, a hardware merchant. Smith used a combination of local stone and brick from his own kiln, and also supplied most of the bricks for the older buildings in Burns.

Operating single-screen theaters like the Desert are fast disappearing in town landscapes. *Credit: author*

Burns has only a few two-story structures. Because of the extra cost, owners generally had specific reasons for constructing an additional story. In small towns, fraternal groups such as the Masons frequently erected two-story buildings, with the intent of renting the ground floor and using the upper story for lodge activities. Fraternal groups usually identified their buildings with their emblem in the center of the structure above the top floor. Three interlocked rings are exhibited on the Odd Fellows structure at 348 N. Broadway, while a compass above a carpenter's square decorates the Masonic building at 406 N. Broadway.

Other builders of two-story structures usually were prominent merchants who thought the town had a future, such as Voegtly or Nathan Brown, whose building stands at 530 N. Broadway. An early settler wrote that Brown, who previously had lived in Walla Walla, Oregon City, and San Francisco, rode through the surrounding valley and said, "This is going to be a good country; I'm going no further." The exterior of his 1896 building, exhibiting fiscal caution, displays six no-nonsense narrow windows and a row of stone dentils on the second story. Its less-dressed rubble sides suggest that the structure anticipated same-height neighbors, which never came, to hide its ungainly parts.

A History of the Courthouse

BURNS EXTENDS SEVERAL BLOCKS BEYOND the Brown building, and then the main street reverts back to a highway heading northbound for the Blue Mountains and Grant County. Harney initially was part of Grant County, but the distance to the county seat at Canyon City, several days away by horse, influenced many citizens to petition for a more locally based government. Supporters circulated a bill in the legislature as early as 1887, but it was not until February 1889 that the state created Harney County, honoring the general who had assisted in opening up eastern Oregon for settlement. Harney City was designated as the temporary county seat, but had to face Burns and three other towns in a general election for the permanent position.

Burns citizens began campaigning vigorously. The May 17th, 1890 *Herald* listed Burns's natural advantages, including that "public buildings erected in Burns are not liable to destruction from cloud-bursts" and that "[the town] is free from the annual mosquito and gnat visitation that afflicts other parts of the county." Other persuasive arguments were "Burns has the only brewery in the county" and "the Burns Brass Band, of 18 pieces, is the only band in the county." Such compelling reasons undoubtedly swayed the voters, for the final election results were 512 votes for Burns, 415 votes for Harney, with the rest of the contenders sharing the remaining 89 votes.

Even before the official count was finished, the June 4, 1890 newspaper reported triumphantly that "the battle is over, and victory perches upon the banner of the Burnsites." The battle was not over. "Burnsites" had to file lawsuits to compel county officers to move to Burns. After the officials had relocated, a court ordered them back to Harney City until claims of suspected voter fraud were resolved. However, Burns citizens, including several town leaders, armed themselves and marched back and forth in front of the building housing the county records, threatening to shoot down the first person who attempted to move the records.

According to a petition filed by a Harney City citizen, several of the Burns men "threatened and still threaten to kill" the sheriff and officers of the court if they moved the records. The

Wooden buildings frequently were the first courthouse a county built. This structure served Harney County until 1941. *Collection of Eugene Luckey*

petition claimed that some of Burns' citizens had made bribes with the promises of money and employment, had intimidated schoolchildren to vote, had furnished whiskey to voters, and had circulated fraudulent ballots to "careless, illiterate and hasty voters." In addition, it stated that Burns "is an unhealthy and sickly place and the inhabitants thereof not law-abiding but notorious and dangerous. Many of the buildings therein of old wood and about to fall in. . . . There is great danger of flood at all times."

However, Harney City citizens themselves were not guiltless. While Harney City citizens claimed that 110 Burns votes were fraudulent, Burns citizens countered that 146 Harney City votes were fraudulent. Finally, almost three years after the initial election, an independent referee ruled that Burns had won the county seat position by a mere six votes.

Perhaps in response to the fear of flooding mentioned in one of the county seat election lawsuits, officials in 1894 located the first Harney courthouse, a two-story wooden structure, on a hill two blocks away from the main street. In the second-floor courtroom, small ranchers fought cattle barons over land ownership. The most famous trial occurred in 1898, when a jury found Edward Lee Olivier, a homesteader, innocent of murdering cattle baron Peter French.

Forty years later, the November 4, 1938 *Burns Times-Herald* called the courthouse "antiquated [and] poorly arranged." Voters were deciding whether the county should construct a new $100,000 courthouse, with 45 percent of the cost to be paid by the federal Public Works Administration (PWA). With such largess, the issue passed, and the county judge immediately traveled to Portland to present a request to the PWA official. But the PWA refused the request; later newspaper accounts blamed either incomplete plans or that the county's part of the funding was not entirely available in 1938.

By 1940, the court began discussing building a modest courthouse entirely with its own funds. Officials and interested leading citizens toured recently constructed courthouses in Tillamook, Linn, and Deschutes Counties. Economy, however, was foremost in their minds. The court even reduced the amount of the lowest construction bid by about five thousand dollars to $63,066. The county moved to the Brown building and, assisted by a grant of over four thousand dollars from the Works Progress Administration, work began on excavating a basement.

Just one month after the invasion of Pearl Harbor, the county court moved into the courthouse, and the community began using the new facilities. One group that announced plans to meet there, the Harney County Wild Life Association, apparently preferred their wildlife dead; according to the March 6, 1942 newspaper, they would "enjoy the new rifle range in the court house basement."

The Courthouse Today

A SIDEWALK AND A BERM ALONG THE front of the courthouse distinguish this block from others along the street. The landscaped square provides a cool respite during Burns's hot summer months, although sprinklers discourage lolling on the grass. Most of the trees provide only shade, but an apricot tree on the southwest corner also bears fruit, which locals pick during summer.

Elms flank the walkway leading to the front of the building, which faces east like the first courthouse. Except for its square, the veterans memorial, and the words on its facade, the building has little to suggest it is a courthouse. A modest budget and a shift in architectural styles from ornate embellishments to nondescript facades were two major factors contributing to the courthouse's austere exterior.

Decoration is concentrated on the central entry, where concrete fluting flanks a tall twelve-pane window over the two front doors. A plastic owl, which replaced a rotted wooden flagpole, guards against birds perching on the ledge over the entry. Another owl stands above the back door, whimsically added not to discourage birds but to match the one in front. During the spotted owl controversy, pranksters painted spots on the back-door owl; it has since been repainted.

The lobby's rose-colored terrazzo floor, one of the few interior extravagances, has become the basis of the courthouse's subsequent color scheme. Benches lining the wall exhibit a similar shade, as does some of the lower half of the lobby walls in order to simulate wainscot. Even the elevator, a recent addition that replaced one of the two stairways to the second floor, sports this warm color on its exterior doors. Using nothing more than a bucket of paint, the maintenance man, Irv Rhinehart, showed that the county cares about the courthouse's appearance.

Even though sheepherding, farming, and logging also were ways of life for Harney County citizens, the pioneer society chose a cattleman on a horse for the seal lying in the center of the terrazzo floor. At the head of the seal, a setting sun bisects the date 1870, the year the county was created. Darrell Otley, whose family were ranchers, designed the seal and was awarded a wrist watch for his efforts.

The courthouse construction budget did not allow much interior embellishment, but employees and officials have added their own decorations which define Harney County and personalize the building. A picture of two cowboys amid grazing cattle, painted by Otley, dominates the far wall. (A rendition of the painting, naturally in a rose tint, is printed at the top of the county's official stationery.) On a side wall, three paintings donated by county employees and Otley also portray ranching scenes.

In the 1910s, Harney, like other counties, paid a bounty for jack rabbits, which were considered a pest to alfalfa and grain fields. The bounty, a nickel a head, financially aided struggling homesteaders. To prevent fraud, the county defined what constituted an acceptable scalp: "both ears and the tip of the nose of the animal, all connected with the natural skin that grew between them, and all whole and intact."

Pictures of Harney County's rangelands are located throughout the courthouse. In the county clerk's office, one prominently located painting depicts the site where the famed cattle baron Peter French was killed. During election nights, interested citizens waiting for the voting results in the clerk's office share a potluck in the nearby break room. While as many as fifteen to twenty people stand around talking, the clerk posts the results on hand-written poster board lying along the long counter in the clerk's office. Unlike metropolitan areas where counting can continue throughout the night, courthouse-loitering residents, many with full stomachs from the potluck, generally will know the election outcome by 10:00 p.m.

In the midst of election night socializing, few probably notice that the piers in the clerk's office have either rounded or squared corners. Those with the squared corners were added after the discovery in 1959 that the aggregate in the reinforced concrete construction was inferior and was causing the seventeen-year-old courthouse to sag. Employees vacated the building for three years while the county court vacillated between tearing it down and repairing it. During that time, the local newspaper even referred to the building and its grounds as "the old courthouse property."

Inside the courtroom, a painting of a cattle roundup towers over the judge's bench. *Credit: author*

The courtroom on the second floor is another place where the Harney County identity is strong. In 1995, a local junior high school art class painted a mural on the wall outside the courtroom. This forest scene, depicting the northern part of the county, contrasts with the rangeland paintings on the first floor. However, inside the courtroom, a painting of a cattle roundup towers over the judge's bench. This picture, like the wildlife scenes on the entry door walls, once hung in the old downtown post office. Another later addition is the elk trophy on the rear wall—the evidence in a case against several hunters who had killed the elk illegally.

The furnishings connect the courtroom to the rest of the courthouse and the community at large. The recorder, witness, prosecution, and defense sit on modern burgundy chairs, a deeper shade of the rose tones found throughout the building. The Edward Hines Lumber Company supplied the clear pine for the spectator benches, and unlike other counties which selected their benches from a catalog, these appear to be locally made. The Hines company also provided the knotty pine used in the judge's bench and jury box—a wood found more frequently in vacation cabins than in solemn courtrooms.

Because Harney County did not receive the PWA funds to help build its new courthouse, the building does not feature a lobby with costly marble wainscot or elaborate ornamentation on the exterior like the courthouses in Linn and Clackamas counties, which did receive PWA funding. The Harney County courthouse is a plain structure, but through the years its citizens have personalized the building with things that speak of the community. Just like their predecessors at the turn of the century, Harney County citizens are aware that the courthouse represents them.

The path to the Morrow County courthouse was planned carefully. Courthouse afficionados should experience walking up the stairway. *Credit: author*

Morrow County

County Seat: Heppner
Courthouse Address: 100 Court Street
Year Completed: 1903
Architect: Edgar Lazarus
Date of County Formation: February 16, 1885

*"The water was 15 feet high in Heppner's streets
and rose over the new courthouse [retaining] wall. .
. . Many people slept in the courthouse last night,
and any place they can make a bed."*

—*Fossil Journal,* June 26, 1903

Playing ball in front of the roller-compacted concrete Willow Creek Dam is a way of life for Heppner youth. The dam, which rises 165 feet and extends between two hills to contain a 125-acre reservoir, can startle first-time visitors. The dam is a mark on the land, a legacy from the flash flood in 1903 that killed almost two hundred fifty people. Other effects of the flood are not as tangible; for years, townspeople lived in fear of a recurrence, and the seeping of the current dam in the 1980s raised an outcry. That one event—the flood almost one hundred years ago—remains a persistent part of Heppner's history.

Heppner's development began relatively late. Early travelers on the Oregon Trail in the 1840s journeyed through the northern part of the present-day county, without noticing the bountiful grasslands in the creeks and valleys to the south. In the early 1860s, ranchers began using these lowlands for their cattle and horses, and later, sheep. George Stansbury, a farmer, purchased land along Willow Creek in 1869 and constructed a primitive cabin. Stansbury extended hospitality to travelers journeying through the region, and the area soon became known as Stansbury's Flat. During that period, ranchers from the hinterlands needing supplies traveled more than thirty-five miles north to towns along the Columbia River. Seeing an opportunity, Jackson Morrow, a La Grande merchant, and Henry Heppner, a freight distributor, formed a partnership to operate a store in Stansbury's Flat. While Heppner secured the merchandise, Morrow constructed a store on the present-day northeast corner of Main and May Street. After the roof and floor were completed, families from as far away as fifty miles came to dance and celebrate.

Morrow and Heppner's store was a magnet, attracting business owners who soon established a blacksmith and a drug store on nearby sites. When residents wanted a new name for the community (apparently Stansbury's Flat was inadequate), they considered such names as "Willows," "I. X. L." (after a famous elixir carried at the first mercantile), and "New Chicago." They finally settled on Heppner, honoring one of the partners who had built the cornerstone of the town.

In October 1875, Stansbury filed the first Heppner plat, which consisted of seven blocks along the flat land bordering the creek. By 1880, Heppner's population of 318 was second-largest in the mid-Columbia region behind The Dalles. Heppner's growth was due in part to its location at the end of several roads, including the Monument road, which extended to the stockland region of the John Day area. Heppner's role as a transfer point expanded when the Oregon Railway & Navigation railroad built a spur line from its main line along the Columbia River to Heppner in 1888. According to *An Illustrated History of Umatilla County and Morrow County*, the railroad enhanced "the values of Heppner realty about fifty per cent," and merchants reported a threefold increase in trade.

In June 1903, disaster struck when a violent cloudburst southeast of Heppner unleashed torrents of water that rushed into Willow Creek. The flash flood formed a wall of water and debris that washed through the town in minutes. According to the June 18, 1903 *Heppner Times*, "Large two-story dwelling houses were picked up and hurled around like a spring top, others were knocked into kindling wood with as much ease as a child would destroy a toy house; the heaviest of implements and farm machinery were hurled along as if they were drift wood; the heaviest track rails were snapped in two like corn stalks, and bent in all conceivable shapes." Bodies littered the streets. Almost two hundred fifty people—about one-fifth of the town's population—were killed.

After retrieving the bodies and cleaning up the muck, Heppner citizens began rebuilding their town. However, Heppner's role as a transfer point gradually diminished as other railroad lines and better roads linked the region. Its location near the Blue Mountains, however, attracted a lumber mill in the late 1930s, which boosted the town's population to 1,600 by 1950. Like any small town dependent on one major industry, the declining fortunes of the mill directly affected Heppner, and its population has decreased.

Visiting the Seat of Morrow County Government

ALONG MAIN STREET BETWEEN WILLOW and May streets, Heppner's one-story buildings, constructed before the turn of the century, generally hide their age behind remodeled storefronts. Gone are the Palace Hotel and The Fair store, both grand multi-story buildings from that time period. The tall structures still standing, with period embellishments on their upper floors, reflect construction in the new century.

The Keeney & Roberts Building, on the northwest corner of North Main and Willow Streets, displays blue-gray stone, the same material later used on the courthouse exterior. Roberts used red stone above his second-floor windows, and then constructed the adjoining Odd Fellows' building with a red stone front. Perhaps the Odd Fellows members wanted a slightly more flamboyant building, because a parapet rises slightly above its blue-gray neighbor. While the Odd Fellows' second floor served as a meeting hall, the upper floor of the Keeney & Roberts Building served at various times as an opera house and offices, and as a morgue after the 1903 flood. On the southwest corner of Main and Willow streets, the Masons constructed their red brick lodge in 1915, which features a parapet like the Odd Fellows structure, but has a more detailed facade.

Contractor Lou Traver built both the Heppner Hotel directly across the street (originally called St. Patrick's Hotel, a name that has since been restored) and the two-story Elks building located further south on the block. In 1933, concerned Heppner citizens met at the Elks building because the county did not have money to pay its school teachers, and there they developed the idea of "Heppner Sheep Skin Scrip," a currency replacement to be accepted by local merchants.

Money was scarce during the Depression in Heppner. The local bank, which occupied the two-story brick building at the northwest corner of Main and May streets, already had failed by 1933. Offices once occupied the second floor of this 1918 bank building, but today a bank occupies the first floor, and the second story is empty, apparently due to "security concerns."

Gilliam and Bisbee, hardware merchants, built the two-story brick building on the northeast corner of Main and May streets after a 1918 fire. Above the second-story windows, faint lettering still reads "AND BISBEE." Although Frank Gilliam's name is missing, his place remains in the area's history as one of the first county commissioners, a three-time county treasurer, and two-time Heppner mayor.

A History of the Courthouse

GILLIAM HAD NOT YET STARTED HIS HARDWARE business when Jackson Morrow introduced a bill to the legislature in February 1885 to create a new county out of the western section of Umatilla. Because Morrow's constituents held him in such high esteem, they decided to name the new county after him. Heppner became the temporary county seat until the permanent location could be put to popular vote at the next general election.

Heppner citizens took the matter into their own hands before the election by donating a site on a hill overlooking the town and contributing money for the building. County officials, themselves temporarily appointed until the election, ordered a courthouse to be constructed in Heppner three months before the vote. This action galvanized the people in nearby Lexington to hold a town meeting, where prominent citizens decried the fiscal wisdom of it as Heppner was not yet the permanent county seat. In an effort to sway voters, Lexington residents themselves pledged $3,000 and a building site for the courthouse.

Although the two communities were only nine miles apart, ranchers frequented Heppner, while farmers, called "bunchgrassers," preferred Lexington. According to Sam McMillan in *The Bunchgrassers*, the June 4, 1886 Lexington *Bunchgrass Blade*, published three days before the election, boasted that "Lexington Blocks the Game of the Heppnerites!" The newspaper also printed a letter from a farmer to "Brother Bunchgrassers" which recounted that "the Heppner merchant says he doesn't want your trade. . . . You have come into that town with your ragged overalls on, expecting to be treated as white men. . . . Have you not, until recently, been met on every side with sneers?"

So that pro-Heppner sheep ranchers could vote, the town's youth rode to the surrounding hills to watch the flocks. Despite this effort, at a counting of the ballots that night Lexington appeared so far ahead of Heppner that at 2:00 a.m. the judges stopped their work, agreeing to resume the next morning. A guard was posted, but according to a story in *The Bunchgrassers*, he was drugged with a cup of coffee, and the next morning all ballots were missing. Citizens took the matter to court, which decided to give Heppner the county seat designation since it already possessed the records.

A wooden two-story courthouse served the county for over fifteen years, but in January 1902, Heppner citizens met at the opera house to show support for a new courthouse. The county court wasted no time; by the next week, the Heppner newspaper reported that officials had selected a site for the new courthouse on the corner of May and Chase streets and that the former quarters would be the county poor house. By the next week, representatives had completed a trip to Salem, Corvallis, Dallas, Oregon City, and Moro to visit their courthouses.

Although the court acted quickly, the outlying areas of Eight Mile, Dry Fork, and Dairyville still had time to protest in the newspaper, writing that the courthouse would be an unnecessary tax burden. Nevertheless, in early February, the court invited architects to submit their plans. Although Charles Burggraf, who had designed the courthouse for Sherman and Wheeler counties, had visited Heppner, the court awarded the contract to Edgar Lazarus, later known for his design of the Columbia Gorge Vista House and the Clatsop County courthouse.

The court reversed its location decision, choosing to build on the original courthouse site, and had the old courthouse moved to the side during construction. To help finance the building, Heppner citizens donated $2,000. By the end of February, workers were grading the site, and by May—just five months after the first Heppner meeting—the court accepted the contract bids.

Over the next nine months, the *Heppner Gazette* furnished details of progress on the structure: "Stone work on the new court house is almost finished" (September 25, 1902); "Work has been commenced on the tower in which will be stationed the town clock" (November 6, 1902). When the November 27, 1902 newspaper listed the subscribers for the clock, Henry Heppner, a frequent town benefactor, was not shown, although Jackson Morrow donated twenty dollars. The January 1, 1903 *Heppner Gazette*, while touting Heppner as the "Metropolis of Morrow County," noted that several stone buildings had been erected, including the courthouse, and hastened to add that the building cost about forty thousand dollars. In March 1903, even though the county was waiting for larger clock face dials, the county court moved into the building.

The Courthouse Today

CAREFUL PLANNING AND INADVERTENT DECISIONS contributed to Morrow County having one of the most memorable courthouse sites in Oregon. Rather than building on level land at May and Chase streets, one block off the downtown, and leave the old courthouse as a poor house (which would symbolically have elevated that institution above the town), officials decided to use the original site. The building is positioned so that May Street leads directly to a long flight of steps which gently curve up to the courthouse front door.

The Morrow County courthouse tower, like those on other courthouses, is an important landmark in the town. *Credit: author*

Along the way to the building, May Street crosses the now benign Willow Creek, which had flooded just three months after the courthouse opened.

The blue-gray stone in the Court Street retaining wall, in the stairway wall and on the building exterior was extracted from a quarry southeast of Heppner, giving the building a local flavor. Unlike the Crook, Baker, and Wallowa county courthouses, which display regularly shaped blocks, Morrow's stone on the courthouse exterior is randomly coursed, with rectangular blocks of varying sizes creating a greater texture. The stone masons, expecting more attention to be focussed on the courthouse, took less care building the retaining wall, leaving an enduring illustration of the available qualities of stone construction.

Light gray stone provides a contrast around the windows and on the entrance piers and quoins. This stone is further distinguished with a smooth band, called a draft line, which encircles the face of the block. For additional variation, regularly laid stone is used in the piers, and smooth stone above the arched entrance.

The courthouse exhibits characteristics of the American Renaissance style, such as a bilaterally symmetrical front facade and a central pavilion, but the architect also deviated from the style. American Renaissance buildings typically have flat roofs and smooth dressed stone; the Morrow County courthouse possesses a hipped roof and roughly dressed stone. To add embellishment, brackets that look like squared, four-toed feet grace the frieze, and bull's-eye windows stand above the roofline. The curve of the bull's-eye windows matches the rounded shape of the tower above, which is supported by clusters of columns and ends in a jaunty finial.

In the central pavilion atop each pier, granite statues representing Liberty and Justice give human expression to the exterior. Both look forward, not down at the populace, perhaps implying favoritism toward none. Both grip a sword, suggesting that the ideals they represent are so important they must be defended. The pans of Justice's scale, which the statue clutches to her body, are not identically rounded, but this should not be interpreted to mean that Morrow County's justice might be skewed.

A clock in a tower added prestige to a county building, but during the turn of the century they were also a necessity. Pocket watches were relatively expensive, and the townspeople could run their lives by the chimes of the clock. The chimes, which ring every hour, reportedly can be heard ten miles away. Although a story has circulated that the clock stopped ringing on the day of the flood, local historians dispute this. Heppner residents must have briefly paused, however, when Lions Club members from the neighboring town of Ione, dismayed at the dirt on the tower, once reported that they were coming to Heppner to "clean their clock."

The clock, however, has only three faces. Apparently as a cost-savings measure, the rear face was never added. The rear also is devoid of ornaments such as the bull's-eye windows, brackets, and contrasting stone around the windows. Ironically, the frugal construction method did not take into account the coming of the parking lot,

The one-story high extension on the back of the courthouse was originally the jail. The original plans show that the floor was to be concrete, but perhaps this was not installed immediately. The November 18, 1905 *Central Oregon Star* noted, "Morrow County jail does not seem to be any stronger than that of Wheeler. For the second time recently Fred Fehrmann dug his way out of prison."

which now forces the unadorned rear to serve as the main entrance. Almost everyone uses the back entrance, including a prisoner who escaped from the courtroom in 1995. He ran out the back door, across the parking lot, and down the driveway, hotly pursued by the district attorney, county judge and emergency services director. He ultimately was captured by the district attorney.

For west-bound escapees and courthouse aficionados, a better route is via the front entrance. The front door, however, is so ill-used that when the county replaced the original double doors, they chose a single modern door more appropriate for a school classroom. Just as a path runs from Main Street to the front door, the architect designed a formal passage inside the building. In the Morrow County courthouse, a corridor opens up to a large hallway with a grand stairway positioned in the center.

Just inside the front door on the left wall, the original certificates appointing Morrow's first county officers display flowery old-fashioned language stating, "Know ye, that reposing special trust and confidence in the capacity, integrity, and fidelity . . . " Nearby, an oil painting of the courthouse is displayed, made by a former treasurer who apparently was so fond of her workplace that she painted its image after she retired.

Others besides county employees have great affection for the courthouse. In the county clerk's office, a needlepoint picture embroidered by a city policeman's wife shows another rendition of the building. Over the years, Barbara Bloodsworth, the county clerk, saved courthouse memorabilia that otherwise would have been lost. Wooden clock hands hung on her office wall; brass spittoons propped open her door. As the keeper of county records, the clerk has one of the original vaults, customized by the words "Morrow County" on the door. By the handle, a warning stating "protected by bank-type gas" might stop some burglars, but likely out of puzzlement rather than fear.

Aspects of Heppner history also are part of the courthouse displays. In the southern hallway, a 1929 panorama photograph taken from a neighboring hill shows the town in snow. In the county judge's office, eight photographs depict the 1903 flood devastation in Heppner. Modern tokens in the county judge's office from that event include a paperweight commemorating the dam's construction and—hidden in the closet—a core sample of the dam.

Like the county judge's office, other offices in the courthouse have fir wainscot, a feature usually reserved only for public spaces such as the hallways. The extensive fir wainscot, described by one employee as being "fourteen miles" long, is nicked and scratched from years of wear. While some employees longingly speak of sanding the wood so that the wainscot would appear new, these marks, an honest patina, give the courthouse a worn yet dignified look.

The courthouse's sounds also speak of its age. When opened, doors squeal; when tread upon, steps creak. A legend exists that a ghost inhabits the courthouse, and although the ghost has never been seen, mysterious footsteps have been heard late at night. In the early 1980s, the district attorney and a colleague working late at night heard the toilet flush in the women's restroom, and after finding no one there, speculated that the ghost had paid a visit. Perhaps the ghost is an old-time female settler, upset that the picture hanging in the second-floor hallway portrays only male pioneers.

In the second-floor hallway, structural support columns have been fashioned to look like Greek columns, and they also provide a handy place to hang the fire extinguisher. With benches placed in the hallway, the room becomes a waiting area when court is in session. Inside the courtroom, the county has removed several spectator benches in order to add bookshelves for law books. At the turn of the century, trials served as a source of entertainment, but now more drama usually can be seen in television programs.

Cushions, in a plaid fabric normally found on living-room chairs, helps to alleviate the jury's discomfort. Like the wainscot throughout the courthouse, the judge's bench shows nicks from the passing years. On the bench, a slice of log serves as the place to pound the gavel, appropriately tying the courtroom to the timber industry.

The courtroom receives natural light from windows on three sides. Besides being a practical design to reduce consumption of electricity, the windows—particularly the front ones— provide a view of Heppner and the surrounding landscape. Early townspeople chose a lofty courthouse site so that their efforts (both fair and foul) would be visible. They selected well.

While other counties have replaced their first courthouses, this building is Sherman County's only courthouse. Off to the rear, the wheat fields for which the county is known are visible for miles. *Credit: author*

Sherman County

County Seat:	Moro
Courthouse Address:	500 Court Street
Year Completed:	1899
Architect :	Charles Burggraf
Date of County Formation:	February 25, 1889

"Few counties in the state are better off financially than Sherman, and it certainly is in condition to build a temple of justice that will be a credit to the county."

—The Dalles Times-Mountaineer, as reported in the Moro Observer, May 24, 1899

Highway 97, one of the busiest Oregon roads east of the Cascades, runs along Moro's main street, but the long-haul trucks and Los Angeles-bound buses stop for a just moment, if at all. Moro started as a farming town, and no other industry has developed to change it. The Sherman County motto, "from bunchgrass to golden grain," describes a transition that occurred more than one hundred years ago, but the golden grain is very much a part of today.

Sherman County's rolling hills were covered with knee-high grass when ranchers first arrived in the 1860s. Many moved on after the bunchgrass was eaten, but others stayed and cultivated a few acres. The news that the grassland could grow wheat, and that a transcontinental railroad would soon locate along the Columbia River, inspired hundreds of farmers to move to the area in the early 1880s.

The farmers, miles away from The Dalles, needed equipment and staples. One settler, Henry Barnum, converted a room in

According to Lewis A. McArthur in *Oregon Geographic Names*, several stories exist about how Moro received its name. One is that it was named by Judge O. M. Scott after his former town in Illinois; another is that it was named after the Moore Brothers, who had an interest in the townsite. Yet another, seemingly less likely, version is that the community was named after the Moors, the Muslims living in northwest Africa. After relating these possibilities, McArthur invites readers to choose their own preference.

his house in the present-day Moro into a trading post, and later a merchandising firm constructed a small store. The partnership of Scott & McCoy continued the store, started a post office, and filed the first Moro plat which consisted simply of two rows of three blocks each bracketing the main street. Moro slowly grew when a hotel began and a blacksmith opened.

The region was part of Wasco County, but the settlers resented the long journey to the county seat in The Dalles, which at one time included a toll bridge across the Deschutes River. In addition, many thought their area was poorly represented in the county. In 1888, when some discussed annexing to Gilliam County to the east, two petitions circulated—one rejecting annexation and the other promoting a separate county. The issue was hotly debated and citizens were divided. According to Giles French in *The Golden Land*, one settler wrote to the local newspaper saying the "majority of those who want a new county are a class of sore-heads."

Support for a new county grew. While serving as state representative, E. O. McCoy, the merchant from Moro, introduced a bill in 1889 to the legislature to create Fulton County, which would honor Colonel James Fulton, a leading local citizen, a former state legislator, and a southern Democrat. When the bill came before the House, J. T. Maxwell, a powerful legislator from Tillamook and Yamhill counties, reminded his colleagues that in 1870 a resolution had circulated to ask General William Sherman, a Unionist fighter, to speak to the legislators. Fulton had convinced the body to veto the idea, and Maxwell, remembering the slight, suggested that instead the new county be named Sherman.

The town of Wasco, now separated from the county for which it was named, became the temporary county seat. Wasco,

Moro, and Kenneth, a small settlement east of Moro, vied for the permanent county seat position in the 1890 election. Wasco, the winner, did not receive the necessary majority and another vote against Moro was scheduled. In 1891, the county extended its southern border, and when the next county seat election was held, the new Sherman County citizens swung the election toward Moro, the town closest to their homes.

With an enormous wheat production in relation to its land size, Sherman was called the "biggest little county on the Pacific Coast" in the 1890s. The January 1, 1898 *The Dalles Times-Mountaineer* also proclaimed it the "largest wheat belt in the world not intersected by a railroad"—a title that did not please local residents. Business owners organized a railroad, initially called the Columbia Southern Railway, to run from Biggs to Wasco. At a meeting held in Moro about extending the railroad line, within two hours residents pledged $5,000 and eight acres for the depot. *An Illustrated History of Central Oregon* relates that when the rails were laid to the Moro depot in December, 1898, there was "considerable excitement, ringing of bells, fanfare of whistles."

The January 1, 1898 *The Dalles Times-Mountaineer* stated, "it is safe to predict that Moro will continue to retain its preeminence as a commercial center. . . . Nature has surrounded it on all sides with rich and fertile agricultural lands, whose golden harvests are year by year, in the usual course of trade, poured into the lap of its commercial population." Optimistic about the town's future, Moro grew to its largest population, 418 people, in 1920.

Changing circumstances prevented the town from realizing those expectations. The rail line was extended as far south as Shaniko, but it lost passengers and freight when the railroad was constructed down the Deschutes River to Bend. Although wheat production has increased at least four times over turn-of-the-century production, farms required fewer and fewer workers due to mechanization. Better roads soon allowed county residents to drive their own cars to larger stores in The Dalles. The railroad ceased taking passengers in the early 1940s, and finally stopped transporting wheat in the mid-1960s. Moro, however, remains the largest town in the county, which is one of the least-populated in Oregon.

Visiting the Seat of Sherman County Government

AT A TIME WHEN THE ROADS WERE POOR and the townspeople did their shopping in Moro, businesses extended in every direction from its center at First and Main streets. Today, small towns like Moro serve as convenience stops along the way to bigger cities, and businesses that once were located along its Main Street, such as a hardware store and barber shop, have disappeared. In Moro, the march of empty storefronts has crept closer and closer to its center.

The buildings still standing in the heart of Moro were constructed for different uses, and the later tenants, with considerably fewer resources than the original owners, have adapted to them. On the northeast corner of First and Main streets, a three-story hotel built in 1921 now serves as an antique store, its second-floor rooms catering not to guests but to tourists seeking old wares.

On the southwest corner, the town's only cafe occupies a former bank space. A county seat with only one restaurant can present practical problems during lunch time. In one large civil case, the plaintiff and his witnesses ate at the cafe, while the defendant and his party had to journey to the sole restaurant in another town. As justice would demand, they switched on alternate days.

Sometimes older buildings give clues to their former uses on the ground floor. *Credit: author*

Half a block west along First Street stands the oldest commercial building in Moro, the former Scott and McCoy store. Originally, this 1883 building abutted Main Street, but when the bank was constructed in 1901, the building, by then a newspaper office, was dragged on skids by horse to its present location. With tongue-and-groove siding, double doors, and a wooden sign on a false front simply reading "Journal," it seems suspended in the past.

Signs and brochures guide visitors to the museum located one block east of Main Street. While the museum preserves aspects of the region's agricultural past, the county's rural life is still very visible in Moro today. Agriculture equipment is still sold in town. During harvest time in July and August, farmers drive truck after truck laden with wheat to the Moro grain elevator, which dominates the town's eastern skyline.

A History of the Courthouse

ALTHOUGH THE CLERK AND SHERIFF occupied a modest county-built structure for several years after moving to Moro in 1892, officials decided to construct an official courthouse in 1899. The person they chose to draw up the plans was Charles Burggraf, an architect who later designed several Oregon courthouses including one still standing in Wheeler County. The contractor's bid of $6,665 was $665 more than the county court had authorized, but Moro citizens banded together and raised the remainder.

The Courthouse Today

UNLIKE MANY OREGON COURTHOUSES, the Sherman County courthouse block lies on the edge of Moro, as if officials wanted to separate themselves from the town. Located near the crest of a hill four blocks from Main Street, the site required townspeople to travel up the rise to the courthouse. Behind the building, the land changes from town to country but the transition is not precise. On the next block west, odors from a horse pasture and a cow barn sometimes waft over to the

The tower was capped with a magnificent cupola painted in alternating dark and light bands. It was removed in the 1950s. *Credit: Sherman County Historical Society*

courthouse. Beyond, wheat fields on the gently sloping hills extend for miles.

A fence once separated the courthouse from the street, but now a knee-high sidewalk, the only one in the neighborhood, forms a concrete barrier. On the south side of the walkway leading to the courthouse, a war memorial pays tribute to those who "gave their lives and those who served." Nearby, a marker covers a time capsule filled with memorabilia to be opened in the year 2039, the county's 150th anniversary. So that Sherman County citizens will not swell with pride over their pedigree, a quote from Plutarch on the marker reminds them that "it is indeed a desirable thing to be well descended but the glory belongs to our ancestors."

Burggraf designed a courthouse with Queen Anne architectural features, which included straight and round topped windows, a corner tower, and varied wall surfaces such as the brick exterior and patterned wood shingles on the tower. While the building has the theme of the style, it does not exhibit much of the intricate Queen Anne detailing, doubtless because of the added cost. Although the May 24, 1899 *Moro Observer* reported that the county could well afford a courthouse, the budget in comparison to other counties was relatively modest.

The building materials also were thrifty. Bricks for the courthouse were made in a nearby field from local clays, and their irregular edges attest to the brickmakers' skill level. Some of the bricks on the building appear scorched at one end, as if the bricks closest to the fire—the clinkers—could not be wasted. Over the years, the temptation to immortalize themselves proved too great to resist for some citizens, who carved their names and dates in the bricks. On the north side, east of the drain pipe about eleven feet up, one brick reads "J. F. N. 1927," while on the south side, above the corrugated roof of the shed, several bricks show "1929" and some now indistinguishable names. To avoid a similar obliteration, the custodian scratched his name, "Lee L. 7-19-90" deeply into the five-foot high brick on the south side by the southwest corner.

The budget did not include a clock tower, so the architect designed a tower capped by a cupola featuring a bell-shaped roof. Originally both the cupola and the tower displayed alternating bands of dark and light paint, although now the tower is simply painted white. Because of storm damage, the county removed the cupola in the late 1950s and the building now seems unbalanced. However, official postcards and coffee cups sold during the county's centennial in 1989 depicted the courthouse with the cupola, in effect denying its present appearance.

Even though the budget was modest, decoration during the Victorian era was important. The arched windows display delicate wooden ornamentation. Instead of a simple lettering, the sheet metal sign displaying "Sherman County" and "1899" features egg-and-dart molding with rosettes at the two extending ends. Beyond the modern glass doors, a filigree knob—now worn—still graces one of the original doors.

Inside, modern carpet and acoustical tile ceiling hide clues to the interior budget, but the walls without wainscot suggest it was minimal. Eight oak-framed, black-and-white photographs, most larger than two by three feet, transform the hallway into a gallery. The photos, displayed at the 1905 Lewis and Clark Exposition, show the county at its finest. One

Photographs placed in the courthouse lobby and stairway landing show past aspects of Sherman County life. *Credit: author*

photograph shows the courthouse, just three years old, sporting the elaborately striped cupola. Another photograph exhibits the soil's bounty; wheat sacks are piled more than eleven feet high at a Moro warehouse.

On the stairway landing, another photograph displays the original meaning of the term "horsepower": more than thirty horses pull a combine. Modern-day farmers and others climbing up the stairs usually head for the county's courtroom. The sign on the door reads "Justice Court/Public Meeting Rooms/Circuit Court," indicating that like other small counties, Sherman County cannot afford to use the room exclusively for one purpose.

Two nine-foot high swinging doors with filigree handles distinguish the courtroom from other offices. Even in the courtroom, however, the furnishings are austere. Walls are devoid of decoration with the exception of bookshelves lining the side and back of the room, which cause the floor to sag. Individual captain's chairs form the spectators' seats, but the county has fastened them together in rows to discourage scooting one out of the line. Negating any attempt at solemnity, the jury sits on black-and-orange high school stadium seating pads that read "Sherman County Huskies."

During harvest time in July and August, farmers disappear into the fields to reap their once-a-year paycheck, and court cases involving juries are not held. During the rest of the year, the county's legal needs are small. Even during the 1980s, the district attorney filled his time by also working as a private lawyer and providing property title searches. The judge is still shared with surrounding counties and usually visits one Friday afternoon every three weeks.

Individual captain's chairs form the spectators' seats, but the county has fastened them together in rows to discourage scooting one out of the line. Credit: author

The simple rooms for the judge and jury, located off the front of the courtroom, physically illustrate the county's limited legal needs. The January 1, 1898, *The Dalles Times-Mountaineer* stated, "After all, the back bone of the county is the farmer. Intelligent, shrewd, hard-working and honest." Although the modern world sometimes intrudes, this statement, made about one hundred years ago, holds true today in Sherman County.

Like other buildings in Enterprise, the courthouse exhibits a stone exterior, but architect Calvin Thornton added greater design features such as the cupola to distinguish it. While the courthouse was under construction, Thornton, who was working on the second floor of a neighboring building, stepped off the scaffolding, lost consciousness, and never recovered.
Credit: Alan Viewig

Wallowa County

County Seat:	Enterprise
Courthouse Address:	101 S. River Street
Year Completed:	1909
Architect:	Calvin R. Thornton
Date of County Formation:	February 11, 1887

> *"[The courthouse] is what the parlance of the day would call a 'humdinger'."*
>
> —*News Record,* May 4, 1910

A newspaper masthead, a statue in the city park, an expanded Northwest Indian section in the bookstore— these are some of the few tributes in Enterprise to the Nez Perce's presence in the Wallowa Valley. Although the Nez Perce fought courageously for the land where they spent their summers, Enterprise is the creation of the white settlers. Whether it is the remoteness, the towering Wallowa Mountains, the relatively undisturbed nature, or a combination of these, the ranchers, farmers, and artists who walk the streets of Enterprise are, like the Nez Perce, drawn to the land.

Ranchers discovered the valley in the 1860s, but the first white settler, William Bennett, did not build a cabin until the early 1870s. In 1881, Robert Stubblefield, a Missouri sheepherder, filed the first homestead claim on the site of present-day Enterprise.

After the population gradually increased in the valley, some settlers began demanding a separation from Union County to the west. In the 1886 election, Frank McCully, a homesteader who had founded the town of Joseph and had advocated independence, won a seat in the legislature. Wallowa Valley citizens had been divided in their votes for the local man, but numerous voters in La Grande and Union, two large Union County towns, reportedly had cast their ballots for him because they did not want to pay for the considerable services, such as roads, soon needed in the valley.

Once in the legislature, McCully astutely became chairman of an influential committee which processed legislation on new counties; by February of 1887, the governor signed the bill creating the county. Wallowa was named after Nez Perce's method of trapping fish with rows of sticks supported by poles stretched across the Wallowa River. Not surprisingly, McCully's town—Joseph—was named the temporary county seat, but the permanent position was to be decided in a later election. Besides Joseph, only Lostine and Alder (now a ghost town) had significant populations, and each was determined to win the coveted position.

Several Union County business owners, calling themselves the Island City Mercantile and Milling Company, also knew the benefits of being the chosen town. They approached first the Lostine and then the Joseph leaders about the company constructing a bank, a general store, and a flour mill if the town would contribute the land. (Apparently they did not believe that Alder had a good chance of winning the election.) Both refused the proposition, saying that the business owners could afford to buy the land themselves.

Upon their refusal, the leader of the Island City Mercantile and Milling Company reportedly stated that it was obvious his company would just build a town of its own. Not long after, Robert Stubblefield and his neighbor, John Zurcher, filed a twenty-one-block plat called Wallowa City, which included a central public square donated by both men. Shortly after the recording of the plat, Stubblefield sold a block to the Island City Mercantile and Milling Company. Not surprisingly, a partner in the Island City Mercantile and Milling Company became mayor of the new town.

However, postal officials refused to locate a post office in Wallowa City, since a town of Wallowa already existed in the county. According to lore, the local citizens held a meeting, but no names were favored until one participant declared that whatever name they selected, "it ought to be an enterprising little town anyway." Robert Stubblefield then proposed the name "Enterprise," which was enthusiastically adopted. The town, a late entrant in the county seat fight, won the position.

Expansionist times in Enterprise did not start until the railroad came to Wallowa County in 1908. With the ability to easily transport lumber out of the county, the local timber industry began. Enterprise boomed. Many of the new buildings were of stone, compelling the May 14, 1910 *News Record* to tout Enterprise as a "Stone City." However, these new buildings were also the last of the major structures erected along Main Street. During the 1920s, the agricultural and lumber markets were poor and the population dropped from almost 1,900 in 1920 to just under 1,400 in 1930. Today, trade and government are the economic mainstays of the town.

Visiting the Seat of Wallowa County Government

Although Enterprise is not quite the "Stone City" envisioned by the newspaper, stone buildings—seemingly on every corner along Main Street—still make the town unusual. The first to build with this material, Enoch R. Bowlby, constructed a stone structure at 107 W. Main Street, undoubtedly as an advertisement for his quarry. Lest anyone forget, he prominently placed his name high on the building. While the front stone blocks are regularly coursed, the blocks on the sides are roughly laid, indicating less care in the stonework. This was typical of older mid-block buildings, both of brick and stone; the owner expected that eventual neighbors would hide its unsightly sides with similarly tall structures. Unfortunately, the building directly to the east remained only one story, and the one to the west, although two stories, never achieved the grand height of the Bowlby building.

Besides the metal cornice, Bowlby also embellished his building with lighter gray stone which form the arched openings on the ground floor. Builders of subsequent stone structures generally selected less elaborate detailing. However, when the Enterprise State Bank erected its structure at 110 W. Main Street, they added fluting on the corner pilasters to suggest its classical nature.

The building standing at 100 W. Main Street is an anomaly with its mix of pressed metal imitating stone along River Street and Bowlby stone along Main Street. Originally, a one-story, wood-frame building stood on the corner before Samuel Litch in 1909 decided to expand the building by adding a second floor and an addition. Because of the weight of the stone on the wood-frame building, he had to use an imitation made of metal sheets on the second floor, but he constructed the two-story addition of Bowlby stone.

The diagonal entrance of the two-story Litch Building faces Main Street and River Road, matching the diagonal entrance of the former Enterprise Hotel on the opposite corner (the hotel once was three stories before a fire burned the upper floor). This building, part of the most extensive block of stone structures, stands as an edifice to the town's "enterprising" nature. In 1903, when city leaders realized that there were no "suitable" lodgings available, the townspeople contributed their money to build the hotel, and when it was completed they celebrated with a large banquet.

Further east on the block stands the largest stone building in Enterprise, built by the Enterprise Mercantile and Milling Company, a descendant of Island City Mercantile and Milling. In 1916, during Enterprise's boom period, the company hired Portland architect John Toutellotte (though for the courthouse, a northeastern Oregon architect was good enough). The ground floor of the three-story building was planned as a large department store, and it was expected to be the finest anywhere between Portland and Boise, but with the poor local economy, the firm failed just ten years later. Today, the building stands as a monument to past dreams.

A History of the Courthouse

AFTER THE 1888 ELECTION, COUNTY OFFICIALS rented the second story of a building on Main Street. Ten years later, citizens proposed to fund half the expense of a courthouse costing between $5,000 and $8,000, but the thrifty court refused, saying that it was cheaper to rent than to pay the interest on their half of the capital outlay. In 1908, after the county court had rented its quarters for twenty years, residents from the town of Wallowa made an attempt at securing the county seat position, and another election was called. According to the May 21, 1908 *News Record*, the Wallowa paper claimed it nearer to the "geographic, habitable and population center of the county," but this was all refuted by the Enterprise newspaper, which went on to say that "all the other claims made in the *Sun*'s article are equally false." After reporting Enterprise's subsequent victory, the June 4, 1908 *News Record* attempted to reconcile the fractured county by noting that "nothing has occurred to call for future revenge," but added that "the people have spoken in clear and unmistakable terms."

To prevent another county seat war, officials decided it finally was time to build a courthouse. After five business owners offered the county court $10,000 for the public square Stubblefield and Zurcher had donated, the county began considering a more grandiose location on the hill east of town. When the court solicited the opinions of three attorneys as to who really owned the square and whether it could be sold, their response was that the "public" owned the square, that it could not be sold, but that county buildings could be erected there. The August 27, 1908 newspaper, reporting the legal opinions, noted that by buying the square from the county and then reselling it, "there is more than one local capitalist who is confident he could clean up several thousand dollars [of] profit."

Once again local citizens offered to contribute $5,000 for the courthouse, but seemingly mistrustful of the county court, they promised to pay only when the walls were up to the second story. Another condition stated that the county build a "suitable" courthouse costing at least $25,000. By dictating a minimum amount, the citizens hoped to have a building that would reflect well on the county and on Enterprise.

S. R. Haworth, a contractor, presented the plans designed by his wife's cousin, Calvin R. Thornton of La Grande, and a month later, his bid of $31,300 was accepted by the court. To supervise the construction of the new courthouse, Thornton moved to Enterprise and also accepted other building projects in the town. In December 1909, while helping to install iron work on a second-floor window at the Litch Building on Main

Street, the fifty-year-old architect stepped backward off the scaffolding and tumbled twenty feet to the street. He never regained consciousness and died three days later.

The courthouse was completed in May 1910, and although the furniture had not arrived, county officials eagerly moved in. According to the May 4, 1910 newspaper, "Deputy Sheriff Crow was the first official encountered by the press representative on entering the new county building. He looked ten years younger than when down in the old building. But before the press representative could remark upon this merry change, Sheriff Marvin appeared on the scene, his countenance beaming like a 60-candle incandescent light and almost happy enough to sing."

The Courthouse Today

IN THE MIDWEST TRADITION, COMMERCIAL buildings located around the courthouse square emphasized the nineteenth-century idea that courthouses were considered important to a town. Although the commercial buildings also extend several blocks west both on Main and North streets, the courthouse, on its own block with green grass and shade trees, serves as the symbolic center of the town.

Residents have honored the two public square donors, Stubblefield and Zurcher, by placing a granite bench carved with their names on the square. In the concrete arch over the northwest corner walkway, other pioneers are listed, and to ensure everyone is included, it adds "and any other settlers whose names are unknown." A nearby Japanese cannon commemorates World War II veterans, while an egg-shaped granite rock more than six feet high is dedicated to Wallowa County veterans who died in wars ranging from World War I through Vietnam. On the northwest corner of the block, a log with a quarter section missing serves as a bench. Like the county's vanishing timber jobs, when the log becomes rotted, this type of native bench also will disappear.

By using stone from the Bowlby quarry, Thornton integrated the courthouse with the rest of the downtown, but at the same time he also distinguished it. With a half basement, two full stories, an attic, and a cupola, the courthouse stands taller than any of its neighboring structures. Instead of a "stone box" such as the Enterprise Hotel on the opposite corner across Main Street, Thornton added details to make the courthouse visually interesting. Two side projections relieve an otherwise flat front side. Above the roofline on the projections, the gabled ends feature semicircular windows surrounded by diamond-shaped shingles. Dormers rise from the roof. The soaring cupola, which holds the town's fire alarm horn, serves as a focal point in Enterprise.

Thornton designed a courthouse that displays no particular architectural style. The building, however, possesses a balanced appearance due to its repeated elements. The semicircular window in the central section above the roofline mimics the windows in the gabled ends. The rounded opening in the main entrance echoes the design in the semicircular windows, and the light gray keystone above the opening follows the keystone pattern in the arched windows.

The exterior design largely remains true to its original appearance, although the county has boarded up a front window for an unsightly air conditioner. The county enclosed the front porch as a heat-saving measure, but the original entry doors are still in place beyond this. Leaded glass in the sidelights border these older doors, while patterned glass in a floral design forms the transom. In the midst of this elegance, a label affixed to one front door states, "Please wipe your feet. Thank you."

Inside, the first office on the left still possesses an original door, with an old-fashioned sign painted on the glass that genteelly reads, "Office of County Clerk & Recorder/ Walk In." A modern, rustic wooden sign above the door tersely states "CLERK." One prominent woman, Marjorie Martin, held the county clerk position for forty-seven years before retiring in 1988. At one time, the office was arranged so that instead of people standing

Marjorie Martin spoke about the courthouse in the January 4, 1996 *Wallowa County Chieftain*. "'It's wonderfully historical. I thought it was delightful to work in. I kind of grew up in it,' said Martin about the old building. She noted that modern courthouses just aren't the same as old ones like the Wallowa County Courthouse. 'It's like a church without a steeple.'"

Photos of past judges, like those on the wall in the Wallowa County courthouse, are a typical courtroom decorating feature. *Credit: author*

at a counter as they do now, they sat in a chair in front of her desk. The requests were not always strictly county business. In the course of doing their regular work, Martin and her employees would also write personal business letters or handle matters with federal agencies such as the Veterans Administration.

Instead of a grand lobby, the wide, cross-shaped hallway, with the rear doors at the end of the corridor and the stairways to the left and right, gives a clear view of the first-floor configuration. Around the corner to the right, above the drinking fountain a computer-generated sign combines high-tech with the Old West by stating, "This is not a spittoon." The doors to the basement are tucked out of sight underneath the stairways. Standing only six feet tall, the doorframe can be perilous, and handwritten signs, seemingly hastily written, warn of the low clearance.

A kitchen still remains from the days when a caretaker lived in a basement apartment. Although the caretaker had the town's most prestigious address, his or her duties were to cook the food for the prisoners in the jail once located in the courthouse. In another room in the basement, the original boiler still operates. Although the boiler no longer burns logs, the custodian must mechanically feed into the hopper the modern-day equivalent—wood pellets—every day except during the summer.

While the basement doors appear small due to their location under the stairway, the diminutive size of the women's restroom door on the second floor seems not to have had similar placement restrictions. The neighboring office door is more than six-and-a-half feet tall and thirty-one inches wide, but the restroom door is just six feet tall and twenty-four inches wide. Perhaps the smaller size suggests that the builders were attempting to hide this "necessity"; however, its size in contrast to the neighboring office doorway only accentuates it.

Double doors on the second floor are the main approach to the courtroom. Six windows face east directly opposite the doors, making the principal view from the courtroom toward the hills—not to the majestic Wallowa Mountains. The unpainted wooden slats on the venetian blinds match the other wood tones pervasive in the courtroom. Only some law books on the bookshelves and two modern office chairs add bright color to the somber tones in the courtroom.

Each wooden jury chair has a graceful slatted back that extends up to reach the back of the head (vinyl seat cushions now prop the jury member up higher). The chairs, affixed to the floor by a single stem, also tip back, so that each juror, with his or her feet on one of the two brass footrests, can relax while contemplating testimony. Long spectator benches, with tiny holes forming a shield encompassing a circle and then a star, line half of the courtroom. Unlike the jury's and the spectators' furnishings, the judge has a simple, nondescript desk, seemingly more appropriate in an old-fashioned office than in a courtroom.

Elsewhere **on the** second floor is the door—now locked—to the attic. Once thriftily put to use as an office before concerns arose about its inadequate fire exits, the attic is now used for storage. With the dormer windows and the ceiling sloping down to the walls, a sense of the building's exterior design can be felt on the interior, making this one of the most interesting rooms in the courthouse.

From the attic windows, one can view Enterprise residents transacting their business in the shadow of the Wallowa Mountains. The townspeople had wanted a "suitable" courthouse, not one that was imposing or overpowering. That remains the job of the county's physical landscape.

Wasco was once the largest county in the United
States, and has an extraordinary heritage with three
standing courthouses. The current courthouse,
constructed in 1914, has been carefully preserved.
Credit: Alan Viewig

Wasco County

County Seat:	The Dalles
Courthouse Address:	511 Washington Street
Year Completed:	1914
Architect:	Charles Crandall
Date of County Formation:	January 11, 1854

*"That Wasco county badly needs a new court
house and jail was again proved Sunday morning
when prisoners succeeded in tearing and cutting a
hole through the ceiling and roof. . . . The prisoners
were able to effect an opening with the aid of only
their hands and a pocket knife."*

—*The Dalles Weekly Chronicle*, May 26, 1911

From the great Northwest Indian trading place to the site
of Lewis and Clark's camp, from the initial terminus of
the overland Oregon Trail to the establishment of Fort
Dalles, from the miner jumping-off point to the great
commercial center of eastern Oregon, the land in present-day
The Dalles has played many historical roles. Much of its history
is due to the area's location along the Columbia River, which
now has been altered forever by mammoth dams. The town
itself has been cut off from the river by later transportation
routes—the railroad and the freeway. However, the city remains
rich with history.

According to *Oregon, End of the Trail,* William Clark, upon
returning from the Pacific Ocean in 1805, wrote in his diary
that what is now The Dalles area was "the great (Indian) mart
of all this country." Upstream, a series of rapids provided
excellent fishing, and ten different tribes came to buy fish from

the Wascos. Because of the daunting Cascade Mountains and the steep cliffs farther west, pioneers on the Oregon Trail stopped to rest at the Methodist mission, established in 1838, before constructing log rafts to float down the Columbia. The federal government built a military fort in 1850 on part of the former Methodist land to protect settlers in central and eastern Oregon and safeguard pioneers on the Oregon Trail.

With a captive clientele of wage-earners at the fort, John Bell, a settler from Salem, opened a sutler's store nearby, selling general merchandise geared to the soldiers. Allen McKindlay & Company built a second sutler's store, located closer to the river near present-day Main and Court streets. Other diversions for the soldiers, such as a saloon, soon followed.

During the early 1850s, the area east of the Cascade Mountains still was part of Clackamas County, with the county seat located in Oregon City. Traveling to the county seat consisted of either following the river route with a portage around the Cascade Falls (now Cascade Locks) or taking the Barlow Trail, a toll road built in 1846. Occasionally, winter weather prevented travel for months.

In January 1854, the Oregon territorial government created Wasco County, the largest county ever established in the United States. Encompassing approximately one hundred thirty thousand square miles, the new county extended as far as the western slope of the Rocky Mountains. Its governing powers were as far reaching: one of the first county acts was to approve the operation of a ferry across the Green River in Wyoming. The county government formally located the county seat at The Dalles in April 1855, and ordered a survey of 160 acres, "or as much as can be obtained without trespassing on the private rights." The officials authorized the county auditor to arrange that the land owned by the federal government be donated to Wasco County. They also hired a surveyor, who devised a long, narrow, sixteen-block plat that extended from the Columbia River to the rocky terraces adjacent to Fort Dalles.

Wasco County's population burgeoned with the discovery of gold in Idaho and eastern Oregon. Rapids further upriver caused steamboats to stop at the town, and swarms of miners journeying from Portland to The Dalles stayed in town to outfit themselves before heading toward the mining region. During the cold weather, miners spent their winter in The Dalles. According to *An Illustrated History of Central Oregon*, the miners "squandered their dust lavishly on whatever caught their fleeting fancy; verily The Dalles was lively."

Gold became so prevalent that Congress decided to build a mint in The Dalles, but before its doors opened, the mining strikes waned and the government canceled its plan. (The mint building, now used as an office, still stands on the block bounded by E. Second, E. Third, Monroe, and Madison streets.) Another economic boom began when financiers extended a railroad line through The Dalles in 1883, and the town served as a major shipping point for agricultural products making their way east.

The Dalles Chronicle on January 1, 1902 reported that the town "has a population of 5,000 people, yet the busy streets and elegant mercantile houses, residences and public edifices give her the appearance of being a much larger city." Twentieth-century changes, however, altered the role of The Dalles. In 1922, the Columbia River Highway, a paved route, connected The Dalles to Portland. Subsequent improvements to the road, culminating in today's Interstate 84 freeway, have diminished the traveling time between the two cities, and The Dalles has lost business to Portland. Dam construction, beginning with the Bonneville Dam completed in 1937, created low-cost electrical power which attracted aluminum manufacturing, now a major employer. Wheat storage and fruit processing are still economically important, as is tourism.

Visiting the Seat of Wasco County Government

THE DALLES SOON REORIENTED ITSELF from facing the road to the fort to paralleling the river, a greater source of commerce. Warehouses and businesses, many run by Chinese workers who came to work in the mines or for the railroad, formerly lined First Street, the closest street paralleling the Columbia. The great 1894 flood cleared away many of these wooden structures, and to deter further flooding, the city raised the level of the street. Although the 1857 structure that stands between Washington and Court streets on the south side of E. First Street appears to be one story high, the street hides the original first floor. Another building, located on the opposite side of E. First Street just to the east, was erected in 1867 and once housed several attorneys and the ticket office for steamboats. The railroad separated this building from the street, but it still bears a faded advertisement on its south side for the *Regulator*, a steamer to Portland which left "daily except Sunday."

Much of The Dalles' commercial area, including Second Street, the main street, has been designated a historical district. Second Street possesses a hodge-podge of styles both old and new (many tourists inquire in disbelief, "this is the historic district?"). The Dalles never suffered through a bust cycle so great that its buildings remained suspended in the past. Although fires and floods cleared many older structures, remodeling has altered others. The 1870 Wingate and Williams Building at 306 E. Second Street outfitted miners heading for the gold fields, but a 1938 remodeling hides a sense of the building's true age. The 1890 Vogt Building at 312 E. Second Street lost its third story to fire in 1891 and its second story to fire in 1962. Its ground floor now shows the style then in vogue at the time of the last fire.

Two past monuments—one to religion and the other to drinking—still flank the commercial district. On the west side, a 176-foot-tall tower marks the 1898 St. Peter's Church, a brick Gothic building at W. Third and Lincoln streets. On the east side, the three-story 1869 brewery along E. Third Street east of Taylor Street suggests the residents' alcohol capacity. One historian, upon noting the juxtaposition, mentioned that "The Dalles has always attracted a wide class of people."

The remaining public buildings indicate The Dalles' historic eminence, although they also can represent a modern-day burden. The Dalles is likely the only Oregon town of 11,000 with a 1,000-seat civic auditorium, located at 323 E. Fourth Street. The American Legion backed its construction after World War I as a memorial to war veterans, but over the years the structure has fallen into disrepair.

Despite The Dalles' standing as the county seat of the largest U.S. county ever created, its first courthouse was scheduled for demolition in 1973. Concerned citizens and one city commissioner went to court to obtain a temporary restraining order. After promising to renovate the building and find a suitable location, residents persuaded the city to save the building, now located at 410 W. Second Street. Over the years since the courthouse was constructed, it has stood in six different locations; its visitors' pamphlet calls it the "roving courthouse."

One of the most dramatic stories of courthouse preservation occurred over the 1859 courthouse. According to the story, destruction was so imminent in the early 1970s that Alf Wernmark, a shoe maker, physically stood between the courthouse and a bulldozer about to raze the building. Although later efforts were less confrontational, the courthouse endures because of the work of dedicated county citizens who believe it is an important historical building.

A History of the Courthouse

IN 1858, FOUR YEARS AFTER THE CREATION of the county, officials commissioned a courthouse to be built on the site at 313 Court Street (now the site of City Hall). Jail space had also become a pressing issue for the county. The army had offered its guard house at the fort for a small fee, but when it was full, the county had to pay to transport its prisoners to Clackamas County. Completed in 1859, the small 25- by 33-foot courthouse, with an outside staircase to the second floor to save space and expense, also housed a jail on the ground floor. The Dalles citizens held public meetings and dances in the second-floor courtroom, and the Congregational Church initially met there on Sundays. They soon moved, as during the service the prisoners on the ground floor would sing ribald songs to distract the churchgoers above them.

Officials again cited the lack of an adequate jail as the reason for building the second Wasco County courthouse in 1882 one block west at 105 W. Third Street. This courthouse featured

According to the October 8, 1914 *The Dalles Optimist,* when the new courthouse opened, county residents "one and all [were] being most enthusiastic in their praise of the beauty of the structure and its finishings and furnishings." The opening was well attended, as "Saturday afternoon and evening had been announced as the real opening day but group after group of visitors arrived all day and until half past 10 at night until Judge Gunning thought he might have to keep open on Sunday."

sturdier brick construction and the extravagance of a clock tower, indicating that the county believed it could afford a more elegant building. This courthouse now serves as a funeral home on the ground floor and a Masonic meeting hall on the second story.

In 1911, the county judge mailed postcards to voters asking whether to repair the building or to construct a new courthouse at the estimated cost of $80,000. After a two-thirds majority chose a new structure, the county judge and local architect Charles Crandall visited courthouses in Spokane, Baker City, Astoria, and other towns to form ideas for their own. When the plans were drawn approximately a year later, the cost of the new building had jumped to approximately $150,000—well beyond the county's savings. The officials prudently decided to spend $50,000 on the building, and then complete it by raising $25,000 in taxes each succeeding year. The grand jury, commenting on those plans, wisely recommended that the foundations, vaults, and jail be erected first.

A jail was sorely needed. Six months after the grand jury's report, prisoners escaped from the "county bastille" by pounding out a brick wall with an iron bar, creating a fourteen-by twenty-inch hole in just five minutes. Two prisoners later attempted a break-out by sawing off a lock on a cell door. One later defended his actions by ruefully stating, "You'd figure on making a getaway too if you had a jail sentence staring you in the face." When the same two prisoners attempted another escape just a month later, the sheriff decided to move all the prisoners to the new jail in the courthouse, despite it being served without water or lights until the next day.

The Courthouse Today

THE WASCO COUNTY COURTHOUSE IS ONE OF the few courthouses in Oregon that sit on less than a full block. Even though the $150,000 courthouse budget was extravagant, the site for the new courthouse was just slightly larger than the 1882 courthouse. Despite visiting other Oregon courthouses such as Astoria and Baker City which were located on their own square, the county chose a smaller site perhaps because of local tradition. The county acquired the two lots east of the courthouse in 1940 to make its ownership at least one-half block.

Nevertheless, the relatively small site undoubtedly posed some problems for the architect in trying to design a magnificent edifice. To have a sufficiently sized structure, the architect placed the south side of the building only three feet back from the property line. The front of the building, the east side, stands forty feet back so that the two-and-a-half-story structure looms above Washington Street without being overwhelming.

To distinguish the building, the architect used Corinthian columns, one of the showiest of the classical styles. The capital of the columns supporting the porch projection exhibits two

A current view of the 1859 courthouse. When the courthouse was threatened with destruction, a resident reportedly stood between it and the bulldozer about to raze it. *Credit: author*

rows of acanthus leaves, a Mediterranean plant used in classical decoration. The entablature, the band of terra cotta located above the second story, is intricately detailed with dentils, egg-and-dart molding, and other embellishments.

The small area of grass on the front does not include the usual war memorials. However, a 1986 addition is a bronze antelope on top of a stone-clad base bearing a plaque that reads, "Dedicated to all who steadfastly and unwaveringly opposed the attempts of the [Bhagwan Shree] Rajneesh followers to take political control of Wasco County, 1981–1985." (During the early 1980s, when this commune occupied a ranch in the southern part of Wasco County, some of its members were charged with numerous crimes ranging from arson to attempted murder to mass poisoning.) One county worker wryly mentioned the statue is indeed a war memorial, of sorts.

Traditionally, counties sell foreclosed properties on the courthouse steps. With twenty-three full steps, the Wasco County courthouse can accommodate a large crowd for this purpose, but on Good Friday, they serve another purpose. A local church, which dramatizes the Passion Play at different places in the town, portrays Christ's trial before Pontius Pilate on these steps.

Until recently, the foyer was home to a framed display with miniature portraits of long-ago county officials surrounding a short history and a photograph of the newly completed courthouse. Black shrouds, made with a marking pen, surrounded four of the officials' pictures to indicate their death. (Presumably, the rest have now also died.) The county clerk has possession of the business card of F. S. Gunning, the county judge when the courthouse was completed. While one side proclaims his county position, the reverse advertises his General Blacksmith and Wagon Shop, and that he is a "dealer in blacksmith supplies" and the "manufacturer of Gunning's harrow teeth weeder."

The county's extravagant budget makes this one of the most lavishly decorated interiors of the county courthouses in Oregon. Rows of columns line the walkway, emphasizing the classical nature of the building. Alaskan marble, in light gray with darker gray trim, forms five-foot high wainscot and the bases of the pillars. Good workmanship meant detailing even in unobvious places such as the corners, where half sections of pilasters were added to keep the uniformity of the wall pattern.

Items of county history are exhibited in the changing displays in two of the three cases in the hallway. The third case, by the county clerk's office, exhibits an intriguing book that lists the names of convicted criminals, including their pictures (alway unsmiling) and their crimes, which in 1930 frequently seemed to be that of operating a still. Occasionally, a county employee will turn the pages of the book, and while the names change, the stony stares remain. Other county records are stored in the vault in the county clerk's office. While most are formal in nature, the first wedding listed in Marriage Book A in 1856 states in faded ink, "This is to certify that the undersigned, a Justice of the Peace . . . [did] join in lawful wedlock William C. McKay and [?] Campbell. . . . Oh! What a glorious time we had."

A metal plate from an old bell system remains on the wall near the clerk's copier machine. Initially, when there was an escape from the jail located on the lower level, a bell would ring throughout the courthouse. The county clerk was to go to his or her post by one door, the assessor to another door, and so forth. Although county officials are no longer routinely

The courthouse has an unusual row of columns which direct the major path through the lobby. *Credit: author*

expected to detain escapees, the county jail is still located in the basement. Unlike other counties that acquire another building or construct an addition when they need to enlarge, Wasco County added to its office space literally by digging a new level under the basement. Prison labor helped with this expansion, at times carrying out dirt in five-gallon buckets.

One route to the second floor is via the grand staircase in the main lobby. On the landing, an amorphous figure on the south wall wainscot created by the cut of the marble is pointed out to believing schoolchildren as the "County Santa Claus." The other way to the second floor is via a modern elevator, which required a slight addition on the west side of the courthouse. Unlike other courthouses where subsequent changes are simply added without concern for their appearance, Wasco County has diligently maintained its courthouse so that any changes have blended with the original building. This even extends to the second-floor trash cans, which have a plastic laminate surround in a marble-like design that matches the wainscot.

At one end of the hallway, the county judge's office displays old bottles, a horse bit, and square nails—all treasures found in the ground underneath the courthouse. At the other end is the circuit court section, which includes the jury room and their restrooms. A bathtub once was located in the "ladies toilet" room.

The circuit courtroom conveys the feeling of a church with its long and narrow shape and with the center aisle flanked by two rows of spectator pews. Largely true to the courtroom's 1914 design, the furnishings incorporate patterns found in the courtroom and elsewhere in the courthouse. The light and dark gray marble wainscot matches that found in the lobby. The oak door and window molding follows the design around other doors in the courthouse. The pairs of Ionic pilasters on the judge's bench mimic the Ionic pilasters on the walls.

Although the pressed-metal ceiling is covered, the county thoughtfully kept the original light fixtures. Metal statues of Washington and Lincoln, a later addition to the courtroom, flank the judge's bench and were a gift from a grateful Italian immigrant who was sworn into citizenship. Another addition is the crack in the northeast corner of the room, the result of a bullet fired by a deputy sheriff at a pigeon flying around the courtroom (he missed).

Mysteriously, the architect designed two jury boxes instead of one. The original plans state that the row of chairs along the window were designed for a grand jury, although in other Oregon courthouses, grand juries sit in the regular jury chairs. With the two jury boxes and narrow room, the plaintiff and defense tables cannot be aligned end to end, and thus are placed to form an "L." The space is so cramped that after testifying, an unfriendly witness has to pass by the side of the defendant and then behind him or her to exit the bar. Sometimes, the witness will spot the balustrade curving outward by the wall and assume that he or she can exit there, only to find himself or herself trapped and embarrassed. To court regulars, this is a frequent source of amusement.

From the courthouse windows, one can see City Hall, the site of the first courthouse, and further west, the clock tower of the second courthouse. With its three courthouses still standing, Wasco is the only county in Oregon that can illustrate its growth through its county buildings. While its days of glory are long past, this courtroom, with its lavish furnishings, suggests the county's former eminence.

The Wheeler County courthouse appears unchanged from the time of initial construction in 1902. For many years, the building served as the exhibit hall for the county fair. Produce was displayed on the basement ledges formed by the foundation, and home economics projects were shown in the courtroom.
Credit: author

Wheeler County

County Seat: Fossil
Courthouse Address: 701 Adams Street
Year Completed: 1902
Architect: Charles Burggraf
Date of County Formation: February 17, 1899

> *"It [the courthouse] underwent complete rewiring a few years ago and the upper floor 'fire escapes' were replaced. These 'fire escapes' were ropes secured to the floor which, in the event of fire, were thrown out the window."*
>
> —*Fossil Journal*, August 26, 1965

The football field behind Wheeler High School is well known to both local sports fans and widespread fossil fans, for bordering the field are Oregon's only open fossil beds. Even on summer evenings, fossil-seekers can be seen digging through rocks, hopeful of finding petrified alder or maple leaves. Since Highway 19 now bypasses Fossil, residents in this town of almost four hundred immediately notice visitors. As the town's life is enacted over a few blocks, a tourist in turn is bound to see the same inhabitants several times a day as they retrieve mail from the post office, transact business, walk their dogs, or pass time people-watching.

Settlers were seeking rangeland rather than fossil beds when they homesteaded in present-day Wheeler County in the late 1860s. Trying to accumulate a sufficient amount of land for survival, many of these pioneers lived far from their neighbors—a situation some may have prized. Popular lore tells of how Andrew Clarno, after hearing that a friend had settled about twenty miles east of him, rode over and said, "Bill, don't you think you're crowding me a little?"

Approximately two miles north of present-day Fossil, Thomas Benton Hoover begun ranching near what became known as Hoover Creek. One afternoon, Hoover and his family heard a roar from a landslide, and upon investigating, discovered the remains of a fossilized elephant. Hoover summoned his geologist friend Dr. Thomas Condon, who sent the specimens to New York City for identification. When Hoover applied for a post office to be located on his ranch, he named it Fossil.

In 1881, Hoover and Thomas Watson started a store at the confluence of Butte and Cottonwood creeks, apparently believing that it was a better location than Hoover's ranch. George and W. S. Thompson soon established a second store nearby and platted the eight-block town of Fossil. Usually, town promoters try to maximize their profits by placing the narrow end of the lots along the main street, but the Thompsons did the opposite by putting the long side along the street, suggesting that they had limited experience in town platting—or perhaps, little greed.

The town grew slowly, but by the turn of the century Fossil boasted 288 residents. In the late 1920s, E. D. Wetmore, who owned 50,000 acres of timberland, started a mill and laid out a town called Kinzua. Fossil, about fifteen miles away, benefitted as some mill employees lived and shopped in Fossil.

After the mill closed in 1978, one Fossil resident stated in the April 1, 1990 *Oregonian*, "When we lost our mill, that was it." The town today has only about one hundred more people than it did at the turn of the century. Many Fossil citizens are retired, and for those who are younger, the government is a major employer. In Wheeler County, cattle and logging make use of the land's natural resources, but with the mill gone, the county's products are processed elsewhere.

Visiting the Seat of Wheeler County Government

FOSSIL'S UNIQUE PERSONALITY IS EVIDENT on First Street, which runs east from Highway 19 toward the town. There, a motel entices visitors with its sign depicting a triceratops snug in bed with the words "Sleep in a Fossil Bed." Several blocks beyond is the first prominent commercial building, two stories tall and crowned with a brick parapet. The upstairs once was used as a meeting place for the Odd Fellows lodge, but Fossil's sparse population cannot support its own fraternal organization and the upstairs remains empty. The county museum now occupies the ground floor space, preserving the old building as well as an assortment of community treasures.

At the blinking red light just one block east, downtown Fossil changes direction and turns south. On the southwest corner of this intersection, an out-of-state bank replaced the Bank of Fossil. Its modern, homey exterior of wood lap siding suggests that the building is vulnerable to break-ins or fires, but underneath the original brick walls remain. Break-ins were contemplated even as the bank was being built. The October 3, 1902 *Fossil Journal* reported that each person watching the construction "is trying to figure out a weak spot so as to be able to tap the vault when he gets hard up."

For almost one hundred years, the Fossil Mercantile has stood on Main Street, first in the two-story brick structure and now in a one-story stone building next door. Although there have been other stores in Fossil, everyone inevitably bought something from the Fossil Mercantile—including the county, which purchased office supplies there when the courthouse opened.

The retirement home, built along Main Street in the late 1980s, is a relative newcomer to Fossil. During winter months, retirees located in the country move into its facilities, but when the home has a vacancy it provides overnight lodging. Although visitors sometimes park along the side street, Fossil residents usually note the appearance of a strange car.

A History of the Courthouse

BEFORE THE TURN OF THE CENTURY, FOSSIL residents were among the strong advocates for a separate county. The new political division was to take land from Crook, Grant, and Gilliam counties, and although Crook and Grant residents were unopposed to it, many Gilliam citizens were against it. According to *An Illustrated History of Central Oregon*, the January 19, 1899 *Condon Globe* stated, "Everyone about here is kicking like a mule downhill against the proposition to cut off a slice of Gilliam county for the purpose of benefitting a little two by four locality."

Despite Gilliam County's views, the bill passed on February 17, 1899. The new county was named after Henry Wheeler, a pioneer living within its boundary who had survived a rifle bullet wound in the face from a Northwest Indian raid. With Fossil designated as the temporary county seat, two Salem attorneys promptly moved into offices in the Odd Fellows building. The March 10, 1899 *Fossil Journal* welcomed them as the "first of a good many business and professional men who are expected to locate in the county seat of Wheeler county this year."

However, residents had yet to vote on the permanent county seat location. Months before the election, the editor of the newspaper in Twickenham, located about twenty miles south, began a campaign for his town to become the permanent county seat. After an article in the Twickenham newspaper expounded on the negative aspects of Fossil, the April 27, 1900 *Fossil Journal* called the Twickenham editor a "cowardly lying cur" and the author of the article a "piddling, contemptible, pettifogging liar." The May 25, 1900 *Fossil Journal* further refuted the Twickenham newspaper's statements, saying, "It is a damnable lie that goods are 25 per cent higher in Fossil than in neighboring towns" and "No one but a disgruntled nincompoop would father that lie, and no one but a disreputable cur would publish it."

The June 1, 1900 *Fossil Journal* made one last effort before the election by printing a picture of Twickenham showing a few scattered buildings and one of Fossil depicting a bustling metropolis. The strategy worked—and Fossil won.

Before the election, Bert Kelsay had offered to donate a block west of the Butte Creek for a courthouse. The March 17, 1899 newspaper reported that "the block is perfectly level, of very rich, deep black soil, capable of producing fine shade trees in a few years. . . . The whole state does not contain a better acre of ground for the purpose." The county court, which occupied a building in town, originally considered constructing a temporary building to safeguard the county records, but after learning that such a structure would cost $4,000, they decided to build a "County Court House." The advertisements for bids specified that the county wanted a brick building which would "conform in size and capacity to the Court House of Sherman County, Oregon." Charles Burggraf was the architect for that structure, and was commissioned to design the courthouse for Wheeler County. The contractor, A. F. Peterson, who also had worked on the Sherman County courthouse, bid the job for $9,025.

A pivotal Wheeler County levy barely passed in late 1996. Had it failed, the county would have had insufficient funds to operate. Wheeler County could have dissolved, but unlike the time when it was created, none of the neighboring counties wanted Wheeler's lands. The last time a county was absorbed by another was in 1862, when Douglas County acquired the former Umpqua County.

The Courthouse Today

FOSSIL NEVER GREW INTO A METROPOLIS with commercial buildings surrounding the courthouse. Today the square, four blocks from the center of town, is surrounded by houses on the front and sides. On the north side more than fifty tea kettles whimsically line one resident's property.

Behind the courthouse, boys once played football in the present-day alfalfa field. One resident remembered that his grandfather, after winning a horse race held there, spent his $100 prize money on a telephone line from his town home to his ranch house. Many older townspeople remember the area directly behind the courthouse as the site of the county fair.

Sheds, standing where the parking lot is now, held the exhibited stock. Even today, while waiting for the fair parade to start before it winds its way through Fossil to the fairgrounds, sometimes twenty to thirty horses mill about on the courthouse square seeking shade.

In the front of the yard, black locust trees line the concrete walkway. Roots supposedly were grafted to these trees so they would have numerous branches. Popular lore also states that the small brick structure behind the courthouse, now used for storage, was an outhouse. However, older Fossil residents do not remember ever using it, and one person stated that another outhouse site was discovered. With two doors and a hipped roof, the building would have been a luxurious facility. Although its use remains a puzzle, one piece of evidence—a roll holder with the word "Toilet"—hangs under the south window frame.

Like Sherman County's courthouse, Wheeler's exhibits a Queen Anne style, including multiple roof shapes, varied exterior material, and an irregular plan. Although the Wheeler County citizens wanted a spacious and commodious courthouse like Sherman County's, with a slightly larger budget they were able to afford a grander building. With both a tower and a turret, it seems appropriate that bats have lived in the courthouse attic. In 1996, a workman removed approximately one hundred bats.

Bats have not been the only entity in the attic. One early twentieth-century photograph in the museum shows women with long skirts standing on the tower balcony, and others peering out the turret window. Frequent trips to raise and lower the flag on the pole above the turret must have been wearing, for the county later constructed a more easily accessible flagpole on the courthouse grounds.

Although Wheeler County's budget was greater than Sherman's, it was not extravagant. To save money, the courthouse was constructed of local brick and stone. Workers sawed the wooden dentils—the only Greek reference on the exterior of the building—and they were not so concerned that the spacing between each dentil be identical.

The courthouse has represented Wheeler almost as long as the county has existed, and it has changed little over that time.

Although the county installed energy-saving aluminum windows in the mid-1970s, they kept the wooden ornamentation above the windows. Oil stoves have replaced the wood-burning ones, but the five brick chimneys on the roof are still in use. In the back, an oil tank does hide the clumsy conversion of a rear entrance into a solid wall.

On the southwest corner of the building, four windows, smaller than the others, provided light for the jail once located inside. While the jail held its share of lawbreakers, it also detained ordinary citizens. In 1924, one county resident, while working on a ranch near Spray, cut the phone lines to elope with the rancher's daughter. Traveling to Goldendale where they were married, they were pursued by the sheriff and the enraged father, but managed to elude them until they returned to Fossil. The groom and his friend, who had driven the get-away car, were both thrown in jail until the charges were dismissed the next day.

Many sheriffs have walked their prisoners through the arched front doorway, under the sheet metal sign proclaiming "Wheeler County, 1901." Six interior steps lead to the main hallway, and at one time the top step was several inches higher than the rest. Because inebriated prisoners usually would stumble there, one former sheriff called it the "drunk step."

Before the steps, a side doorway leads to the basement. The assessor's office, now refurbished, once served as the wood shed. Even as late as the early 1970s, part of the sheriff assistant's job was to carry wood up from the basement. The basement, however, once served another function. During fair time, while the courtroom displayed home economics projects, the inside ledges formed by the basement foundation were used to exhibit produce.

By the time the courthouse was constructed, Fossil citizens were used to the idea of a jail. H. S. Goddard, an early physician, wrote in the October 17, 1941 *Fossil Journal* that when the first town jail was built, it was a puzzle to some. Despite its being "a cute little house with a solid door and two very small windows," some residents "speculated whether it was some sort of civic attraction or had a useful purpose. When its use was discovered, some were so disgusted that they tried to burn it and be rid of a thing that could take away their liberty."

The linoleum, designed to look like a carpet, adds a homey appearance to the jury room. *Credit: author*

Although the county has maintained the exterior, the interior hallway has been painted in a contemporary baby-blue. Modern-day luxuries such as indoor plumbing have enabled installation of a drinking fountain. One former employee noted that the drinking fountain in the hallway generally is not used by the locals, perhaps because they recall the time when a bat flying around the main hallway landed on the drinking fountain, and the sheriff whacked it with a broom.

Traditionally, the sheriff collected the taxes before the position of treasurer was created; now, both officially share one office. The demise of the jail in the back corner has created some awkwardness, as prisoners scheduled for trial upstairs wait in this office in front of the bill-paying public. One handcuffed suspect jumped out of the adjacent office window and escaped.

The escapee was caught, and undoubtedly was tried in the second-floor courtroom. There, the otherwise plain judge's bench is embellished with decorative brackets and given stature by its elevation. Sitting in a chair on the judge's platform, a witness is exposed without a shielding balustrade separating him or her from the jury and the attorneys. Against one wall lies a judge's ornate leather retiring couch, and although this was at one time a standard piece for any sophisticated courthouse, it seems out of place with the plain furnishings.

The jury seats reportedly are from an old movie theater in town. The backs of the seats show the wear of many hands, as movie-goers must have steadied themselves to sit or rise. With red seat cushions, curved wooden arm rests, and red and silver stripes on the metal row ends, they recall the ornate movie palaces of the 1920s. Such flamboyance is unusual in a rural courtroom with bare walls except for a clock and a fire extinguisher.

In thinly populated counties, a judge "rides the circuit," visiting several counties over a period of time. In Wheeler County, the circuit court judge comes only when needed, and sometimes a month or two will pass before the county requires his or her services. In summertime, presiding in the Wheeler County courthouse can be a difficult task, as the courthouse is well known for its wasp problem.

Wasps also are a problem in the jury room, located off the courtroom. In the winter when the radiators are warm, the sleeping wasps awaken. However, not all perceive this as bad; one former sheriff speculated that the jury might return with the verdict faster.

The courthouse's only remaining wood stove, located in the jury room, is no longer operable, and now juries are warmed by portable electric heaters. The jury room shows an effort to make it comfortable. Floorboards are painted a light blue, and a later-added linoleum piece, exhibiting a pattern that resembles a carpet, lies under the jury table. Wooden bookshelves, obviously constructed by local workers, are laden with law books.

In 1902, Wheeler County residents constructed what remains today the most elaborate building in the county. At the time, the county was still young, and they hoped that the courthouse would show their faith in a prosperous future. However, the years have not been easy for Wheeler County, and it has struggled to maintain not just its economy but its existence. The courthouse, having remained standing almost one hundred years, exemplifies the hopes and dreams of those early settlers.

❖

Other Operating Courthouses

Coos County
Address:	250 N. Baxter Street, Coquille
Year Built:	1954
Architectural Firm:	R. D. Kennedy

Curry County
Address:	29821 Ellensburg Avenue, Gold Beach
Year Built:	1957
Architectural Firm:	Raymond O. Marks

Gilliam County
Address:	221 S. Oregon Street, Condon
Year Built:	1955
Architectural Firm:	Morrison & Howard & Wesley Roman

Grant County
Address:	200 S. Canyon Boulevard, Canyon City
Year Built	1952
Architectural Firm:	Burns, Bear, McNeil & Schneider

Hood River County
Address:	309 State Street, Hood River
Year Built:	1953
Architectural Firm:	Roald, Schmeer & Harrington

Jefferson County
Address:	657 C Street, Madras
Year Built:	1961
Architectural Firm:	Roald, Schmeer & Harrington

Klamath County
Address:	316 Main Street, Klamath Falls
Year Built:	1998
Architectural Firm:	Kaplan McLaughlin Diaz

Lake County
Address:	513 Center Street, Lakeview
Year Built:	1953
Architectural Firm:	Morrison & Howard

Lane County

Address:	125 E. Eighth Street, Eugene
Year Built:	1959
Architectural Firm:	Wilmsen & Edicott

Lincoln County

Address:	225 W. Olive Street, Newport
Year Built:	1955
Architectural Firm:	Burns, Bear, McNeil & Schneider

Malheur County

Address:	251 B Street, Vale
Year Built:	1958
Architectural Firm:	Roald, Schmeer & Harrington

Marion County

Address:	100 High Street N.E., Salem
Year Built:	1954
Architect:	Pietro Belluschi

Umatilla County

Address:	216 S.E. Fourth Street, Pendleton
Year Built:	1954
Architectural Firm:	Roald, Schmeer & Harrington

Union County

Address:	1101 Fourth Avenue, LaGrande
Year Built:	1996
Architectural Firm:	Barber Barrett Turner

Yamhill County

Address:	535 E. Fifth Street, McMinnville
Year Built:	1963
Architectural Firm:	Schmeer & Harrington

Glossary

arch

American Renaissance—An architectural style characterized by bilateral symmetry, a flat roof, rectangular windows, smooth-dressed stone or brick, and classical ornamentation.

arch—A curved structural member used to span an opening.

Art Deco—An architectural style that incorporates such elements as multi-colored surfaces, rounded corners, a stepped or flat roof, stylized sculptures, and geometric ornamentation such as chevrons and sunbursts.

battlement—A parapet (see definition below) with alternating solid parts and openings (usually associated with castles).

bracket

brackets—Projecting member supporting eaves, door and window hoods, and other overhangs. Can be plain or ornamental.

bull's-eye—A circular window.

bull's-eye window

capital—The upper decorated part of a column.

chevron—A V-shaped decoration generally used as a continuous molding.

column—A cylindrical structure, usually a supporting member in a building.

capital

Corinthian

Corinthian—One of the several styles of classical architecture, characterized by slender, fluted columns (see "fluting," below) and an ornate capital with acanthus leaves (a common Mediterranean plant) and an elaborate cornice (see definition below).

cornice—The uppermost main division of an entablature (see definition below), or an ornamental molding running around the walls of the room just below the ceiling.

cupola—A small structure surmounting a roof or tower.

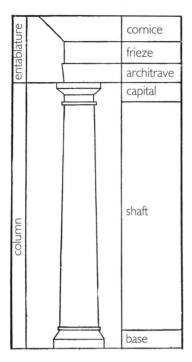

the parts of a column

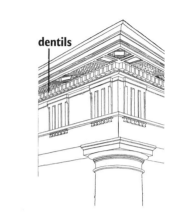

dentils

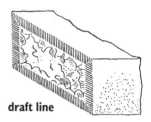

dormer

dentils—A band of small tooth-like blocks found in cornices, moldings, etc.

dormer—A window projecting from the slope of the roof.

draft line—A narrow, dressed border around the face of a stone.

egg-and-dart molding—A continuous decorative band consisting of alternating egg-shaped and dart-shaped ornaments.

entablature—The upper section of a classically styled building resting on the columns. Horizontally divided into a cornice, frieze, and architrave (see illustration above).

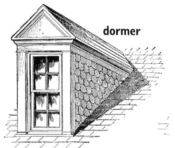

draft line

egg-and-dart molding

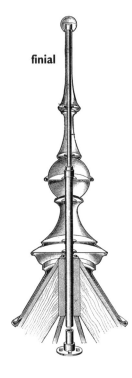

finial

escutcheon—A protective plate surrounding a door handle.

finial—An ornament at the end of a spire.

fluting—Vertical concave grooves on columns and pilasters; the reverse of reeding.

fret—An ornamental design consisting of continuous lines arranged in rectangular forms.

gargoyle—A water spout projecting from the roof gutter of a building, often shaped in figures and sometimes used only for decoration.

escutcheon

fluting

Georgian—An architectural style characterized by a bilaterally symmetrical facade, arched windows, pedimented doorways, and columns in the classical order.

gargoyle

fret

gnomon—The object on a sundial that projects a shadow to indicate the time.

Half-Modern—An architectural style characterized by a flat or stepped roof; a brick, stucco, or marble exterior; rectangular windows; and classical proportions; but simplified to geometric forms and stripped of ornamentation.

hipped roof—A roof that is pitched on all four sides.

hipped roof

hood—A decorative or sometimes protective cover found over windows and door frames.

International—An architectural style characterized by a functional approach to design with unadorned geometric forms, smooth or stucco plaster surfaces, a flat roof, and windows placed flush with wall surfaces.

hood

Ionic—One of the several styles of classical architecture characterized by a fluted column with a base and a capital embellished with two pairs of spiral ornaments called volutes.

Italianate—An architectural style that displays low-pitched roofs with widely overhanging eaves having decorative brackets underneath, and tall, narrow windows.

keystone—A wedge-shaped member, usually stone or brick, found in the center of an arch.

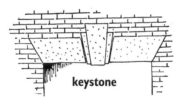

keystone

low relief—A carving or casting moderately protruding from a background surface.

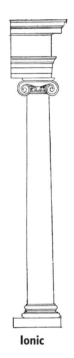

Ionic

molding—A continuous decorative band that serves as an ornamental device on either the exterior or interior of a structure.

newel—An ornamental post supporting the hand rail at the head or foot of a stairway.

parapet—The part of a wall that extends above the roof.

pavilion—A prominent portion of a facade, usually central, identified by projection, height, and special roof forms.

newel

pediment

pediment—A wide, low-pitched gable surmounting the facade of a classically embellished building; used ornamentally over doors and windows.

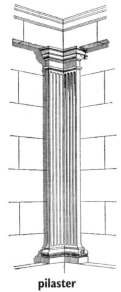

pilaster

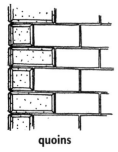

quoins

pier—A rectangular vertical support structure.

pilaster—A rectangular column attached to the wall for ornamentation.

Queen Anne—An architectural style using an asymmetrical facade shape, patterned shingles, varying window styles, and other devices to avoid a smooth-walled, balanced appearance.

quoins—Cornerstones on a building, extending up the wall and distinguished by size or texture.

randomly coursed—A stone masonry course with blocks varying in size.

reeding—Parallel, convex moldings; the reverse of fluting.

Richardson Romanesque—An architectural style characterized by a massive appearance; masonry walls; and rough-faced stonework, towers, and arched and flat-topped openings.

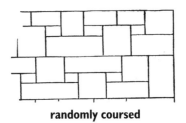

randomly coursed

rotunda—A building rounded both outside and inside.

terrazzo—Flooring of marble or stone chips set in mortar and polished.

transom window—A small window or series of panes above a door or window.

Tuscan—One of the several styles of classical architecture characterized by simplicity, with no fluting on the columns, and unadorned capitals.

wainscot—A facing or paneling applied to the walls of a room, generally on the bottom half.

water table—A ledge that protects the foundation from rain running down the wall of a building.

Sources Consulted

General

Biedermann, Hans. *Dictionary of Symbolism*. New York: Penguin Group, 1994.

Blumenson, John J.-G. *Identifying American Architecture*. 2nd ed. New York: W. W. Norton, 1979.

Brooks, Howard C., and Ramp, Len. *Gold and Silver in Oregon*. Portland: State of Oregon, Department of Geology and Mineral Industries, 1968.

Bureau of Municipal Research Service. *Population of Oregon Cities, Counties and Metropolitan Areas 1850–1957*. Eugene: Bureau of Municipal Research and Service, 1958.

Carey, Charles. *General History of Oregon*. 3rd ed. Portland: Binfords & Mort, 1971.

Center for Population Research and Census, *Population Estimates for Oregon 1997*.

Clark, Rosalind. *Architecture Oregon Style*. Portland: Professional Book Center, Inc., 1983.

Cooper, J.C. *An Illustrated Encyclopedia of Traditional Symbols*. New York: Thames and Hudson, 1995.

Culp, Edwin. *Stations West*. Caldwell: The Caxton Printers, Ltd., 1972.

Cyclopedia of Architecture, Carpentry and Building. Chicago: American Technical Society, 1907.

Ferriday, Virginia Guest. *Last of the Handmade Buildings*. Portland: Mark Publishing Company, 1984.

Harris, Cyril M., ed. *Illustrated Dictionary of Historic Architecture*. New York: Dover, 1977.

Lever, Jill and Harris, John. *Illustrated Dictionary of Architecture 800–1914*. 2nd ed. London: Faber and Faber, 1993.

Lockley, Fred. *History of the Columbia River Valley from the Dalles to the Sea*. Chicago: S. J. Clarke Publishing Company, 1928.

McArthur, Lewis. *Oregon Geographic Names*. 5th ed. Portland: Oregon Historical Society, 1982.

Oregon Employment Department. *Regional Economic Profile Region 1–14*. Salem: State of Oregon Employment Department, 1996.

Pare, Richard, ed. *Court House*. New York: Horizon Press, 1978.

Phillips, Steven. *Old House Dictionary*. Washington D.C.: The Preservation Press, 1992.

Reps, John W. *The Forgotten Frontier*. Columbia: University of Missouri Press, 1981.

Whiffen, Marcus. *American Architecture Since 1780*. Cambridge: The M. I. T. Press, 1981.

Woodbridge, Sally. *Details, The Architect's Art*. San Francisco: Chronicle Books, 1991.

Workers of the Writers' Program of the Work Projects Administration in the State of Oregon, compilers. *Oregon, End of the Trail*. Portland: Binfords & Mort, 1940.

Baker County

Baily, Barbara Ruth. *Main Street, northeastern Oregon*. Portland: · Oregon Historical Society, 1982.

Baker City Centennial Album. 1974.

Baker County Plat Books. Baker County Courthouse, Baker City, Oregon.

Hiatt, Isaac. *Thirty-One Years in Baker County*. 1893. Reprint. Baker City: Baker County Historical Society and The Powder River Sportsmen's Club, Inc., 1970.

Historic Baker City, A Walking/Driving Tour. Baker: Historic Baker City, Inc., 1985.

History of Baker County, Oregon. Baker County Historical Society, 1986.

Shaver, F. A.; Rose, Arthur P.; Steele, R. F.; Adams, A. E.; compilers. *An Illustrated History of Baker, Grant, Malheur and Harney Counties*. Spokane: Western Historical Publishing Company, 1902.

Van Duyn, James N. *National Register of Historic Places Inventory— Nomination Form: Baker Historic District*. State Historic Preservation Office, Salem, 1978.

Wisdom, Loy Winter. *John William Wisdom*. Baker: Loy Winter Wisdom, 1974.

Newspapers: *Baker City Herald* (Baker City)

Benton County

Benton County Courthouse History. Corvallis Area Chamber of Commerce, n.d.

Benton County Plat Books. Benton County Courthouse, Corvallis, Oregon.

Corvallis, Benton County, Oregon Building and Structure Inventory Form. Corvallis Preservation Society, Inc. 1983–1984.

Fagan, David D. *History of Benton County, Oregon; Including its Geology, Topography, Soil, and Productions*. Portland: A. G. Walling, 1885.

Gallagher, Mary Kathryn. *Historical Context Statement, City of Corvallis, Oregon*. City of Corvallis, 1993.

The Historical Records Survey. *Inventory of the County Archives of Oregon, No. 22 Linn County (Albany)*. Portland: The Historical Records Survey, 1939.

Kight, Pat and Burk, Daniel. *The Flight of Time*. Corvallis: The Benton County Board of Commissioners, n.d.

Johnson, Edwin A. *History of Benton County Courthouse*. Unpublished manuscript, Benton County Clerks Office, 1984.

Mengler, Richard. Transcription of oral interviews. Oregon State University Archives, Corvallis.

Mengler, Richard. Transcription of speech given July 1987. Oregon State University Archives, Corvallis.

Powers, David W. *National Register of Historic Places Inventory—Nomination Form: Benton County Courthouse*. State Historic Preservation Office, 1977.

Stadsvold, Cy. *Benton County Courthouse Study*. 1977.

Strand, A. L. Letter to Thomas Vaughan. (April 10, 1968) Oregon Historical Society Vertical Files, Portland.

Newspapers: *Benton County Herald* (Corvallis), *Corvallis Gazette* (Corvallis), *Gazette-Times* (Corvallis)

Clackamas County

Erigero, Pat. *Historic Oregon City, Main Street Walking Tour*. Oregon City: City of Oregon City, 1983.

Erigero, Pat and McLaughlin, Debora. *City Of Oregon City, Architectural and Historical Inventory, Downtown Oregon City*. State Historic Preservation Office, 1983.

Lynch, Vera Martin. *Free Land for Free Men*. Oregon City: Vera M. Lynch, 1973.

Milln, Nadiene. "The First Paper Mill in the Northwest." *Clackamas County Historical* (1968–1969) 46–48.

Mockford, Stuart B. "Jails of Clackamas County." *Clackamas County Historical* (1962–1963) 33–39.

Smelser, June. "A History of the McLoughlin Home." *Clackamas County Historical* (1960) 27–55.

Welsh, William. *A Brief History of Oregon City and West Linn, Oregon*. Oregon City: Crown Zellerbach Corporation, 1941.

Wollner, Craig. *Electrifying Eden*. Portland: Oregon Historical Society Press, 1990.

Newspapers: *Enterprise-Courier* (Oregon City), *Oregon City Enterprise* (Oregon City), *Oregonian* (Portland)

Clatsop County

Astoria Sesquicentennial 1811–1961 Official Program. Astoria, 1961.

Clatsop County Courthouse Plans. Clatsop County Courthouse, Astoria, Oregon.

Clatsop County Plat Books. Clatsop County Courthouse, Astoria, Oregon.

Cleveland, Alfred A. "Social And Economic History of Astoria." *The Quarterly of the Oregon Historical Society* (March, 1903–December, 1903) 130–149.

Cronin, Kathleen. "Life and Death of An American Town." *Mainstream* (August 1958) 1–28.

Dennon, Jim. "Captain George Flavel." *Cumtux* (Summer 1991): 20–30.

Gault, Vera Whitney. *A Brief History of Astoria, Oregon, 1811–1900*. 4th ed. Astoria: Vera Gault, 1989.

"The Historic Flavel House." *Cumtux* (Summer 1991): 3–19.

Hummasti, Paul George. *Finnish Radicals in Astoria, Oregon, 1904–1940: A Study in Immigrant Socialism*. New York: Arno Press, 1979.

Hummasti, P. G. "Ethnicity and Radicalism: The Finns of Astoria and the *Toveri*, 1890–1930." *Oregon Historical Quarterly* (Winter 1995–96): 362–393.

Mattila, Walter. "The 'Finnogonians'." *Finlandia Pictorial* (May 1959) 5–29.

Miller, Emma Gene. *Clatsop County, Oregon*. Portland: Binfords & Mort, 1958.

Miller, May S. My Father, A. G. Spexarth. Astor library vertical files, Astoria.

Morrell, Joyce Simpson. "The Astoria Labor Temple" *Cumtux* (Spring & Fall 1991): 13–17; 34–38.

Oathes, Bonnie Susan and Goodenberger, John E. *Astoria Downtown Area Historic Resource Survey and Inventory Report*. State Historic Preservation Office, 1990.

Oregon Historical Records Survey. *Inventory of the County Archives of Oregon, No. 4 Clatsop County (Astoria)*. Portland: The Oregon Historical Records Survey, 1940.

Oregon Insurance Rating Bureau. *Astoria Conflagration, Astoria Oregon, December 8, 1922*. Reprint n.d.

Scully, Susan M. *National Register of Historic Places Inventory—Nomination Form: Clatsop County Jail (Old)*. State Historic Preservation Office, 1982.

Tetlow, Roger T. *National Register of Historic Places Inventory—Nomination Form: Clatsop County Courthouse*. State Historic Preservation Office, 1983.

Newspapers: *Astoria Daily Budget* (Astoria), *Astoria Evening Budget* (Astoria), *Daily Astorian* (Astoria), *Morning Astorian* (Astoria), *Oregonian* (Portland), *Oregon Mist* (St. Helens)

Columbia County

Columbia County Plat Books. Columbia County Courthouse, St. Helens, Oregon.

MacColl, E. Kimbark with Stein, Harry H. *Merchants, Money and Power, The Portland Establishment 1843–1913*. Portland: The Georgian Press, 1988.

Oregon Almanac. Salem: Oregon State Immigration Commission, 1912.

Rees, Judith and Demuth, Kimberly. *National Register of Historic Places—Nomination Form: St. Helens Downtown Historic District*. State Historic Preservation Office, 1984.

SHPA Channel 9, St. Helens. "The Old Columbia County Courthouse." Television program, 1991.

Synder, Eugene. *Early Portland: Stump-Town Triumphant*. Portland: Binfords & Mort, 1970.

Newspapers: *Chronicle* (St. Helens), *Oregon Mist* (St. Helens), *St. Helens Sentinel-Mist* (St. Helens)

Crook County

Beckham, Stephen Dow. *State of Oregon Inventory Historic Sites and Buildings: Crook County*. State Historic Preservation Office, 1976.

Brogan, Phil F. *East of the Cascades*. Portland: Binfords & Mort, 1964.

Crook County Commissioners Records. Crook County Courthouse, Prineville, Oregon.

Crook County Courthouse Plans. Crook County Courthouse, Prineville, Oregon.

Crook County Historical Society. *Echoes From Old Crook County Volume II*. Prineville: Crook County Historical Society, 1992.

Crook County Historical Society. *Prineville/Crook County General Information and Historical Tour Guide*. Prineville: Crook County Historical Society, n.d.

Crook County Historical Society and A. R. Bowman Memorial Museum. *Echoes From Old Crook County*. Prineville: Crook County Historical Society, 1991.

Crook County Plat Books. Crook County Courthouse, Prineville, Oregon.

Due, John F. and Rush, Frances Juris. *Roads and Rails South From the Columbia*. Bend: Due and Juris, 1991.

Juris, Frances. *Old Crook County: The Heart of Oregon*. Prineville: Frances Juris, 1975.

Shaver, F. A.; Rose, Arthur P.; Steele, R. F.; Adams, A. E.; compilers. *An Illustrated History of Central Oregon Embracing Wasco, Sherman, Gilliam, Wheeler, Crook, Lake and Klamath Counties*. Spokane: Western Historical Publishing Co., 1905.

Newspapers: *Bend Bulletin* (Bend), *Central Oregonian* (Prineville), *Crook County Journal* (Prineville), *Prineville Review* (Prineville), *Oregonian* (Portland)

Deschutes County

Brogan, Phil F. *East of the Cascades*. Portland: Binfords & Mort, 1964.

Deschutes County Plat Books. Deschutes County Courthouse, Bend, Oregon.

Gribskow, Joyce. *Pioneer Spirits of Bend*. Bend: Joyce Gribskow, 1980.

Hall, Michael. *National Register of Historic Places Multiple Property Documentation Form: Historical Development of The Bend Company in Bend, Oregon*. State Historic Preservation Office, 1992.

Hatton, Raymond. *Bend in Central Oregon*. Portland: Binford & Mort, 1978.

Heritage Walk, A Pathway to the Past. Bend: Deschutes County Historical Society, 1993.

Vaughan, Thomas, ed. *High and Mighty*. Portland: Oregon Historical Society, 1981.

Williams, Elsie Horn. *A Pictorial History of the Bend Country*. Bend: Elsie Horn Williams, 1983.

Zisman, Karen and Donovan, Sally. *National Register of Historic Places Inventory—Nomination Form: O'Kane Building*. State Historic Preservation Office, 1986.

Newspapers: *Bend Bulletin* (Bend)

Douglas County

Beckham, Stephen Dow. *Land of the Umpqua: A History of Douglas County, Oregon.* Roseburg: Douglas County Commissioners, 1986.

Bureau of Municipal Research and Service. *Population Trends in Roseburg.* Roseburg: City Planning Commission, 1959.

Douglas County Plat Books. Douglas County Courthouse, Roseburg, Oregon.

Harbour, Terry. *Roseburg Cultural and Historical Resource Inventory* Vol. 1. State Historic Preservation Office, 1983.

Historic Douglas County, Oregon 1981. Roseburg: Douglas County Historical Society, 1982.

Kadas, Marianne. *Roseburg Business District Historic Context and Cultural Resource Inventory.* State Historic Preservation Office, 1991.

Know Your County Government. Roseburg: Douglas County Planning Department, 1990.

Rasmussen, Marie. *Douglas County Court House 1856–1976.* Douglas County Museum Vertical Files, Roseburg.

Riggs, Bonnie Wallace. "The Night Our Town Blew Up." *The Saturday Evening Post* (July 2, 1960) 17–46.

Newspapers: *News-Review* (Roseburg), *Oregonian* (Portland), *Plaindealer* (Roseburg), *Roseburg News-Review* (Roseburg)

Harney County

Brimlow, George Francis. *Harney County, Oregon, and Its Range Land.* Portland: Binfords & Mort, 1951.

Court transcripts, copy of. Typist unknown. Burns library vertical files, Burns.

Fitzgerald, Maurice. *Harney County, Its Early Settlement and Development.* Burns library vertical files, Burns.

Gray, Edward. *Life and Death of Oregon "Cattle King" Peter French 1849–1897.* Salem: Edward Gray, 1995.

Harney County Plat Books. Harney County Courthouse, Burns, Oregon.

Hatton, Raymond. *Oregon's Big Country.* Bend: Raymond Hatton, 1988.

A Lively Little History of Harney County, A Centennial Souvenir Album 1889–1989. Burns: Harney County Chamber of Commerce, 1989.

Jackson, Royal and Lee, Jennifer. *Harney County, An Historical Inventory.* Burns: Harney County Historical Society, 1978.

Shaver, F. A.; Rose, Arthur P.; Steele, R. F.; Adams, A. E.; compilers. *An Illustrated History of Baker, Grant, Malheur and Harney Counties.* Spokane: Western Historical Publishing Company, 1902.

Newspapers: *Burns Times-Herald* (Burns), *Herald* (Burns)

Jackson County

Atwood, Kay. *Blossoms & Branches; A Gathering of Rogue Valley Orchard Memories.* Ashland: Kay Atwood, 1980.

Atwood, Kay. *Historic Overview and Architectural Development of Medford Oregon, 1846–1946: A Historic Context.* City of Medford, 1993.

Atwood, Kay. *National Register of Historic Places Inventory—Nomination Form: Jackson County Courthouse*. State Historic Preservation Office, 1985.

Dunn, Joy, ed. *Land in Common, An Illustrated History of Jackson County, Oregon*. Medford: Southern Oregon Historical Society, 1993.

Jackson County Chamber of Commerce. *Historical Notes on the Fruit Industry of the Rogue Valley Oregon*. Medford: Jackson County Chamber of Commerce, 1959.

Jackson County Planning Department. *Jackson County Cultural and Historical Resource Survey*. State Historic Preservation Office, 1992.

Jackson County Plat Books. Jackson County Courthouse, Medford, Oregon.

Kramer, George. *Jacksonville Courthouse Complex Historic Structures Report*. Southern Oregon Historical Society, 1995.

Kramer, George. *Survey of Historic and Cultural Resources, Downtown Commercial Area, Phase I & II*. State Historic Preservation Office, 1994 and 1995.

Medford Commercial Club. Medford, Rogue River Valley, Southern Oregon. Medford: Medford Commercial Club, 1910.

Snedicor, Jane. *History of Medford*. Southern Oregon Historical Society, ca. 1930.

Walling, A. G. *History of Southern Oregon comprising Jackson, Douglas, Curry and Coos Counties*. Portland: A. G. Walling, 1884.

Newspapers: *Medford Mail Tribune* (Medford)

Josephine County

Booth, Percy. *Grants Pass, The Golden Years*. Grants Pass: Grants Pass Centennial Commission, 1984.

The Grants Pass National Historic District and Historic Building Tour. Grants Pass: Grants Pass Daily Courier, 1995.

Hill, Edna May. *Josephine County Historical Highlights I*. Grants Pass: Josephine County Library System and Josephine County Historical Society, 1980.

Josephine County Commissioners Records. Josephine County Courthouse, Grants Pass, Oregon.

Josephine County Courthouse Plans. Josephine County Courthouse, Grants Pass, Oregon.

Josephine County Plat Books. Josephine County Courthouse, Grants Pass, Oregon.

Kramer, George. *National Register of Historic Places Registration Form: G Street Historic District*. State Historic Preservation Office, 1992.

Kramer, George and Chappel, Jill. *Historic Resources Survey and Inventory of the Central Business District: Grants Pass*. 1992.

The Oregon Historical Records Survey. *Inventory of the County Archives of Oregon, No. 17 Josephine County*. Portland: The Oregon Historical Records Survey, 1939.

Street, Willard and Elsie. *Sailors' Diggings*. rev. Wilderville: Wilderville Press, 1992.

Sutton, Jack. *110 Years with Josephine, The History of Josephine County, Oregon*. Grants Pass: Josephine County Historical Society, 1966.

Walling, A. G. *History of Southern Oregon comprising Jackson, Douglas, Curry and Coos Counties*. Portland: A. G. Walling, 1884.

Newspapers: *Daily Courier* (Grants Pass), *Douglas Independent* (Roseburg)

Linn County

Avery, Marilyn and Robert. *National Register of Historic Places Inventory Nomination Form: Albany Custom Mill*. State Historic Preservation Office, 1979.

Clark, Rosalind. *National Register of Historic Places Inventory— Nomination Form: Albany Downtown Commercial Historic District*. State Historic Preservation Office, 1982.

Clark, Rosalind, *National Register of Historic Places Inventory— Nomination Form: Straney & Moore Livery Stable*. State Historic Preservation Office, 1979.

Edgar Williams & Co. *Illustrated Historical Atlas of Marion and Linn Counties of Oregon*, Reprint. Salem and Albany: Marion County Historical Society and Friends of Historic Albany, 1981.

Historic Albany Seems Like Old Times. Albany: Albany Visitors Association, n.d.

Historical Records Survey. *Inventory of the County Archives of Oregon, No. 22 Linn County (Albany)*. Portland: The Historical Records Survey, 1939.

Holmgren, Virginia C. *Chinese Pheasants, Oregon Pioneers*. Portland: Oregon Historical Society, 1964.

Linn County Plat Books. Linn County Courthouse, Albany, Oregon.

Mullen, Floyd C. *The Land of Linn*. Albany: Floyd Mullen, 1971.

Nuttig, Fred. *Old Time Albany*. Reprint. Albany: Richard Milligan, 1982.

Newspapers: *Albany Democrat-Herald* (Albany), *Albany Greater Oregon* (Albany), *Benton County Herald* (Corvallis), *Moro Leader* (Moro), *Oregonian* (Portland), *Oregon Journal* (Portland)

Morrow County

French, Giles. *Homesteads and Heritages: A History of Morrow County, Oregon*. Portland: Binfords & Mort, 1971.

Hedman, Arnie and Belsma, Ronnie. *National Register of Historic Places—Nomination Form: St. Patrick's Hotel*. State Historic Preservation Office, 1982.

Historical Records Survey. *Inventory of the County Archives of Oregon, No. 35 Morrow County (Heppner)*. Portland: The Historical Records Survey, 1937.

Kilkenny, John F. *Shamrocks and Shepherds: The Irish of Morrow County*. 2nd ed. Portland: Oregon Historical Society, 1981.

Lynch, James E. and Derickson, Partick M. *National Register of Historic Places—Nomination Form: Morrow County Courthouse*. State Historic Preservation Office, 1984.

McMillan, Sam G. *The Bunchgrassers: A History of Lexington, Morrow County, Oregon*. Portland: Irwin-Hodson Co., 1974.

Morrow County Extension Units. *Yesteryears of Morrow*. Heppner: Heppner Gazette Times, 1959.

Morrow County Plat Books. Morrow County Courthouse, Heppner, Oregon.

Parsons, Col. William and Shiach, W. S. *An Illustrated History of Umatilla County and of Morrow County*. Spokane: W. H. Lever, 1902.

Reelford, J. et al. Summary of April 18th, 1888 Meeting of Lexington Citizens. Morrow County Museum Vertical Files, Heppner.

Wetherford, Justine. "The Morrow County Court House," *Morrow County Chronicles* VI (1987): 3–9.

Newspapers: *Central Oregon Star* (Fossil), *Fossil Journal* (Fossil), *Heppner Gazette* (Heppner), *Heppner Times* (Heppner)

Multnomah County

Abbott, Carl. *Portland, Planning, Politics and Growth in a Twentieth-Century City*. Lincoln: University of Nebraska, 1983.

Bosker, Gideon and Lencek, Lena. *Frozen Music, A History of Portland Architecture*. Portland: Western Imprints, 1985.

Cost Planners, SERA Architects, and The Resource Group. *Focus Study: Multnomah County Courthouse*. Multnomah County, 1996.

DeMarco, Gordon. *A Short History of Portland*. San Francisco: Lexikos, 1990.

Eckardt, Wolf Von. "A Pied Piper of Hobbit Land." *Time* (August 23, 1982) 62–63.

Journal Voucher Fountains, Statues & Memorials incl. letters from concerned citizens. Oregon Historical Society Vertical Files, Portland.

MacColl, E. Kimbark with Stein, Harry H. *Merchants, Money and Power, The Portland Establishment 1843–1913*. Portland: The Georgian Press, 1988.

Moseley, Carl. *National Register of Historic Places—Nomination Form: Multnomah County Courthouse*. State Historic Preservation Office, 1978.

Multnomah Courthouse Plans. General Services, Multnomah County Courthouse, Portland, Oregon.

Neuberger, Richard. "The Cities of America, Portland, Oregon." *The Saturday Evening Post* (March 1, 1947) 23–108.

O'Donnell, Terence and Vaughan, Thomas. *Portland: A Historical Sketch and Guide*. Portland: Oregon Historical Society, 1976.

The Office of General Services. *The Portland Building*. Portland: The City of Portland, 1982.

The Oregon Historical Records Survey Project. *Inventory of the County Archives of Oregon, No. 35 Multnomah County* Vol I & II. Portland: The Oregon Historical Records Survey, 1940.

Sights and Scenes at the Lewis and Clark Centennial Exposition, Portland, Oregon. Portland: Robert A. Reid, 1905.

Synder, Eugene. *Early Portland: Stump-Town Triumphant*. Portland: Binfords & Mort, 1970.

Synder, Eugene. *Portland Potpourri: Art, Fountains and Old Friends*. Portland: Binford & Mort, 1991.

Walking Tour of Portland's Parks. Oregon Historical vertical files.

Newspapers: *Oregonian* (Portland), *Oregon Journal* (Portland), *Wall Street Journal* (New York)

Polk County

Beckham, Stephen Dow. *State of Oregon Inventory Historic Sites and Buildings: Polk County*. State Historic Preservation Office, 1976.

History of Polk County Oregon. Monmouth: Polk County Historical Society, 1987.

Newton, Sidney. *Early History of Independence Oregon*. Independence: Sidney W. Newton, 1971.

Polk County Centennial, Souvenir Booklet and Program. Dallas: Centennial Committee, 1947.

Polk County Plat Books. Polk County Courthouse, Dallas, Oregon.

Newspapers: *Capital Journal* (Salem), *Itemizer-Observer* (Dallas), *Polk County Itemizer* (Dallas), *Polk County Observer* (Dallas), *Sun-Enterpise* (Dallas)

Sherman County

Due, John F. and Rush, Frances Juris. *Roads and Rails South From the Columbia*. Bend: Due and Juris, 1991.

French, Giles. *The Golden Land*. Portland: Oregon Historical Society, 1958.

Moore, Patty. "Our County Is Formed." *Sherman County: For The Record* (Fall 1983): 3–10.

Shaver, F. A.; Rose, Arthur P.; Steele, R. F.; Adams, A. E.; compilers. *An Illustrated History of Central Oregon Embracing Wasco, Sherman, Gilliam, Wheeler, Crook, Lake and Klamath Counties*. Spokane: Western Historical Publishing Co., 1905.

Sherman County Plat Books. Sherman County Courthouse, Moro, Oregon.

Newspapers: *Dalles Times-Mountaineer* (The Dalles), *Moro Observer* (Moro)

Tillamook County

Baker, Fred, compiler. *Illustrated and Descriptive Edition of Tillamook County, Oregon*. Tillamook: Tillamook Chamber of Commerce, n.d.

Beals, Arthur G. *The Autobiography of Arthur G. Beals*. Tillamook: Tillamook Publishing Co., Inc., 1952

Building of "The Morning Star." Tillamook County Historical Society Vertical Files.

Collins, Dean. *The Cheddar Box*, Vol. 1. Portland: The Oregon Journal, 1933.

Levensque, Paul. *A Chronicle of the Tillamook County Forest Trust Lands*. Tillamook: Tillamook County and Paul Levensque, 1985.

Orcutt, Ada M. *Tillamook: Land of Many Waters*. Portland: Binfords & Mort, 1951.

Oregon Almanac. Salem: Oregon State Immigration Commission, 1912.

The Oregon Historical Records Survey Project. *Inventory of the County Archives of Oregon, No. 29 Tillamook County*. Portland: The Oregon Historical Records Survey, 1940.

Tillamook County Creamery Association Information Kit. Oregon Historical Socity Vertical Files.

Tillamook County Courthouse Plans. Tillamook County Courthouse, Tillamook, Oregon.

Tillamook County Plat Books. Tillamook County Courthouse, Tillamook, Oregon.

Tillamook History. Reprint. Tillamook: Tillamook County Pioneer Association, 1991.

Tillamook Memories. Tillamook: Tillamook County Pioneer Association, 1972.

Newspapers: *Tillamook Headlight* (Tillamook), *Tillamook Herald* (Tillamook), *Tillamook Headlight–Herald* (Tillamook)

Wallowa County

Baily, Barbara Ruth. *Main Street, northeastern Oregon*. Portland: Oregon Historical Society, 1982.

Coffman, Lloyd W. *Wallowa County, Oregon, a Capsule History*. Enterprise: Wallowa County Centennial Press, 1987.

The History of Wallowa County, Oregon. Wallowa County: Wallowa County Museum Board, 1983.

An Illustrated History of Union and Wallowa Counties. Spokane: Western Historical Publishing Co., 1902.

Wallowa County Plat Books. Wallowa County Courthouse, Enterprise, Oregon.

Newspapers: *News Record* (Enterprise), *Wallowa County Chieftain* (Enterprise)

Wasco County

Dodds, Linda and Schneider, Ted. *National Register of Historic Places Inventory—Nomination Form: The Dalles Commercial Historic District*. State Historic Preservation Office, 1985.

Drake, Anita. *The Autobiography of Lulu D. Crandall*. The Dalles: Fort Dalles Museum, 1990.

Lundell, John. *Governmental History of Wasco County Oregon*. The Dalles: John Lundell, 1970.

Mills, Randall V. *Sternwheelers Up Columbia*. 1947. Reprint. Lincoln: University of Nebraska Press, 1977.

Oregon Historical Records Survey. *Inventory of the County Archives of Oregon, No. 33 Wasco County (The Dalles)*. Portland: The Oregon Historical Records Survey, 1941.

The Original Wasco County Courthouse, 1859. The Dalles Chamber of Commerce, n.d.

Shaver, F. A.; Rose, Arthur P.; Steele, R. F.; Adams, A. E.; compilers. *An Illustrated History of Central Oregon Embracing Wasco, Sherman, Gilliam, Wheeler, Crook, Lake and Klamath Counties*. Spokane: Western Historical Publishing Co., 1905.

Wasco County Plat Books. Wasco County Courthouse, The Dalles, Oregon.

Weeks, James. *One Part of the West*. The Dalles: Original County Courthouse Preservation, Inc., 1978.

Newspapers: *The Dalles Chronicle* (The Dalles), *The Dalles Optimist* (The Dalles)

Washington County

Benowitz, June Melby. *From Log Cabin to High-Rise, The Washington County Courthouse, 1849–1988*. Hillsboro: Washington County, Oregon, 1988.

Hillsboro, Washington County, Oregon. Hillsboro: Hillsboro Commercial Club, n.d.

McLaughlin, Emde and O'Brian, Cole. *City of Hillsboro Cultural Resource Inventory*. State Historic Preservation Office, 1980 and 1985.

The Oregon Historical Records Survey. *Inventory of the County Archives of Oregon, No. 34 Washington County (Hillsboro)*. Portland: The Oregon Historical Records Survey, 1940.

Washington County Plat Books. Washington County Courthouse, Hillsboro, Oregon.

Newspapers: *Hillsboro Argus* (Hillsboro), *Polk County Itemizer* (Dallas)

Wheeler County

Beckham, Stephen Dow. *State of Oregon Inventory Historic Sites and Buildings: Wheeler County*. 1976.

Finding Fossils in Fossil. City of Fossil, n.d.

Fussner, F. Smith, ed. *Glimpses of Wheeler County's Past*. Portland: Binford & Mort, 1975.

The History of Wheeler County Oregon. Condon: The Times Journal, 1983.

Shaver, F. A.; Rose, Arthur P.; Steele, R. F.; Adams, A. E.; compilers. *An Illustrated History of Central Oregon Embracing Wasco, Sherman, Gilliam, Wheeler, Crook, Lake, and Klamath Counties*. Spokane: Western Historical Publishing Co., 1905.

Wheeler County Commissioners Records. Wheeler County Courthouse, Fossil, Oregon.

Wheeler County Plat Books. Wheeler County Courthouse, Wheeler County, Oregon.

Newspapers: *Fossil Journal* (Fossil), *Oregonian* (Portland)

Index